Work, Sister, Work

WORK, SISTER, WORK

Why Black Women Can't Get Ahead and What They Can Do About It

Cydney Shields
and Leslie C. Shields

Foreword by Eleanor Holmes Norton

A BIRCH LANE PRESS BOOK
Published by Carol Publishing Group

650.1408956555w

A Birch Lane Press Book
Published by Carol Publishing Group
Birch Lane Press Book is a registered trademark of Carol Communications, Inc.
Editorial Offices: 600 Madison Avenue, New York, NY 10022
Sales & Distribution Offices: 120 Enterprise Avenue, Secaucus, NJ 07094
In Canada: Canadian Manda Group, P.O. Box 920, Station U, Toronto,
Ontario, M8Z 5P9, Canada
Queries regarding rights and permissions should be addressed to:
Carol Publishing Group, 600 Madison Avenue, New York, NY 10022

Manufactured in the United States of America
ISBN 1-55972-147-2

10   9   8   7   6   5   4   3

Carol Publishing Group books are available at special discounts
for bulk purchases, for sales promotions, fund raising, or
educational purposes. Special editions can also be created to
specifications. For details contact: Special Sales Department,
Carol Publishing Group, 120 Enterprise Ave., Secaucus, NJ 07094

Library of Congress Cataloging-in-Publication Data

Shields, Cydney.
    Work, sister, work: how Black women can get ahead in the
workplace / by Cydney Shields and Leslie C. Shields.
        p.   cm.
    "A Birch Lane Press book."
    1. Vocational guidance for women--United States. 2. Afro-American
women--Employment. I. Shields, Leslie C. II. Title.
HF5382.65.S54   1993
650.14'089'96073   dc20   92-39837
                                                    CIP

To Our Mother,
Sylvia Lorraine Shields,
whose faith encouraged us to become

CONTENTS

FOREWORD

by Eleanor Holmes Norton,
Congressional Delegate for District of Columbia
and the first woman to head the Equal Employment Opportunity
Commission

Until recent years, racial discrimination in America forced a Darwinian adaptability to the workplace by African Americans. Historically, only a tiny fraction of the rich pool of jobs in our country has been available to black women and men. They went after those jobs with a vengeance, sometimes working two demeaning jobs to earn one inadequate salary. While European immigrants crossed the oceans to a country hungry for labor, blacks had to cross borders within their own country in search of any work they could find and took whatever was left.

African American women were all but lost in the shuffle of the workplace. In the illuminating pages of this book, two sisters, Cydney and Leslie Shields, coax black women out of the background to take ownership of the jobs to which their energy and talent should entitle them. Only in the 1960s were African American women able to branch out into the formal economy away from their predominant job— housework in other women's houses.

Not to worry. Black women have found their way on their own and, as the authors demonstrate, black women have done very well at it. Yet this book has much to offer. Race and sex barriers are broken, not down. Those looking for all the help they can get will find much of it in these pages.

The authors pay African American women the respect due their diversity. **Work, Sister, Work** is at once a useful reference and a source of practical advice. It is objective and yet is often intimate. Facts and flair, do's and don'ts, criticism and self criticism—they are all here. This book speaks rather than tells.

The book's immediacy and its usefulness may be attributable to its origin in workshops the Shields sisters held for working women. The authors seem to have listened as much as they spoke. As a consequence, they have been able to find the black woman's voice. For example, their "old school thinkers" for whom race is foremost are heard, but so are the "new school" women. Neither is discredited. Both are real.

Yet the author sisters do not shrink from the toughness required to survive in today's competitive work environment or take refuge in race or sex. This is no racial or gender apologia. Nor is it a mournful tale of rejection. The authors know how to comfort, they also know how to spur.

African Americans face an undeserved challenge as they struggle belatedly to find their rightful places in the American workplace. For that workplace is far more competitive and demanding now than it has been historically for most Americans because the traditional national economy has now become global. It was easier to find jobs, to become middle-class, and to accumulate wealth in the old national, industrial economy that was resolutely hostile to blacks in every part of the country. Now black and white Americans are competing not only with each other but with workers of nations throughout the world.

The authors understand the error of approaching this dilemma as though history has passed black people, and especially African American women, by. Equality has become possible of late. This volume offers help before it is too late. While public officials and private employers grapple with workplace fairness, black women must do what they have always done—**Work, Sister, Work**.

ACKNOWLEDGMENTS

Never measure the height of a mountain
until you have reached the top.
Then you will see how low it was.
—Statesman Dag Hammarskjold

You can never be too thankful, and you can never give enough thanks. First thank God Almighty. We then owe a debt of gratitude to a lot of friends, family, and organizations, too many to name individually, who believed that the mountain was not too high and that this book could and should be written.

Thank you, Gail Williams, for planting the seed. Thank you to three very supportive sisters, Allyson, Cynthia, and Stacy, to our father Del and our brothers-in-law, Al and Garnie.

We especially thank the Honorable Eleanor Holmes Norton, and the truly dynamic black women who not only shared their thoughts in letters to our readers (we can't wait for you to read them), but their time in lengthy conversations. For allowing us to use their reports and statistics, we thank the Executive Leadership Council, the Bureau of Labor Statistics, the Urban League, and Wider Opportunities for Women. Thank you to Maxine Carpenter for use of her résumés.

To our good friends (you know who you are) who read and read our manuscript and played critic, we are deeply appreciative. And thank you for not getting tired of hearing us say we were too tired to write another word.

Last, but not least, we thank our agent, Nina Graybill, our editors, Denise O'Sullivan and Hillel Black, and Carol Publishing Group.

Again, thank you, thank you, thank you, to our readers.

INTRODUCTION

Why Can't She?

If someone wrote a song about you it would probably be titled "Work, Sister, Work." You can't remember a time when you weren't working. You think it's your calling. You enter the workplace charged with energy and enthusiasm; but once there you feel alone, angry and misunderstood. It's no secret you are troubled. Your vulnerability destroys any confidence you may have had; and without it your ability to get ahead is limited. Most of all, you are tired.

Many studies document your dissatisfaction with career advancement. White women speak of a "glass ceiling" getting in the way of their career advancement. But the ceiling over a black woman's head is concrete.

Your history? It's about getting and keeping a job. While you are usually forced to work, developing or planning a career is not something you think about. You often remain trapped in an endless cycle of underemployment. But you are hopeful that with trends pointing to a "new work force," this may change employment and career opportunities.

Black working women, like yourself, are still struggling to define their place in the business community. It took a good friend and advice from over four thousand black women, who passed through our "Black Women Can Win!" series, to spur us to write down the strategies for how black women can get ahead in the workplace.

In spite of our history, however, we've come a long way. Years ago a black woman's primary occupation was as a domestic worker. Grandmothers will say black women were keepers of the sweepers. Go ahead, say it, a clean-up woman. In 1940, 60 percent of all black women were employed as domestic workers. Fewer than 5 percent had white-collar jobs. By 1980, only 4.7 percent of black women were employed in domestic work while 50 percent held white collar jobs. Between

1983 and 1986, the percentage of executive, administrative, and managerial jobs black women held increased from 4.9 percent to 6 percent. In professional areas, black women held 10.7 percent of positions in such areas as medicine, science, teaching and engineering.

Black women represent a major segment of the labor force, yet they do not feel as though they are a significant part of it. In 1992, there were over six million black women in the work force. Although hard-working, they are concentrated in low-paying service and clerical jobs and earn less than their white counterparts. Black women are also less successful in moving out of traditionally female jobs and normally start their career in lower status jobs. Ultimately, black women share more difficulties in the labor market than others of the same education and experience.

Black women have reason to be excited about employment gains, but all of our sisters don't and won't share employment success. In 1992, half of us were still working in low paying clerical and service occupations; over 6 percent were precision product craft and repair workers. Black women represented 35 percent of all retail and personal services sales workers, but only 16 percent of all executives and managers. The largest number of black women in management were in government service, mainly in management-related occupations as opposed to line executives and administrators. Our shocking under-representation in corporate management is said to result from the "double whammy" syndrome of being female and black.

There is talk that the nineties and the years beyond will hold promise for the black woman. Experts project that by the year 2000, two of every three entrants to the work force will be women. Black women like you are expected to increase by 2.4 million. This is good news as businesses will be forced to reach out to black women to fill needed positions.

Perhaps in all the ways that matter the "new work force" will catapult you to a distinctive position. A few doors will open; you will be allowed upstairs and, finally, pull down the barriers. But your survival and advancement will demand that you invest now in yourself by getting an education, training and career assistance. If you expect to succeed, you must recognize the importance of preparing for a changing work force and take action to meet the challenge, or be left behind.

AUTHORS' NOTE

Before you go any further, we'd like to introduce you to some of Black America's most outstanding and promising black working sisters. We just couldn't wait to tell you, so we decided to use these few pages to give you a peek inside the letters you will read at the end of each chapter.

You'll meet a brigadier general who is one of two of the highest ranking African American women in the United States military. She began her career thirty-three years ago and has five honorary doctorate degrees. She also is the first female in the U.S. Army to qualify for and be awarded the Expert Field Medical Badge. Included in our "star" lineup are three women (from CNN, Sara Lee Corporation, and NYNEX Corporation) who were cited by *Ebony* magazine as among the most influential Black Americans. One of these same sisters is an author who once worked closely with Martin Luther King, Jr. Then there's the lawyer turned professional orator who has over seventy-five keys to American cities. There's the sister who didn't let childhood arthritis and a wheel chair keep her from learning to walk again and pursuing a career in nursing.

We think you'll also enjoy letters written by sisters who garnished careers against great odds. Would you believe that we found a former secretary who is an established, self-taught fashion designer and never took a course in drawing? If that doesn't surprise you, we'll also tell you about another former secretary who became a columnist for a Pulitzer prize-winning newspaper, and about a former sales clerk who is now an advertising manager and involved in producing commercials. Out of bad comes good could be the story of two women, one once homeless, and the other who watched a mother suffer from Alzheimer's disease, yet turned tragedies into triumphs and started their own businesses.

There's one truly courageous sister who went out on a spiritual limb to launch a successful cosmetic business; another who was called into career by her desire to "help her people and who also established the annual Christmas store for poor children;" two sisters who, while in their thirties, became successful franchise owners; a cartoonist who became syndicated in over seventy-five newspapers even though she was told she would probably fail; the CEO who worked for a famous heart surgeon; the educator whose outspokenness paved the way to her becoming head of a national teacher's association; the corporate VP who didn't take luck for granted or leave her career to chance; the career counselor who pulled herself out of the clerical pool and into management; the government manager who is on loan to a national black woman's organization; the cultural affairs officer who turned a desire to serve the black community into a career; the enterprising entrepreneur who began a business as a way to send herself through school; the sister who took the nation's capitol by surprise by revolutionizing radio programming and becoming the owner and operator of not one but four radio stations.

They are some of the very special women we met along the way to writing this book. Their experiences are varied yet similar. Whatever their story, we're sure you'll find a story that is not unlike yours.

Chapter 1

BREAKING
THE SILENCE

In sharing your stories, you told us that you maintain a code of silence or only whisper among yourselves about your experiences in the workplace. You said you had to, for fear of the consequences and because you felt no one cared to listen. So, when we decided to write, *Work, Sister, Work*, we didn't know what you were going to expect of us. We also weren't sure if we should first tell you to stop carrying around your bad experiences or get you to focus on your weaknesses and motivations. Then we tossed around the idea of just concentrating on solutions to your career problems or on the key ways black women hamper their own career. We just didn't know where to begin. Finally, we agreed that if this was to be a true self-help book (one that would help you in making career decisions), you needed to understand, early on, a black woman's situation in the workplace. What better way than through the eyes and personal experiences of other black women....

On a beautiful Saturday afternoon in September, we gathered with sixty-five other black women in a Philadelphia hotel. They all came to attend our workshop, **"Black Women Can Win!"** A broad spectrum of professions and industries is represented by the participants. Some are lawyers; a number are secretaries; one is a lobbyist; another is a bus driver; there is an accountant; three are government administrators there's a teacher with six of her high school students; a librarian; four recently unemployed women, two pharmaceutical sales representatives and many others, from office clerks to senior managers.

Scanning the room, we are reminded of the diversity of black culture. There were women of many shades of color and outfitted in both European and ethnocentric dress. Some had their hair styled in the "wrap," while others wore gheri curls, cornrows or classic cuts that were either straightened or permed. Yet they were all there for a common purpose, to gain strategies on how to get ahead in the workplace.

The women openly shared their testimonies of the black woman's situation and the black experience, which sparked heated, but enlightening, dialogue as the women revealed thoughts they had never shared in a public forum. As the first woman spoke about why black women weren't getting ahead, we watched the facial expressions. All heads nodded in understanding.

Our introductory discussions ignited a division in the room that was like a parting of the Red Sea. Two schools of thought emerged. The "old school thinkers" represented the traditional view by some black people who felt their efforts at navigating through the workplace are hindered by the way whites treat blacks. Black women, they feel, are locked out by corporations that are not always hospitable to blacks. The "new school thinkers" held the view of today's conservative blacks that the attitudes of black women and problems with black/black relations are the major roadblocks to black women's success. They also said that a lot of black women think they can get ahead only through the civil rights door and that black women need to focus on self-help.

FIRST, SOME WORDS FROM
THE OLD SCHOOL THINKERS

"I want to get ahead, but I feel trapped. I'm trying to move up in the workplace, but I don't know what to do. I feel like a stranger in someone else's house. Some people make me feel at home, while others treat me like an unwelcome guest. I don't have anyone whom I can confide in, which makes it more tough." These thoughts were expressed by a young woman who could have been no older than nineteen.

"Tell me about it," interrupts another woman. "You know, my boss has never taken the time to know me. At least not in the way I have seen him talk with my white colleagues. He will look past me, speak to someone white and not blink his eye at me. There's only been one time that I can recall having a half-decent conversation with him. It was when he learned that my sister was in law school. But his real concern wasn't about getting to know the personal side of me. He was really anxious to know how my sister scored on her LSATs. Each time he saw me after that, he'd ask the same question."

One of the secretaries, sitting in the back of the hotel room, stood up and said, "Sometimes, I feel like there is an invisible sign above my head, reading 'Yield, black woman on board: make her feel different.' I am constantly asking myself, 'What did I do?,' and 'Where did I go wrong?' I don't always get the answers, but I keep reminding myself it's a different world." She continued tapping her right index finger against the palm of her left hand, reciting a list of her problems. "I have to learn how to fit in when I'm not helped to move into the mainstream of a company; accept that good isn't always good enough; deal with sisters who aren't always sisters; and make sure I choose the right battle, or I may not win the war."

The accountant, a "new schooler," shakes her head as if she can't believe what she is hearing and questions the other woman's use of the word *war*. "War's a strong term."

"I agree," comments the secretary, "but sometimes I feel like a soldier. There are days when I feel like I'm waiting for something to happen, but I don't know what it is. I worry about how to take a fall and what to do when the first shots are fired at me. I fear what a soldier fears: I have a fear of failing, impending battles, and those who may use my color to make me an enemy. I don't know. I think I need some basic training."

"You got that right," adds another one of the secretaries. "That's why when people ask me how's work, I tell them it's nothing but a paycheck. It might mean more if it wasn't such a struggle. I want to get ahead, and I want the same things as everyone else. But I seem to face more obstacles and resistance. I have a boss who treats me like a misfit and approaches me with the attitude of 'how dare you' for expecting working America to provide liberty and justice for all."

Two of the lawyers give each other a look, and then one adds, "There's justice, all right. That's the problem. It's just us, alone coping with the barriers of color. I entered the work force like everyone else. I needed a job, and I wanted to make lots of money. There are days when I feel like I accepted an adventure. I know the feeling of being in the wrong place. It's a terrible way to learn prejudice. I experience all kinds of combat zones and work through many battles. With each step I climb, I must watch my back. There are people who refuse to help me up or pull strings for me. I also feel alone."

The accountant hesitates, then ask a question, "Why do you feel that you have no one?"

The lawyer rolls her eyes, but nevertheless responds to the question. "That's not the type of loneliness I'm referring to. How do I explain it without sounding like I'm a racist? When I think about being black in the workplace, I just don't think about being equal. I think invisible. Sometimes you see us, more often than not you don't. And, do you want to know why? We're invisible. I'm a member of a race nobody wants to know. There are a lot of us, yet we're still kept hidden. Explain to me why I have to strain my neck to look for blacks at the top. You know where you'll find us? At ground or basement level. We're either sweeping floors or typing in the word processing pool—with degrees! There are only a few other places you'll find us, and there are certain jobs we'll always be doing: cleaning, nursing, teaching, and cooking. If we're not invisible, we're isolated. We're isolated from the corporate mainstream. We're isolated from the Board. We're isolated from different positions. We're isolated from each other. Even when they include me in a major project or task, I still don't feel a part of it. They seem to either talk over me or around me."

A number of women agreed with these sentiments and further expressed their discontent with the accountant's attitude. Throughout the room we heard: Do you know how it feels to be unacknowledged? People look at black women, and you know what? They don't see us. You know how I know? They don't want to hear what we have to say, and they don't ask for our opinions. We're an exclusion. When we try to talk about our problems, they don't take us seriously. White people think there isn't a problem. I want to say, do you think we made this stuff up?

At this point, we decided to interrupt the discussion and turn the first half of the workshop into a focus discussion regarding the issues being raised. We asked the group, "In light of what is being said, it is possible that some blacks are oversensitive to the issues of color in the workplace?" An overwhelming chorus of no's were heard from the "old school thinkers."

"No, I don't think so," a bank manager responds. "It's hard to explain that you feel your color is preventing you from making it, especially when a company has Equal Opportunity signs posted everywhere. I call these EEO signs 'Uh-Oh' signs: Caution, black woman on site. No one seems to understand what I go through at work. If the organization emphasizes equality, I may work for the one person who makes me feel different. Mine becomes a private struggle, because I work for an institution that doesn't recognize that it has individuals who discriminate. Granted, I've been very lucky during periods of my worklife. I've worked for companies which don't mind providing growth and opportunities to black women. When I've been unlucky, I've received less money and less responsibility, all because of the color of my skin. I'm tired of hearing that the problems of blacks are our own making or that we take things too personally."

"How can you not take things personally," the lobbyist said, "when you see so few black faces among management or when you have to work harder than your white peers to receive the same recognition? Not only that, when I do more, I get less. So, someone's going to have to tell me here, today, why I shouldn't be a little upset because the color of my skin determines how high I can go. Look how long it takes for a black woman to reach the top of her industry. The disparities are overwhelming. I can start on the same day, in the same position, with the same skills, the same education, and a similar background as a white person, and the company won't move our careers at the same pace. Blacks and whites in the workplace are truly on different tracks.

What amazes me is the naïveté of my white friends who believe that affirmative action and quotas have removed barriers for blacks. A white woman who is hired in the same position as me doesn't always start on the same stair. She's allowed to advance five steps ahead, while a black woman in the same position starts two steps behind. We take steps back in terms of promotions, salaries, and opportunities. We are twice as likely to be unemployed. For every dollar a white male earns, a black female earns about sixty-five cents. In professional specialities, such as medicine, science, teaching, and engineering, 10.7 percent of working black women hold jobs in these areas compared to 14.6 percent white women."

"People think black people are looking for special treatment," the bank manager adds, "but we just want to get rid of the unequal treatment. If our ceilings were glass, we'd be able to see what others are doing. I also want to comment on what the sister just said. It's true. The track they put black women on is not an express. Unlike white women, we don't get to skip stops. Our careers are derailed by excuses the company makes to us about not having enough education, experiences or skills. We're not placed under the wings of a chief engineer to help guide us. When people accuse me of trying to be white, I tell them I don't want to be white. I mean, if you had choice between flying or catching a bus, what would you do? Why travel coach when you can go first class. To be honest, yeah, I want to be on the white track. It's wider and longer, with more destinations. A white woman doesn't have to remain in her position as long as I do. The track she's on is also less rigid about educational requirements and skills. She doesn't have to demand to be considered, and she's given more money for starting the same job as another black who was hired long before her. Hers is a high option career plan."

The same thoughts were not repeated by everyone. The teachers and government employees seemed unable to identify with the problems that the corporate women shared. Depending on their industries, or if they were in a unionized organization, some black women emphasized that there are few, if any, problems with concrete ceilings where they work. Women who work for legal, banking, or commercial real estate firms suggested that they faced the most obstacles.

We then switched the discussion to the issue of both black and white biases and perceptions:

"I used to think that I wasn't prejudiced," says the pharmaceutical sales representative. "But some of my prejudices stem from experiences. When you're in sales everyone gets assigned to a certain territory. Depending on how good the territory is, the more money you can make. But most of the time, companies assigning the worst territories to blacks. If you're black, they assign you to the black neighborhoods and areas that are low income or crime-infested. As a result, most of us aren't always fortunate enough to make bonus. At the big sales meetings, the whites collect the top sales awards. What I'm trying to say is sometimes you can have so much happen to you that you begin to believe that some prejudiced white person is behind every bad thing that happens to you."

"I agree that we have our own prejudices and hang ups, but what about the biases?" asks a sales clerk. She takes the absence of responses from the group as a sign that it's okay to keep talking and says, "You know what bothers me?" she continued in a tone of voice that told everyone she was pissed. "Why do whites feel the need to emphasize that they have a black neighbor, cook, or friend in order to make me feel comfortable? It's like they're doing it to prove that they don't have prejudices. And when we attend a wedding of a white colleague, the first thing you hear from his or her family or guests is, 'You must work with Sue or Bobby, right?' I'm also tired of being the black life expert. I'm always asked if I know how to fix soul food or for my opinion of Jesse Jackson. My worst experience was when a white guy on my job had his hair permed. It had turned real coarse. When we asked him what had happened, he looked at me and said I probably would understand. Then he turned to everyone else and said he had eaten watermelon."

Similar concerns about myths and wrong perceptions were expressed by other members of the group. There was a prevailing feeling that most whites do not understand the black experience. One sales clerk talked about how her coworkers assume all blacks are Baptists. Another woman said her white friends are amazed that blacks don't have to wash their hair every day and, they can't figure out how blacks can comb their hair straight one day and wear it curly the next. A few talked about other myths that nonminorities share about blacks, for example, the perception that all blacks like rap music or grew up in the ghetto.

"I can live with the cultural misunderstandings," a financial manager said. "I can't live with the surprise I see in the eyes of whites when they meet an intelligent black person. If you are a member of what they view is the talented tenth, they think t gives them a license to put down blacks in your presence. They seem to feel that your intelligence or expertise qualifies you to be one of them, so now they can tell you everything that they ever thought about black people. I hear comments like, 'You're different,' or 'So and so doesn't act like you; did you grow up in the inner city?' Some of my white colleagues just don't get it. They don't understand how uncomfortable they make me feel. I often feel like an extra. I'm a part of the one percent who are asked to join committees or other special task forces. Every conference I attend and the majority of organizations I join have only two or three blacks. In a way, that also helps me. White people, in those instances, will go out of their way to make me feel like I'm a part of what's going on. They seem glad to have a black join their organizations or become involved in their projects. I usually try to let them see a side of black people that they may not know exists. I put extra effort in everything I do. I always feel I have to prove myself to let them know that blacks are just as hard-working."

"But working hard is no guarantee that people will respect your ability," the office manager counters. "There's still that element of surprise. If I'm in the reception area when an appointment arrives, and the person is white, they always assume I'm the secretary. They appear thrown off when they request to see the office manager, and I announce I'm her. There have been times when white females and I are standing in the reception area at the same time, but vendors will ask which one of them is the office manager."

"There are two experiences regarding the differences between whites and blacks that stand out in my mind," a personal representative said, describing her perception of the issue. "I once overheard two white personnel representatives screening résumés. They joked with me about how they could tell which applicants were black by looking at the names. It made me wonder if that was a way we also get screened out of jobs. I had another experience that made me realize whites and blacks live in two different worlds. When another black personnel representative's father died, a few of the whites attended the funeral and talked about it as if they were in culture shock. They were surprised that my colleague's family had passed out a printed program and that the family marched into the services. I recall a white colleague of mine saying that she didn't know all this went on at black funerals and that the services would be so long. I think that's why companies need to have more cultural diversity programs. It's really another name for sensitivity training, but at least it gets you thinking about the differences between people. Some things are done without malice, but sometimes you have to bring them out in the open and make people aware of the impact of what they do and say."

"Try suggesting that to a company," a customer service manager exclaims. "They don't think there's a problem, so we're forced to talk about it among ourselves. And that creates another problem, because we've been conditioned to not talk to each other. The blacks in my company always joke that when whites see two or more blacks together, they think it's a conspiracy. It's always assumed that we're up to something when we get together. My boss once asked me if there was a problem with the blacks, because he heard that two managers and me were meeting in my office at lunch. The only thing we were doing was talking about refinancing our bills. Now, I feel so uncomfortable that I avoid mingling with blacks on my job except when it's strictly business. It may sound like a poor solution, but I feel like I'm attacked from every end right down to the food I eat. I'm even doubly careful about whom I hire. I have a 50/50 staff, half white and half minority. That way no one can accuse me of an African takeover."

A marketing director summed up these sentiments. "I wish that non-minorities would understand that most of what bothers black people is our pride. We just want to be recognized. It hurts to be treated like an outsider. When I was a secretary, one of my bosses said that I needed to understand that blacks are supposed to get along with blacks and that whites are supposed to get along with each other. When I begged to differ, he told me he noticed how well I got along with the girls in word processing. They, too, were black."

NOW, WORDS FROM THE NEW SCHOOL THINKERS

"It's not just whites that need the diversity training," adds a data processor, voicing a different type of concern. "We need it, too. I've seen so much over the years. I think whites need to learn how to understand blacks, but blacks also have to change their mindset. No one can question, there's racism. It's built into our society. Traditionally, we have been the underdog. However, our problems aren't all about laws, but miseducated individuals and our attitudes. If you look around this room, some of us are succeeding and some of us are not. I feel very strongly that there's a direct relationship between our attitudes and the level of our success. We have to learn how to create our own opportunities. We can't keep turning everything into a black issue."

"I know just what you mean," the bus driver said. "I have black friends who are constantly late for work. When they're written up, they say it's because they're black. When they're given extra work that they can't handle, they say whites want them to fail. It's like they own all volumes of the "It's Because I'm Black" book. Ladies," she adds with emphasis, "I have worked for over thirty years, and I can't say that everything bad that happened to me was a result of racism. I've seen a lot of discrimination in my time, but I can't blame all my failures on being black. Some things stemmed from my own attitudes. My point is that everything's not always a 'them versus us' issue. I don't have a lot of education like some of you, but I learned a long time ago that there's no reason for me to walk around like black women are everyone's target. Some of us are so hostile that people are afraid to approach us. Let's do each other a favor and unload some of our hostilities. It's weighing us down, and if we're not careful, it's going to cost us more than a job."

"I say we need to forget yesterday, and focus on today," another sales representative adds. "We also need to learn when to let go, and when it's time to fight a battle. When I first graduated from college, my father admonished me that there were times when I was going to have to eat crow. He also told me that I would know when it was appropriate to bring problems of discrimination out in the open. He said a white person looking on the outside doesn't see what a black person sees. They think everything's okay. Meanwhile, we're working for a racist bigot. Well, I worked for a racist bigot, once. And I chose to tell it like it is. I did it the right way. I filed a grievance with the Personnel office. I spoke up about the bigotry, racism, and discrimination. The Affirmative Action Officer did the right thing. He cautioned me against the seriousness of my charges and the potential effect on my career. He tried to tell me the problem wasn't the company, but the man for whom I worked.

"I understood what he was saying, but my conscience wouldn't let me back down. The bigot I worked for had made a lot of derogatory comments about blacks, and told one of my friends that we needed to take the cornrows and our garb back to Africa. That's when I lost it. I knew what I was giving up by stepping forward. I was scared, but I counted the cost. I had a choice, piss my boss off or get promoted. I didn't have to think twice about it. I didn't get promoted. But even though that one incident occurred, I looked at it as isolated situations with one white person who had a problem. If we could learn to become less defensive and get out of the white against blacks color rut, we might do better. I try to take everything that happens to me on a case-by-case basis. It's not the organizations that hurt some of us. It's the individuals in the organizations we have to enlighten."

The teacher agrees that racial struggles are no longer with institutions. "It's funny how things have changed. No one has brought up tokenism. There was a time when certain companies practiced years of overt racism, but it's not that way anymore. Now, the racism is subtle and practiced by individuals. There's also economic racism. There are people who don't want some black person or immigrant to take their job away, when that job is what feeds them. As a result of the sixties' civil rights movement, companies felt obligated to hire blacks. A lot of us moved up, but we were tokens.

"I once worked for a company that benefited from certain political influences in a predominately black city. They offered me a job that seemed promising. I remember, though, that they only allowed me to attend the Urban League Conventions, but I couldn't attend the Chamber of Commerce functions. As a matter of fact, I represented the company at most major black functions, receptions, and dinners. At the few nonminority functions they allowed me to attend, they introduced me to only a small number of people who, by the way, were all black. Those were the functions where they needed to showcase the one black woman on staff. Was I upset? You're darn right. But I also was a hypocrite. I wanted the privilege that went with being a minority, but sometimes I didn't do anything to earn those privileges. Now, we all know the days of being a token are over. But what we need to do is stop worrying about being equal, and learn how to be better. It's time for us to move on and get with the program."

"You are so right. Tokenism had its benefits," the marketing director recalls. "It offered visibility. It gave certain black workers exposure and presented them with new opportunities to develop. It worked when a company used it to correct a practice of keeping blacks from moving up the organization. It failed when a company employed it as a tactic to cover up discrimination. But some of us got caught up in the privileges of that period and grew dependent on what someone else was doing. A lot of blacks yell about black empowerment but become all unbent when the government says it's going to take something away from us. That I can't understand. We need to learn how to first help ourselves. You can ask for a hand up, without looking like you always have your hands out. There is a difference."

"This might be a little off the track of what we're talking about, but my problems in the workplace all have to do with black people," the accountant says about black/black relationships. "I have a dual heritage, in the sense that my father is white and my mother is black. I struggle with blacks who often call me an Oreo because I have white friends. They also suggest that I've sold myself to the other side, or make me feel like I'm supposed to pick sides. Blacks cry about prejudice and discrimination as if it's a whites-only act. But look how we treat each other. We're the real racists, as well. I never used to be able to say this, but I get along with whites better than blacks. Blacks say and do things to each other that we would never do to a white coworker. We say anything to each other, and we say it loud. It doesn't matter who's around."

A health care administrator agrees. "You know, we don't need white people to pull us down. Blacks do it to each other. When I was promoted to my position, some of my former black coworkers called me one day and asked if I was getting lighter. At first I thought they must be kidding, but they weren't. Then I got mad. It seems that as soon as some of us get to the top, other blacks dream up charges against those who are making it. I think some of us don't want to see our sisters succeed. We also have unrealistic expectations of blacks in management. We think because a black has moved up that we're supposed to hire everyone who is black. Remember the seventies when a lot of blacks were getting into Islam? Every time a brother tried to sell me a *Mohammed Speaks* or a bean pie, he called me sister. But I would always tell them that having black skin doesn't make anyone a sister or a brother."

"You're on the money," an administrative assistant comments. "Why is there such a disconnection in the sisterhood? Black women used to be more supportive, but we're at each other all the time. Whites will be mad with each other at ten, and go out to lunch together at twelve. Not black people. Mad at ten, we're mad for life. And when a sister dresses nice, we says she thinks she's cute. Or, we try to pull each other down. I'm going back to school, but most of my black friends, who only have a high school education, ask my why I'm doing it or question what it's going to get me. There's a black woman in management who has been helping me, and I'm proud of where she is. But my friends call her the Head Nigger In Charge and say that she doesn't deserve her job. When I ask why, they say she thinks she's white."

A systems analyst talks about the self-help issue. "We're just so defensive. We act like we loathe each other. Some of the dark sisters don't like the light sisters, and vice versa. The educated blacks don't like the uneducated blacks. And what does that really get us? I am truly, truly happy that the government is trying to do away with quotas and affirmative action. We don't need them. We need to stop worrying about what others are doing and work on ourselves. Many of you think working for a white company is a struggle, but try working for an all-black company. I go through many of the same things that some black women experience in white companies. I can't afford to wait around for someone to do something for me. A lot of us think help has to begin with someone else, and I disagree. I've changed my thinking. And I'm feeling and doing better because of my positive attitude."

"I would like to add something else," another secretary says. "I think blacks, and anyone else who is not treated fairly, should fight for what is right. I don't think that we should ignore the obstacles that are put in front of us. But we have to make sure that what we think is happening isn't just in our mind. We can't worry about what others think of us. We should focus on what we know to be true within ourselves. We need to get it together, and get serious about our work lives."

A nurse had the last word. "I know our time's up, but I just had to say something. I used to think that everything was about blacks versus whites. I, too, have shifted my thinking. If you want to say I'm a part of the new conservative black, I won't argue with you. Please, though, just hear me out. I used to be very militant, and my mouth always got me in trouble. I refused to listen to anyone who suggested that blacks need to look at themselves. I thought there was only one truth about how black people can get ahead, affirmative action. I can't remember when, but I started reading books and articles written by other blacks who were advocating self-help. It made sense. Self-help should come first. Obviously, if affirmative action was working we wouldn't be complaining. So, I've decided that I'd rather get things on my own and stop using the white excuse for where I'm not. I remember hearing Maya Angelou once say, 'It takes courage to recreate yourself every day.' She's right, and each of us has to start concentrating on our personal development, figure out what we want, and move forward. Our career isn't always going to be what we want it to be, but we can work on it."

As the seminar came to a close, we came to terms with why some black female executives were hesitant to discuss or respond to our requests for an interview concerning their triumphs and troubles in the workplace. When they didn't return our numerous calls, or answer our letters, they left us with the impression that talking about issues affecting black women might not be a good idea. We wondered if they feared we were doing an expose for "20/20" or "A Current Affair." We concluded that they may feel it is safer to keep the door closed—a type of denial laced with the fear that discussing racial matters would open a Pandora's box.

One entrepreneur, who initially consented to sharing her success story, was advised by her agent that it might not be in the best interest of her business. We honored her request to pull her story. Another executive from a Fortune 100 company responded to our call with this one statement: "There's nothing I could possibly offer to black women, so I suggest that you find someone else." One other said she "neither had the time nor the inclination to address something that should probably be left alone." When we tried to contact the President and CEO of a firm she founded, her secretary expressed surprise that we had not heard from her boss. She said, "You mean, she hasn't responded? I did give her your package. I'll talk to her again." A week later, we made a second call only to be told by the same secretary, "I did give her the message. Look, I'm really sorry. Don't take it personally. Maybe you can find someone more willing." A government administrator agreed to talk with us, but on a personal level. She said, "I still have a job to keep, but I'd love to talk with you off the record. I have seen a lot and have my own theories about the lack of success of black women. And some black people might not like what I have to say."

Unreturned call after call, we felt letdown and confused. We couldn't pinpoint the problem. Were these women resistive based on selfishness or fear? Eventually, one of the executives who was also featured in a major black magazine seemed to offer us the answer. We asked her the same question that we had addressed in our correspondence to others. She said, "I understand why you're contacting women like me. There are fewer and fewer of us who meet the qualifications to get to the top. Therefore, people often want to know how we feel. So, that I can make the corporation happy, I need to first set some ground rules. I will give you my personal time, but I need to let you know that I have indicated to my company that I will not talk about this anymore." When we asked her why her company would have problems with her giving advice on her triumphs and troubles, as well as how other black women can get to the top, she said, "They feel it's not good, for public relations purposes." Six times we scheduled phone interviews with her subsequent to that conversation. Either she was out of the office or said she was on another line or in a meeting. The last time, she contacted us to schedule the appointment. When we called her, she said she had just picked up our number and would call back in five minutes. To this day, we have never heard from her.

As time moved on, we heard from famous black women whose time commitments did not allow us to conduct interviews with them, but who sent short notes encouraging us to write this book. We did hear from seven of the women who had graced the pages of major black publications; and many others, whose stories have never been told, you will read about throughout the book.

Betty Winston Baye
Columnist and Editorial Writer
Courier-Journal
Louisville, Kentucky

When I was a girl, I had my fantasies, but one fantasy I never had was that one day my prince would come, and I'd be spared the need to work.

But I'm not complaining.

I believe my parents did absolutely the right thing in preparing me to work and take care of myself.

So, I'm a working woman and proud of it.

I leave it to others to judge whether I'm successful or not. But ask if I'm happy and fulfilled as a writer and journalist, and you'd get an unqualified yes. And, what makes me happiest is knowing that God isn't done with me yet.

Advice?

First, understand that your personal and professional happiness isn't up to your bosses, your coworkers, your family, friends, or even whomever you're in love with at the moment. Whether you're fulfilled is up to you, especially if you've made the choice to do what you're doing. As for me, I decided some time ago that when what I'm doing no longer fulfills me, I'm going to take the necessary steps and make whatever sacrifices are needed to find something else to do, even if that means going back to school, getting a second job, or doing volunteer work.

Racism and sexism?

My sisters, I consider these twin, despicable, evil givens, that have little possibility of being eliminated in my lifetime. Meanwhile, there is no doubt that racism and sexism will slow you down. But, you simply cannot afford to let them stop you dead in your tracks. If the situation is real bad, sue. But if it's something you can get a handle on, handle it by doing all you can to get around and over the perpetrators.

Perhaps, I'm old-fashioned, but to me being black and female simply means I've got to get up earlier, jump higher, and run faster. Of course, it isn't fair, but then, nobody ever promised me a rose garden.

Now, let me say that being a writer isn't my first career. I've spent most of my adult life as a clerical worker. For about four years in the late sixties, I dabbled in the arts, thinking that I wanted to be an actress. Actually, I had hoped to become a diva. Unfortunately, I realized that I simply didn't love acting enough to devote the energy required to be good. Regardless of what show business seems to be from afar, it's hard work, and what separates the women from the girls is one's willingness to strike a balance between show and business.

But until the late 1970s, my primary goal was to be the baddest secretary or administrative assistant a boss could have. In that field, I could be a diva. If I ever left a job, I did so under my own steam, and always believed that if need be, my excellent track record would make it possible for me to return.

Because I had only a high school diploma when I did clerical work, I had to labor doubly hard to convince my mostly college-educated bosses, who over the years were black and white and male and female, that they needed me. I did things to get noticed. For example, I didn't always race for the door when workdays officially ended, and sometimes, as much as I hate getting up, I'd come to work early on weekends. But whether early or late, I was constantly absorbing information. I wanted to be informed, but I also wanted to be in positions to anticipate what my bosses might need. I also volunteered for special projects, not because I just loved working, but because I wanted to develop additional skills, get broader exposure, impress the higher-ups, and cultivate my growing reputation as a go-getter.

I had a work ethic that I brought with me from childhood. Fortunately, it was that work ethic and my willingness to give every task the best I could that resulted in me getting good secretarial positions that included travel. I got proficient at organizing meetings, conferences, banquets, and fund-raisers. In time, my bosses literally couldn't say no when I scouted out training opportunities and asked them to pay for it.

Advice?

Always—but *always*—ask people above you how they got there and what they think you can do to move yourself. Secure people actually are quite flattered knowing that you respect their achievements. And don't just ask questions, but really be interested and listen to those who've already traveled down the road you want to go.

Another thing, don't just have one mentor, but plenty in various fields, as well as mentors, maybe parents, grandparents, or old aunts and uncles, who have no fields at all, but who've got old-fashioned common sense. And never let a mentor drift out of your life if you can help it. Stay in touch even if it appears that person's area of expertise isn't precisely relevant to whatever you're doing or aspiring to do at the time.

If you're serious about having a career instead of just a job, it's important to get some college, and preferably at least one degree, under your belt. Of course, there are successful people who've never gone to college, but that is getting to be less and less true. The fact is that it's a jungle out there in the professional world. And, my dear sister, you'll find out quickly, if you don't already know, that your blackness, your cuteness, your determination, your eagerness, and even your willingness to work your butt off sometimes aren't enough to get the door of opportunity cracked. What you need is something, like a degree, to help give you an edge, or at least a fighting chance against the competition that increasingly will be college-educated or bilingual. It really is a whole new ball game, and a corporation can easily have its "quota" of "minorities," and yet not have one African American.

Although a college degree may not land you precisely the job or career you want right away, simply being in an environment where higher education is going on is likely to put you in touch with people who are at least thinking big things even if they haven't achieved them yet.

One other thing: Ignore the "dream killers." I'm talking about people, some of them well-meaning, who'll tell you what you "can't do" and what you can't dream. If you absorb such ideas, you're dead in the water and no matter how bright you are, how many degrees you have, or how many languages you speak, you'll lose out.

Finally, my sisters, I wish you luck. Remember, that swimming in the mainstream ain't easy. But think about this: Nothing about being black in America has ever been easy. Yet, our people have persevered; survived; and some have even thrived. The most important thing is to believe in yourself!

Sincerely,

Betty Winston Baye

Jacqui Gates
Director, New York Metro Customer Management Organization
NYNEX Mobile Communications Corporation
Orangeburg, New York

I just had to get my pen and write to you about the latest. Although I've lived forty very full years, I'm always amazed at how the process of learning continues. And despite my fourteen years in the corporate sector, I see the "D" in discrimination is still capitalized. I guess what hurts the most is that our brothers are still underestimating what we bring to the table. When will they take us seriously?

Just recently I was in the midst of a "benchmarking" discussion—you know, what we used to call corporate networking—and a very talented and seasoned brother, who is with a Baldridge award-winning company, was giving me some hints on how to structure my new telemarketing organization. I shared with him a couple of strategies that I had implemented during my first two months of directing this department, and he marveled by saying, "I see Cliff (my husband) trained you right." W E L L!!! It was as though I was jolted into a state of reality:

—the reality of 1980 was the black male corporate director who promoted a white male with similar credentials and lousy interpersonal skills over me.

—the reality of 1984 was my promotion to a key corporate position and the black male retiring vice president was nonsupportive because I was a young, multi-talented and well-liked black female who was his heir apparent.

—the reality of 1989 was when the one white male who, for ten years had been like a brother both personally and professionally, allowed his boss, a white female who has a reputation as a foe of people of color, to make him choose between her and me (and you know he looked out for himself...)

The reality is support between genders is not always a given. AND YES, FACING REALITY HURTS! It hurts because despite my achievements and/or contributions I'm constantly being measured by a yardstick that differs from the norm. YOU KNOW WHAT I MEAN...

> Commitment to career is neglect to family.
> Sisterhood differs from brotherhood.
> Paying dues is always a longer duration.

I can remember when I first graduated from college with a Bachelor's of Art's degree, a.k.a. the key to open all future doors. It took five months before a professional door opened for me as a family counselor. And of course, that door opened because of "who I knew" or as one of my mentors phrases it, "who knows you." After four years of working for a non-profit community-based organization, I learned about the corporate world. Little did I know that transitioning from the public sector to the private sector would be no easy task. So after rigorous networking coupled with the understanding that I possessed "transferable" skills I found an ideal opportunity at a company that had an effective affirmative action officer willing to interview me. My success thereafter was because of my ability to stretch myself beyond the confines of a job description. I volunteered for company-sponsored employee activities and always accepted special assignments aimed at targeted business goals. Volunteering automatically increased my visibility, widened my base of knowledge and complemented my technical expertise. My presence always mirrors my positive attitude, which is characterized by: faith, hope, optimism, courage, initiative, generosity, tolerance, tact, and kindliness.

But since I have chosen the corporate sector to spend a significant portion of my work life, I have had to also learn how to play the game. I have accepted the fact that as an African American I have to live between two worlds. At first, I thought I had to exist between two worlds—one white, one black. But as my maturity evolves, I cannot ignore the "world of woman" that impacts my entire survival, both personally and professionally.

Personally, I strive to be a role model for my daughters and the female protégées that I have been blessed to mentor. Our relationships have been built on honesty so that they will always expect the bitter as well as the sweet. To my son and the numerous young men whom I have counseled, I solicit a consistent level of respect that can be extended to all women in their lives.

To my mate, I share the African proverb, "I am because we are. We are because I am."

Professionally, there is no simple formula for a black woman's success. However, if we can acknowledge that life's not fair and if we take the profile for success and wrap it in a subtle cover of femininity, never trade away our caretaker instinct nor our legacy of spiritual strength and survival, we too *will* rise!!! But unless we rise united—pushing one another, lifting one another—success will not be ours to celebrate.

By the way, did you implement the quality initiative we last discussed?

I'm anxious to hear the results.

Sincerely,

Jacquelyn (Jacqui) Gates

Chapter 2

THE BURDEN OF HER COLOR

Let's clear the air. We are not combative reactionaries, ready to fly off the handle at any moment. We are not hostile to corporations. We are not raging feminists. Nor are we anti-white or anti-men. To find clues to the issues concerning black women in the workplace, we went to the source—the workplace. We asked you, black women from every sector of the business community, "What happened? How did your career get to where it is?"

Some Facts and Projections About Black Working Women

- Historically, black women have worked outside the home and as a means of survival.
- One out of every two black women is in the U.S. labor force. Currently, there are over six million black working women. By the year 2000, that number will increase to over 8.5 million.
- Black women represent the major segment of black employment.
- Black women can expect to spend 27.8 years of their lives in the labor force.
- Black women are the lowest paid race/sex subgroup.
- Of all black working mothers, 53 percent are living in poverty.
- Black women, on average, spend only 16 years of their expected lifetime of 74 years with a husband, primarily due to divorce or separation.
- Black women are less likely to remarry.
- Black women are more likely to be married to a black man who is not college-educated. In addition, because black men make considerably

less than their white counterparts, black women (when married to a black man) tend to be key contributors to the finances of their household.

• Nearly three out of four divorced black women are working or looking for work. In addition, black divorced women have the highest labor force participation rate among all black women.

• Over half of all black women are employed in clerical and service occupations.

• During the past decade, the largest sources of employment for black women were as retail sales workers, nursing aides, secretaries, cashiers, cooks, elementary school teachers, janitors and cleaners. Excluding elementary school teachers, these occupations offer low pay, require little training or few skills, demand little work experience, and offer very limited chances for advancement.

• Black women make up only 3 percent of corporate management and less than 1 percent of female corporate officers.

• Of the most lucrative occupations (lawyers, physicians, engineers, computer systems analysts, scientists, teachers at colleges and universities, managers in marketing, advertising, and public relations, natural scientists, and registered nurses) for women in 1990, only 2.5 percent of the total persons in these occupations were women. Among all women employed in these jobs, only 6.6 percent were black women.

• Black women account for only 1 percent of the over four million total persons employed in the skilled trades. When employed in the trades, they are likely to be working as electrical and electronic equipment assemblers, butchers, meat cutters or dressmakers.

• Less than 20 percent of all black employed women, sixteen years or older, have completed four or more years of college.

• Black women with a college degree are more likely to advance and experience low levels of unemployment, compared to less educated black women.

• The median income gap between white and black college-educated women workers has widened over the past decade, from the early 80's through today.

• Compared to white women, black women are more likely:
  – to be employed
  – to have less education
  – to earn less per week
  – to head their household

- to assume more financial responsibility and work outside the home, when married
- to live in poverty with their children (in fact, black working mothers are three times as likely as white women to be living in poverty)
- to hold down clerical jobs
- to remain in marriages for fewer years
- to work after the birth of their first child

Source: Bureau of Labor Statistics, Department of Labor
        Bureau of the Census
        National Urban League
        Wider Opportunities for Women

Our burden is a heavy one to bear.

We learned that many of us experience more troubles than triumphs in our work life. It seemed that what others considered bitterness was really disillusionment. A number of you expressed concerns that black women are not taken seriously. You feel:

★ you pass through corporations unacknowledged and unnoticed
★ isolated and lonely
★ your uneasiness is often seen as defensiveness
★ your distrust has nothing to do with having bad attitudes or being unapproachable

These feelings, you explained, are due to your uncertainty and wariness concerning your chances of advancement. Yes, some of you seemed angry. Perhaps, because you feel unheard. You are angry because of the silence; mad that you feel compelled to hold it in; and steaming because no one has ever asked how you and other black working women really feel.

A BLACK WOMAN'S LADDER

Not everyone understands the ladder that you climb. As a black woman, you must be twice as good to get on the first step and twice as good to move up it. Your career ladder is steep, and it's long. You're not allowed to skip steps. And when you climb, you often find it necessary to watch your back.

Of the five hundred black working women we interviewed, almost all feel the way you do. They are underemployed and say that advancement is denied them because they are black. They also revealed that black women are more likely to be subjected to the double burden of their race and gender. Interviews with black female managers revealed comments similar to this one:

> "I sense regardless of how well I perform on my job, I can never do enough to convince my white coworkers that I am just as competent. I did not expect the fact that I am black to be a barrier. Management at my company was reluctant to accept blacks at any level."

Dissatisfaction with career advancement and opportunities is not limited to black females at management levels. Nonmanagers interviewed spoke about high levels of frustration. When asked about their perceptions of their career status and mobility, 72 percent of the women surveyed shared they are not where they want to be. Nearly 80 percent said they think their chances of advancement are poor. All expressed a need for strategies for surviving in the workplace. The following comments are also illustrative of the feelings other black women reported:

> "We are treated in a menial way. In our office most of the blacks are in dead-end positions. It is like we are invisible people."

> "In my agency, white women with only a high school education have become managers and supervisors while black women with undergraduate degrees remain line workers."

> "My manager is a first-class chauvinist and is preparing for the day when the South will rise again. He has shown us time and time again that black women will not move out of clerical positions."

BEYOND RACE AND COLOR

Someone might ask you, what's all the commotion about? After all, weren't you offered equal opportunity and affirmative action? Why are you feeling that you can't get ahead? Is the real story that you aren't advancing because you don't know how to survive?

Before we could talk about strategies for survival, we decided to scratch the surface and go beyond race and color. We conducted one thousand surveys. We interviewed black women everywhere—in our travels, at bus stops, airports, and during our workshops—we even encouraged relatives and friends to break their silence. We made one request, however. We didn't want to hear only about how race or discrimination is holding us back. We wanted the "big" picture to piece together all the reasons why black working women feel they aren't taking command of their careers.

THE TROUBLE WITH BEING BLACK AND A WORKING WOMAN

Well, we asked for it, and you gave it to us. We heard everything from personal to political reasons, with racial barriers leading the pack. So here they are, the thirty-five most common complaints, those you said are behind black women's troubles in the workplace:

Racial Barriers:

▶ Companies put blacks on different career tracks.
▶ Inequities and special treatment are given to others.
▶ The system promotes economic and class racism.
▶ Black women are seldom given positions with decision-making power.
▶ Information, guidance and opportunities are deliberately withheld from blacks.
▶ Blacks are not given the same chances because of the perception that we are inferior.
▶ We're black-balled once we speak up about the problems of racism and discrimination.
▶ Those who have power are hesitant to be seen helping blacks.
▶ Blacks blame too much on race and not enough on ourselves.
▶ Carryovers from slavery: absence of trust in anyone who is white.

Personal Problems:

▶ We're complacent and play it too safe.
▶ We allow pride to keep us from asking for help.
▶ We are handicapped by quota systems and affirmative action.

▶ We have poor interpersonal skills.
▶ We allow family commitments and relationships to limit our success.
▶ We have low self-esteem and poor self-images.
▶ We have negative and defensive attitudes, as well as tend to personalize everything that happens.
▶ We lack finances and other resources.
▶ We tend to depend on others to get us ahead.
▶ We have poor follow-through.

Unprofessional Development:

▶ We're not risk takers.
▶ We're fearful and insecure about our ability to perform.
▶ We don't want responsibilities that go along with moving up.
▶ We don't take advantage of what's around us.
▶ We lack written career goals.
▶ We're unclear about what we want, so we tend to stumble forward.
▶ We don't stay on top of what's going on within the organization or our industry.
▶ We don't keep our skills current.
▶ We don't have business maturity.
▶ We don't recognize the importance of mentors and networking.

Cultural Hurdles:

▶ "Crab Syndrome": We are unwilling to support each other.
▶ We struggle with the differences between where we work and where we live.
▶ We are not aware of our own prejudices.
▶ We are not skilled in adapting to a different environment.
▶ We are not understood by other races.
▶ We feel uncomfortable being black in mostly white workplaces.
▶ We are expected to be hypocrites to our race.

You might think, with such sad conditions surrounding black women, that we are trying to discourage you or make you feel your situation is hopeless. In fact, we hope you'll feel just the opposite. If you do find yourself feeling anything but encouraged, then we urge you to keep on reading. While many books were written on how to succeed in the workplace, none addresses the driving and restraining forces of minorities, especially African American working women.

One study did, in fact, address these forces. The Executive Leadership Council in 1991 released a study of fifty senior African American executives, over 70 percent of whom are employed by Fortune 500 executives, and with annual incomes ranging from $100,000 to $700,000. Most of us couldn't imagine making that kind of money. In addition, you may think that such executives, regardless of their color, should have few, if any, problems getting ahead in the workplace. But they did. Before we tell you about their problems, here's some background information about the study's executives:

- The majority of these executives started their careers in government, the military, and education.
- 40 percent said no blacks serve on their company's board of directors; 44 percent said there was only one; 6 percent said two or three.
- Most provided the following factors as contributing to their success:
  — parental relationships, especially with mother
  — level of education
  — religion and church involvement
  — early family experiences
  — community involvement
  — participating in organized social activities, like youth organizations, sororities, and fraternities.

While most of the executives didn't get to the top "by any means necessary," they did define the following forces as having a great impact on their success:

DRIVING FORCES

Corporate Life—The executives identified the most critical skills needed by African Americans to succeed as:

★ the ability to communicate to "bridge cultural gaps, overcome racial obstacles, and gain acceptance by their white counterparts"
★ the ability to lead, to "exert influence" to avoid backlashes and labels such as "pushy," "too aggressive," "difficult to work with," and "going too far"
★ the ability to use interpersonal skills to establish "trust and comfort" and "overcome the barriers of being perceived as 'different' and to be recognized as capable of accomplishing corporate assignments"

★ the ability to understand the organization environment to recognize the true "power brokers" and the "culture." The female executives indicated this ability is also necessary for those of us in "company environments that are not supportive of female executives, especially those laden with double standards and preconceived ideas regarding the capability of women to do the job."

★ the ability to work hard and be ambitious to not only "prove their worth but survive in competitive corporate environments"

Personal Life—The executives identified the most critical aspects of personal life to help African Americans to succeed as:

★ Core Values and Ethics—The participants said these must be based on a "sense of responsibility, honesty, trust, integrity, and a strong work ethic."

★ Early Family and Social Experiences—The study participants indicated that these are key to "developing and nurturing their strong value system, their drive for education, appreciation for hard work, and their self-sufficiency."

★ Education and Experience—The study participants emphasized that "education is the key to opportunity, achievement, and a successful career."

★ Health—The executives pointed out that good health promotes a "sense of well being" and enables them to cope with the stresses of the workplace.

Community Life—The executives identified the most critical aspects of community life to enable African Americans to succeed as:

★ Strong Sense of Community with the African American Community—They stressed that this is key to their ability to "balance their personal life with corporate responsibilities."

RESTRAINING FORCES

Corporate Life—The executives identified the most critical aspects of corporate life that hinder African Americans from succeeding as:

★ **Racism**—The executives said that the racism they experienced tends to be subtle and kept hidden by the individuals who practiced it in their organizations. They also described it as "elusive and heavily masked."

★ **Sexism**—The executives said that sexism usually takes the form of "old boys' networks," "concrete ceilings," "derailment," and "pay differentials."

★ **Old Boys' Network**—The executives talked about being on the outside of informal and formal information networks. The network, they said, was nothing more than a means of excluding African Americans from "receiving information, participating in informal decision-making, and gaining the competitive edge because they do not live in the same community, ride the train together, belong to the same country club or play golf together as members of the network."

★ **Concrete Ceiling**—Most executives felt that the African Americans who break the "concrete ceiling" are the ones who have worked in their corporations for years, built strong ties with their colleagues and key decision makers, and whose ways and behavior most closely mirror the culture of the organization in which they work.

★ **Derailment**—The study participants referred to derailment as being "passed over for promotion each time a position is available." The most commonly cited reasons for derailment, they said, are perceptions that an African American does not fit in or is not ready to move up. Another study of nineteen top executives (conducted by McCall and Lombardo in 1983) gave reasons such as "personal flaws, including insensitivity, arrogance, overambition, betrayal of trust and managerial inadequacies such as overmanaging, poor staffing, inability to think strategically."

★ **Pay Differentials**—When you compare women to men, or minorities to majority workers, the executives said gaps will usually be found. This, they said, often leaves them with feelings of frustration and anger that affects their productivity.

★ **Restructuring and Downsizing**—It was interesting to learn that the executives felt that exposure to "old boy networks" and favoritism often made them more vulnerable to experiencing layoffs, "concrete ceilings," or derailment.

★ **Company Culture**—Descriptions by the executives of their corporate culture ranged from actively supportive to unsupportive, unyielding, lonely, covertly racist, to a sense of isolation, of being the "only one."

Personal Life—The executives identified the most critical aspects of personal life that hinder African Americans from succeeding as:

★ **Value Conflicts**—The executives talked about feeling caught between two worlds. They also described their struggle to find a marriage between black culture and corporate culture. They referred to conflicts "between not wanting to be too isolated from African American support systems and needing to be accepted by and fit in with the individuals who can facilitate or restrain their corporate advancement."

★ **Generalist vs. Specialist**—The executives also emphasized that "there is a tendency in some corporations to limit African Americans to staff areas of responsibility, thus precluding their preparation for the top corporate positions." They also indicated that "one generally moves up the ranks from junior to middle to senior management within a specialized skill area. However, the higher up one goes, the more one needs to acquire general management skills."

★ **Health Issues**—"The effects of smoking, drinking, lack of exercise, being overweight, and not getting sufficient rest" were the concerns mentioned most often.

Family Life—The executives identified the most critical aspects of family life that hinder African Americans from succeeding as:

★ **Hard Work and Long Hours**—The executives stressed that this interfered with their ability to maintain harmonious marital relationships and raise children. Concern was also expressed regarding "the breakdown of the family structure in America and the need for African American executives to help counteract this trend in their homes and communities."

Community Life—The executives identified the most critical aspects of community life that hinder African Americans from succeeding as:

★ **Geographical Isolation from an African American Community**—A number of executives shared that it's a lonely world in their corporations, because they are removed from black communities, support systems, and cultural activities that the black community normally provides. Some of the executives admitted that having been in such a situation before, they would not put their family through the experience again.

★ **Demands Placed on Them by the African American Community—** Some of the executives referred to this as the "black tax." They indicated that the black community often has expectations of black achievers that are not easily met because of the competing demands of a hectic worklife.

WHAT CAN YOU DO ABOUT YOUR DRIVING AND RESTRAINING FORCES?

Over a four-year period, thousands of black women in the Washington, DC, area have passed through our workshops, which have covered a number of topics from "Taking Charge of Your Career" to "Turning Your Image Around." Along the way we met some women who really didn't have any idea about what they wanted in a career, much less how to go about developing one. A large majority felt they were losing ground in both their personal and professional lives because of the burden of their color.

We wrote this book to help you look at the driving and restraining forces that are specific to black women's career success. In the study we conducted, we found that many black women have more restraining than driving forces operating in their life. Not only is this book intended to help you develop some driving forces but to help you find the best ways to knock down the restraining forces that are obstacles to your advancing career.

Twenty Out, Twenty In

Perhaps you brought the wrong attitude to the workplace. Maybe you joined the workforce like a naive soldier thinking, "Twenty in, twenty out," not expecting "front line" treatment, casualties, or losses. When problems occurred you thought, "I'm a black woman. How can they do this to me?"

Unpleasant events will occur in your life as a black woman. The burden of color is often present. And when it is, it can be a very hurtful experience, triggering so many emotions we didn't know were with us: Self-doubt. Confusion. Anger. Fear.

We feel we have to put up with so much. We want to talk about it, but we feel no one will listen. There's also the other side of our problems, the things that we bring upon ourselves. But we tend to blame some of our failures on others. Yet, what other people do to you doesn't let you off the hook. You can't get ahead by laying every problem of yours at someone else's feet. You owe it to yourself to assume **all** your rights to a successful career. If you do not take an active role in your career, don't assume someone else will help you get ahead.

Patricia Russell-McCloud
Attorney/Professional Orator
President, Russell-McCloud & Associates
Atlanta, Georgia

If there's one driving force that has propelled my career from a law clerk, to Senior Managing Attorney and Chief of the Complaints Branch, Broadcast Bureau, at the FCC, to becoming a sought-after, hard-hitting public speaker, and establishing my own firm, it's this: **I didn't wait to be chosen!**

Black women are often taught that we can move only into predesignated slots. We're thankful to be selected as vice president, but don't focus upon being the president. We also don't consider that if we are effective as someone's left or right arm that we are just as capable of becoming the woman in charge.

I felt this same way, for a long time. I wasn't venturesome or visionary. I believed that it was enough to just remain in a good, government job. But that attitude wasn't productive to my career. At the same time, I looked around and observed that white males had their own club and requirements for inclusion. By the way they interacted, I knew it was a closed society and that I would have to find my own way to the top.

Forced to deal with this hard-core reality, I became more intentional about my pursuits. I stopped playing it safe, approached my boss, asked for what I wanted, and requested the training to become a manager. From then on, I decided that I wasn't going to spend my life responding to someone else's agenda. I also regretted that I had not demonstrated more courage earlier. If I had, my climb could have been reduced by several years.

I put my FCC years behind me, in 1983. I was tired of being in the "first and only" category. And being tired of working for somebody else made me do something about it. I was confident that I could put to use in my own business the same skills that I had used at the agency. So, I took risks and stepped out of my comfort zone. I asked myself, "Pat, are you bad enough to risk what you have to, to do something on your own?" I answered yes.

You might say that was a heavy burden to place on myself. Yes and no. I didn't expect to fail. I knew that I was a gifted orator and had mastered the spoken word, as a lawyer and since the age of eight, speaking nationally at churches and numerous other forums. That gift was my advertisement and gave me my introduction as an informative and inspiring speaker on a diversity of subjects.

I often tell aspiring professionals that "in the cool of the evening, when you lay your head next to your pillow, I want you to be satisfied with your life." While it has its twists and turns, somewhere in your life you should have a sense of oneness with your self. Don't focus on systems that may block you, but empower yourself with the proper mindset. Be introspective, and get rid of the "what if's." Ask yourself where you really want to be, and go for it.

First, identify the places, positions, and opportunities in the work place that you desire. Align yourself with someone who can help you. Articulate where you want to be. Make sacrifices, and take tougher assignments. Remember, you have to be viewed as making a contribution that your organization can't do without. Finally recognize that everyone's not your cheerleader and that the pie doesn't get larger in the workplace. There are just more people clamoring for it. So, don't let anyone keep you from getting your share. Follow your dream. Time is at your heels.

Sincerely,

Patricia Russell-McCloud

Chapter 3

THE SURVIVAL
CHALLENGE

A Chinese proverb says women hold up half the sky. As a black working woman, you feel as though your sky is falling. Until now, navigating your career has been everything but smooth sailing. At times, you pull into the wrong ports or declare mutiny when others try to capsize your career. Even when you jump ship, you discover the waters are rough and more than you can handle. Other times, you dropped anchor, fearful of making a move. "Help," you cried. "Can a black woman survive in the workplace?"

When you think about it, career success depends on the means of your survival. You have to work with what you have, even when what you have doesn't seem like much. There is so much to worry about: looking with your eyes, but seeing with your mind; thinking and deciding; the doing; figuring out what others are doing; and making sure the right person sees you. It really comes down to looking out for your own well-being, even when your career is limited by the kind of job you hold or the amount of your paycheck.

YOU'RE NOT ALONE

In a national study conducted by the National Career Development Association, 79 percent of black Americans surveyed said they would seek more information about their careers if they were starting over. 46 percent reported experiencing job stress, and indicated that they perceived some form of discrimination on the job. Obviously, you're not alone. Both black men and black women are seeking career solutions and the key to a successful climb in the workplace.

The Stresses of Survival

There are a number of books written about how to succeed in the workplace. None, however, discusses the stresses that are unique to black working women. Your personal life, home, work, time, and a lot of other things, are the kinds of stresses that may hamper your career mobility. You try to cope with the clouds that are over you. But it's not easy, is it? Every time you think your career is surviving, there's a tug of uncertainty. You convince yourself that you are holding up. You're employed and giving a job your best, although you're not really where you want to be. You feel you're either placed at the bottom of the totem pole or given positions without the responsibility that goes with the title—a job in name only. Your career clock ticks always, yet you haven't gone anywhere. You stand in line waiting for your name to be called. Only your turn never comes. You think about looking for a new place to work. You tell yourself that anywhere is better than where you are. But then, here comes the uncertainty again. Do you stay, or do you go? You wonder if you're really hanging on instead of holding on. Your mind seems undecided. You become a desperate job seeker, grabbing at anything you can find. Your worklife becomes an "around the world" journey. Something isn't right. What is it that you really want? And why aren't you already there? You take a deep breath, but are confused. You didn't realize things had gotten to the point that you need to do something different. Maybe you should have known better. You realize you've been working in a state of denial. You know you're trying. Aren't you?

The Survival Challenge

You're probably wondering what survival has to do with work. One reason is that your career hasn't landed. Second, you don't have a choice. You survive, or your career dies. The hardest part is when you don't know what to do. Emotionally and spiritually you may already feel drained. Your brief moment of hope has faded. You don't know how to play the game, much less follow the rules of the road. At the same time, someone may be running interference without your knowing it. You start asking yourself the universal why: Why don't I fit in? Why don't people accept me? Why am I losing my identity? Why are there so many boundaries? Why aren't my needs being met? And, why doesn't anyone respect my values?

Well, there are no simple answers. To survive, you've got to make it through the journey, and learn how to persist "in spite of." That means you have to keep moving on and plowing your way through. Sadly, you're still searching for the place where you and your career parted company, or trying to figure out why it never came together. You know you should do something, instead of harping on the problem. It's now or never. Take the time to start identifying the conditions that are keeping you down and preventing you from becoming a runaway success.

CONDITIONS THAT MAY HINDER YOUR SURVIVAL

You've got a number of things coming at you in all directions. Then, there's you. You have to have the will to survive and the conviction to endure a tough journey. You need to be healthy, both physically and mentally. If you're not up to it, you're not going to make it through the journey. You may already be tired of being allowed to hold only certain positions, being left out of major decisions, not having access to key information, not receiving equitable pay, or working for companies that claim they are doing things right (but aren't doing the right thing).

1. *Your Condition*
   Are you in condition to make the journey Your career may be in trouble because you're not together. You're not ready to move up, much less change jobs. You have some unfinished business, only it's with yourself. You're fed up, yet you're also playing the victim. In addition, your employer was fed up with you long before you became tired of the job. Physically, your image needs an overall inspection. Psychologically, you are emotionally down, and you can't handle it when race becomes an issue. You feel isolated, insecure, frustrated, or have low self-esteem. With the right attitude, you can replace what is lacking and change the areas that are not right in your life.

2. *Home And Work Conditions*
   You probably hear a lot about the balanced life. You may wish you had one. Home and work will affect your ability to satisfy your career needs, especially when an environment is not supportive of

your goals or when the two compete. If only you could just keep your personal life separate from your work life. But you feel pulled in two different directions. When it comes to your job, you also want to know if it's hostile inside. That's so you'll know how to prepare and what to expect. There are so many things to contend with, like the diversity of the culture, black and white issues, the mood in the office, personalities, the soundness of the company, finances, and conflicts between home and work. On top of that, you don't always know if you're going to be given a warm welcome or a cold reception. It makes coming to work more stressful. At times, you feel that staying at home has better appeal than going through the trouble of holding down a job. But when you're at home you often feel just the opposite.

3. *Time Conditions*

You may own one of those "round tuit" stickers. When something happens in your career, you tell yourself you'll get around to it when you can. You wait, and wait and wait. You may think there's no harm in waiting, but if you don't do anything about it now, your career will move on without you. Timing is everything when it comes to predicting your probability for success. The longer you wait to get it together, the worse off your career may be.

4. *Sociopolitical Conditions*

Politics and people. Two main ingredients to corporate success. Without the help of certain people, you won't get ahead. You have to learn how to play the game, distinguish friendly support from hostile support and watch for signs of those who are antagonistic to your success. Remember, just because you're paranoid doesn't mean no one's out to get you.

5. *Conditions You Bring Upon Yourself*

Think about who's the one behind your career troubles. It could be you. You may have a wrong attitude or be doing things which are putting your career at risk. On the other hand, other people may be hazardous to your success.

SO, HOW DO YOU SURVIVE?

Do you do something low-down and dirty, with the feeling that a black woman's got to do what she's got to do? Not really. The bottom line is you must take personal responsibility and own your own career. Although you're not powerless over others, you do have power over your career. And no one's going to take better care of it than you. While the black working women's problems do have a lot to do with the environment, people, or politics, we also lack self-empowerment.

Typically, black women who are not self-empowered:

1. Have unhealthy attitudes about themselves and lack self-confidence.
2. Stay trapped in unhappy jobs.
3. Were raised in families who feel a career is staying on a job until retirement.
4. Blame others for their failures.
5. Show reluctance to take risks.
6. Faced major setbacks in their personal life, especially in the areas of finance.
7. Are complacent and don't take a vested interest in their careers.
8. Never developed a written career plan.
9. Lack mentors and support systems.
10. Quit when they can't handle problems.
11. Lack business maturity and sophistication.
12. Are confused about what they want and how to execute a job search.
13. Either appear needy or put on an air that they don't need help.
14. Take sides against themselves.

Test Your Survival I.Q.

Do you (Check yes or no):

Yes No

- ☐ ☐ Have career goals that are only in your mind?
- ☐ ☐ Wait for others to tell you what to do or to help you get ahead?
- ☐ ☐ Feel confused about what you want?
- ☐ ☐ Believe that what you are doing isn't getting you to where you want to go?
- ☐ ☐ Lack self-confidence and feel unhappy about where you are?
- ☐ ☐ Allow your personal life to interfere with your goals?
- ☐ ☐ Pay little attention to how your actions are perceived by others?
- ☐ ☐ Worry about what others think of you?
- ☐ ☐ Feel other people are behind your lack of success?

☐ ☐ Stay in a bad mood or tend to feel irritable?
☐ ☐ Prefer to do things on your own, because you'd rather not involve other people in your business?
☐ ☐ Tend to react immediately to problems?
☐ ☐ Have difficulty admitting when you don't know something?
☐ ☐ Find it difficult to persist because you feel unnoticed or unacknowledged?
☐ ☐ Need help in understanding the corporate culture and office politics?
☐ ☐ Lack an ongoing informal or formal support system?
☐ ☐ Seldom network through organizations?
☐ ☐ Feel uncomfortable in situations where you're the only black?
☐ ☐ Need to turn your image around?
☐ ☐ Tend to leave jobs because of problems, rather than to pursue new opportunities?

Total number of yes statements checked _____
0–1   Go on, girl! You've got it together.
2–5   You're doing all right, but you have some room for improvement.
5–9   You're a borderline survivalist. You're walking on a very thin line. We'd get some help if we were you.
10–20   You've got a "dial 911" method of survival. Your career needs to be rescued.

Are You Sabotaging Your Chances of Survival?

Maybe you feel you're in good standing with your corporation. But if you're waiting for things to happen and guilty of unprofessional development, you're really not surviving. Sabotaging one's career isn't always a deliberate act, but you may be what's in its way. Things like going after dollars, poor follow-through, or not seeing signs that you're on the outs will interfere with your road to success. So will lack of follow-up, procrastination, or getting advice and not using it.

WAYS YOU MAY BE SABOTAGING YOUR CAREER

It's hard to be alert to what's going on around you when you refuse to take responsibility for your actions. Let's look at common ways black women allow race and other problems to get in the way of their career:

BLAME SHIFTING Sometimes, we blame the wrong person for our career's state of affairs. It's easier to say "It's them" then to say, "This one's on me," or "I'm the one at fault." We tend to shift the responsibility for our problems to someone else. It's another way of saying "It's not my fault," or "Not me." Blaming others allows us to use excuses like, "The problem with black folks is white folks," "I'm too old," "It's because I'm black," "It's not my fault," "They're discriminating against me," "No one likes me," "I have no one to support me," "It's too late," "I can't," or "I already tried." These excuses (when you know the problem is you) become your alibi for your lack of career success. If you fail, you don't have to feel bad because you have someone other than yourself to blame.

As a black woman you may have been taught that your failures in the workplace would have everything to do with color. However, this isn't always the case. For example, your work may not be up to par. Your approach to people may be wrong. You may be defensive or have some hidden prejudices.

Ways to Overcome Blame Shifting

Make a list of all the people, inside and outside of work, whom you hold responsible for the state of your career. Next to each name, write down why you feel that person is in your way. At the same time, make a list of the ways you are failing your own career.

Few people recognize when they're the real problem. In the workplace, you can experience the same things again and again and delude yourself into thinking that someone else is the source of your problems. If you're going to navigate your way through the workplace, you have to learn when the problem's you. In every work situation, observe how you're being perceived. Recognize that the workplace has a culture of its own. Blacks sometimes blame their uncomfortableness with the difference in culture on something else. The presence of your own prejudices, fear of losing your identity, or other attitudes about race, can keep you from facing the truth about yourself. For these reasons, you need to do a little "reality testing" from time to time.

LACK OF FOCUS If you play tennis, you know that the key to hitting the ball is to keep your eye on it. When you don't, you swing, but you don't hit. With regard to your career, your focus may be too narrow. You could also be confused, because you're focusing on the wrong things. You may be unclear about what you want or where you're going. In most cases, a person who doesn't have clear goals often loses sight of them, or doesn't see as far into the future as someone who does.

On the other hand, you can know what you want. But you become distracted or let something else get in your line of vision. For instance, one of our clients set a goal to obtain a job as an illustrator at a print shop. She hoped that this would be a stepping stone to obtaining a position with an advertising agency. At the same time she was offered the illustrator's position, she obtained another position offering more money. She took the job with more money and turned down the other job. It didn't take long before she was calling us to admit that she had made a bad mistake by making money her motive.

Keys to overcoming lack of focus:

☞ Keep your eye on your goals.
☞ Be clear about what you want.
☞ Write down the reasons that you need to succeed.
☞ Concentrate on where you're going, instead of living for the moment.
☞ Establish priorities.
☞ Work on one goal at a time.

IGNORANCE As a black working woman, you may feel that you're not always let in, that you don't always know what's going on, or that you're kept in the dark. That's a common complaint of black women. But it's important that you participate in other activities or link yourself to someone who is informed.

Become resourceful and learn where reliable sources of information can be found. Information is power. So, do your homework and gather as much information as you can to give you a fair advantage. When you can't determine fact from fiction, get a second opinion. Black women often talk themselves out of good careers because of ignorance and what they don't know.

LISTENING TO PROPHETS OF DOOM AND GLOOM When Dr. Martin Luther King, Jr., talked about having a dream, people listened. Try sharing yours. Some black people don't know how to show support. They'll ask you why you are doing something or what something's going to get you. They'll also either put you down, or give you more reasons for why something won't work than why it will. When our youngest sister decided to return to college and obtain a law degree, people tried to discourage her. Some people told her it's too late, she isn't analytical, or there are too many lawyers. Had she listened to the skeptics, she might not be halfway through obtaining her degree.

You can't believe everything everyone tells you, and watch out for those who offer you the color crutch. The color crutch is when someone tries to discourage you from pursuing a job by telling you a company either doesn't hire blacks or has too few. They think they're doing you a favor by providing you a way out of what they view is a no-win situation. But they're not. They are steering you away from obtaining your goals.

Anyone who isn't rallying behind you isn't a friend to your success. Surround yourself with people who help build up your confidence, and avoid those who try to tear it down. Pick your own cheerleaders and people who are sincere when they tell you, "you can do it." Stop talking to anyone who is negative. Remember, you can do bad by yourself. Misery still loves company, and there are people who will criticize what you're doing because they see you're trying, and they're not.

SELF-DOUBT

The Bible says, "As a man thinketh, so is he." In other words, what you think, you become. Garbage in, garbage out. Sometimes, you can be so down on yourself that you don't see what you're doing to yourself. Either you're convinced that you can't do something, or you convince yourself that someone won't let you do it. Instead of putting yourself in win-win situations, you think, "No way." Take the issue of race. Some of us view every white person in the office as an enemy. As a result, we become defensive or antagonistic. We expect problems, but we're actually creating added hurdles. And what we get often amounts to what we expect.

GIVING IN TO FAILURE

One thing can go wrong in your life, and it can make you feel your whole world is falling apart. You give up, and it's all in your mind. As a result, you don't try because you already failed once. Apparently, you're not aware that a lot of successful black women didn't get lucky the first time around. You're going to have "learn and burn" experiences. But you just have to tell yourself that the next time, you'll know better. You can't view setbacks as dead ends. Stay grounded, even when you don't go right the first time.

BEING CLOSED-MINDED Have an open mind. You have to understand that the same things aren't always going to be important to different people. No one's going to see everything the way that you do. And everyone's not always going to be equal in the same situation. Black people are starting to discover the role that professional counselors can play in changing their lives. In general, though, many of us still have a problem with seeking professional help. You may think, "I don't want anyone in my business," or have the attitude of "No one can tell me anything." You either think you know it all (and you don't), or you pretend you do. Don't be afraid to admit that you don't know something. And learn to trust others, including white people.

You are adamant that you won't get ahead because you're black or a woman. You think everything is either all black or all white. You also convince yourself that you won't do well on a job because you're not ready or unprepared. You set yourself up to fail, without even really trying. But when it comes down to it, your ability to succeed lies in what you think about yourself. You can only go as far as your sense of who you are and what you feel you are capable of achieving.

MEETING THE SURVIVAL CHALLENGE

Black empowerment became the buzz word of the black community during the eighties. We're not sure who coined it but its emphasis is that if blacks expect to have some power, we must begin to take control of our economic future. In other words, we have to look out for ourselves.

Perceptions, on and off the job, still exist about black people. We're often viewed as lazy and always looking for a handout. This myth has been carried overseas to Japan, with some of the Japanese feeling that we are prostitutes of the system and welfare junkies. These attitudes suggest that unless it's given to us, black people won't get anything. Because we are looking for someone else to do it, some of us have a "hit or miss" approach to planning our career. We are passive and feel it's a matter of "*que sera, sera,*" what will be, will be. We want to learn how to swim but we don't want to get into the water. Part of this complacency goes beyond not wanting to get our feet wet. There's no energy in us to keep our motor running. The oil's dry and we're lax. We see no urgency in doing anything.

The good news is that black women are coming out of this state of denial. You, too, must face the reality that you alone are responsible for your survival. As we said earlier, to succeed you must come to the aid of your own career. But you will never truly survive, until you admit that you have not been managing your career. Only then can you begin to take charge and meet the survival challenge.

Elynor A. Williams
Vice President of Public Responsibility
Sara Lee Corporation
Chicago, Illinois

I have traveled a deliberate, long, and winding road during the course of my career. Sometimes, I've had to pull over for directions. Other times, I changed my course or found another way to succeed. I also took many twists and turns along my journey. At age fifteen, I graduated from high school. At nineteen, I completed college and became a teacher. I left the comfort of home and a teaching position and moved to New York with a $500 raise and a new job. My career has also encompassed a variety of experiences. I was a writer and researcher for Cornell University; a publicist for General Foods Corporation; a communications specialist for the North Carolina Agricultural Extension Service; a senior public relations specialist for Western Electric Company; and director of corporate affairs for the Hanes Group, which is now a part of Sara Lee Corporation. I have also hosted my own radio show; written a newspaper column; volunteered in the community; run for public office (I lost an election for state representative by just twenty votes).

Someone might conclude that my career has had more hits than misses, or that I somehow managed to always slip between the cracks. But don't believe that. I have not had an easy journey. Often, my most well-paved roads have turned to gravel. Although I traveled some hard roads, I learned to take good advice and how to benefit from constructive criticism. I was also an overachiever and reared by parents who taught me to do the best that I can if I wanted to get something out of life.

My first rule of success is that you must be clear in determining what it is you want out of life. Put your sights on the kind of career that's going to afford you the things that you want, whether it's spending more time with family or having more money. A lot of women are starting to say that a career is too demanding, and they're beginning to see that it's not all that they want for their life.

Second, know yourself in the best way you can. That's an evolutionary kind of thing. You never should ignore yourself totally, because if you're not changing you're not growing. I started out wanting to be a fashion designer. I gave up that to obtain a degree in home economics and ended up teaching school. I decided teaching wasn't what I wanted to do, so I changed careers. I was working for a company as an editor when I decided that I needed to return to school to sharpen my skills. I obtained a master's degree in communications arts and started working in public relations, which led to what I'm doing now.

Third, don't ever say that you can't change and hone skills in new areas. While working for a large Fortune 500 company, I was told that I couldn't write or speak. I decided to test that and found out I was pretty good in both of those areas. I started working with one of the best writers on the team who complimented me on my writing. I then went back to my performance appraiser to question whether his was an accurate assessment. I learned that you can't take someone else's opinion of you as the final word. I also found it useful to take good criticism and advice. When others challenged my abilities, I let that spur me on to do better.

Fourth, choose a support system that will give you good advice and love you whether or not you make mistakes. It's good to know when you're down that there are people who will make you feel good about yourself. African Americans often have low self-esteem because of years of continuous racism. But that's no excuse. You can't continue to have a chip on your shoulder because of it. You have to be able to walk through that and find opportunities to do what you want. If you dwell on the racism, it becomes self-defeating. See racism as a challenge to go further ahead. If you consider yourself disadvantaged, you will never be able to achieve anything. The people in your support system can help you stop internalizing everything. They'll tell you you're okay.

Fifth, be willing to take risks and pay your dues. But also determine how much of that you need to pay. There are two schools of thought concerning career mobility. One says that you should stay with a company as long as you can. Another says move when you are no longer getting what you need. When I found myself hitting the concrete ceiling on a job, and couldn't see ahead of me, much less reach it, I left. I returned to school or went where the opportunities were. I didn't, though, leave anyone with bad feelings about me. When there was a challenge, I told myself I won't leave here crawling; and I never did. I always left standing tall.

If you really want to move up, be prepared to go where the opportunities are. I often hear young kids out of college say that they're not leaving Chicago. But you have to be prepared to go where the opportunities are if you are serious about growth and having a career. If you want to stay in Chicago, and all they're offering is hamburgers, that's what you're going to have to eat. I'm not saying that you can't bloom where you're planted, but a lot of upward mobility has to do with a person's ability to take risks and willingness to move.

Finally, set goals for yourself. I decided I was going to be a vice president. To get there, I went back to basics. I made sure that I was noticed for doing the right things. I found a support system that worked and looked out for me. A lot of times, we can't see where we are, and where we need to go, but other people can. I also knew my limitations, skills and strengths. Most importantly, I found a way to make a living doing what I like to do.

Sincerely,

Elynor Williams

Saundra Mitchal
Vice President of Marketing
Neutrogena Corporation
Los Angeles, California

I once heard someone say that "luck happens when preparation meets opportunity." In a way, that's my career credo. Through a variety of circumstances over the years, various job opportunities became available—opportunities that represented promotions or, equally important, opportunities that would provide the exposure necessary to prepare for a promotion. When those opportunities arose, I would "ask" for the job. Having worked hard at whatever it was I was doing, I felt "prepared" for the opportunity and was comfortable asking to be seriously considered for the move. In more cases than not, I got the job—then began preparing for the next move.

I've always been the one to guide my career instead of waiting for someone else to say this lady's doing fine, let me see that she's given the right exposure and moved up. Taking personal responsibility for what does or doesn't happen in my career has guided my success. While I didn't launch my career alone, I received well over 60 percent of my promotions because I asked for them. Yes. I worked harder than others and prepared myself for where I wanted to go. Whenever I felt that I was ready to move up, I wasn't gun-shy about approaching my superiors about what I needed to do to get to the next tier. I held the attitude that there must be something that I'm not doing by evidence of the fact that I hadn't received a promotion. So, I learned to ask for what I wanted.

My career gave birth in personnel, as an employee relations specialist, at Bristol-Meyers. Early on, I looked around the organization and figured out that no one who was in a very senior level position had come up through the personnel ranks. The people who were running the company were, for the most part, from a marketing, sales, or career path. That's when I decided to make a switch. It didn't come easy. I met resistance and was turned down several times. There was the feeling that I didn't have the experience, coming from personnel. Ultimately, through a lot of insistence that the decision makers at least give me the opportunity to fail, I was offered a job as a media planner. That position gave me entrée and exposure to marketing.

I can point to numerous other catalysts to my career. I was reared by a mother who insisted on good grades and that I work hard. I enjoyed the benefits of completing an M.B.A. at a time when corporations were anxious to hire women and minorities. I even moved to the "Big Apple" to increase my résumé value and broaden my experiences. I learned that people who moved there, either rightly or wrongly, believed themselves to be competitive. Competition made me work harder, so that I could keep up with my peers.

For you to succeed you don't have to sign up for twelve-hour days, but work hard. Learn the most that you can, and be the best at whatever you are doing. Be prepared for the next move by doing all that you can at whatever level you are. Talk to your peers and counterparts, and ask them why they're doing well. Find out from your managers what qualities they look for when promoting employees. Have a reliable support system. Early in my career, people told me not to go to New York because it's too big, too fast, and I was from a small town and wouldn't make it. But part of my motivation was to prove everyone wrong. I figured if eight million people could make it, so could I.

If you're sincere about succeeding, then don't be tempted to sit back and rest. Take some risks, and remember, no one can become successful without making a few mistakes.

Sincerely,

Saundra Mitchal

Chapter 4

SUCCESS PLANNING:
"DON'T WAIT

**FOR YOUR SHIP TO COME IN,
SWIM OUT TO MEET IT."**
—Source Unknown

Years ago, like you, we struggled with our own career climb. With our mother's encouragement and wisdom, we made some changes in the way we were trying to get ahead. She warned us that we didn't have reliable transportation and that we were on the wrong road. Mom knew what she was talking about. Now, years later, we find this is a typical situation facing most black women. They share the dilemma we once faced, and they don't know how to get ahead from where they are. Administrative assistants with secretarial skills don't know how to move into management, or nonprofit workers have difficulty figuring out how to move into the private sector. You, too, may have your eyes on something better, but you keep asking yourself, "How do I get there, from here?"

We took the advice of the matriarch of our home. She said "You have to make choices." She explained, "Wherever you are in your career, you're on a stepladder in your organization. You have to figure out how to get on the step you covet. If someone else is on that step, you have to either find another step or wait your turn. If the step is unoccupied, you have to find the best way to move ahead or you may be pushed down."

If you're new to the work world, you may be on step one trying to advance to step two. Or, you may be a grade seven trying to become a grade ten, or a junior analyst trying to become a senior analyst. But like many black women, whether you get ahead or fall behind is a matter of your approach. You decide what you want, then you go for it. And it takes preparation and planning if you expect to advance to the next step(s) on the staircase of your career.

One other pivotal factor is your focus. You know that you want to do something, but you don't know what that something is. You think to yourself, "If I choose the right career, I'll have a promising future," instead of, "If I plan to get ahead, I need to succeed in my planning."

In the last chapter, we talked about blame-shifting and the excuses black women make about that state of their careers. All too often, we tell ourselves, "I'm not where I want to be." If this sounds like a familiar statement, it's best to ask yourself, "Why?" Examine what you've tried before and find out why it did or didn't work. Don't always hang your career on the "excuse noose." Stop telling yourself that you can't get ahead because it will take too long, you're black, you're too old, you lack the right education, you're in the wrong field, you have no money, or you are a single parent.

THE BLACK WORKING WOMAN'S ROAD MAP

When we first entered the business of helping black women get ahead in the workplace, we did what other career counselors and consultants now do. We focused on career planning, as if picking a career was like pulling a slot machine and hoping you hit the jackpot. We faced some painful truths in our own careers. By our own mistakes, we quickly learned that choosing a career wasn't good enough. We realized there's more to moving up than trying to find the "perfect job." One of us found her way up the corporate ladder by accident. The other enjoyed a comfortable, lengthy career in academia before charting new waters. We were both guilty of the same thing, picking one career, sitting back and settling in. But something was missing. We had fallen into the habit of playing it safe and weren't really driving our career. The missing ingredient? You guessed it, success planning.

A prime example of a success planner is our friend, whom we'll call Cynthia. She's a high-level executive in a major corporation. It seems as if whatever she touches turns to gold. We refer to her weapon of success as vision. Cynthia's not one to agonize over her career decisions, but she sure is farsighted. She constantly evaluates where she is now in relation to where she wants to be in the future. She also doesn't involve herself in anything that isn't going to either benefit her career or put her in a position to get something else. She says her method of planning is similar to the old "Oil of Olay" commercials. Remember how the model would talk about her beautiful skin and say something like, "My beautiful skin? It didn't get like this; I had to work at it." Cynthia says that she thinks through most of her career decisions, and every year concentrates on what she needs to do to move into the next position. She says her needs may be new skills or education, more networking, politicking, or anything else that will close the distance between where she is and where she wants to be.

Success planning is that reliable transportation we talked about earlier. It carries you to your destination. It's also a map of your vision of where you would like to be and the steps you need to take to get there. Again, we're not just talking about merely picking a career, but about charting your course to success. Remember the theme song from the movie, *Mahogany*—"Do You Know Where You're Going To?" The reason you may not be taking charge of your career is that you honestly don't know. You don't know what you want. If you know what you want, you don't know how to get it. If you know how to get it, you don't know which way to go. If you know which way to go, you don't know who can help you. On and on you go, drifting in and out of jobs, often only surviving by accident.

THE BENEFITS OF SUCCESS PLANNING

In the children's classic storybook, *Alice in Wonderland*, the Cheshire Cat told Alice that which way she should go depended a lot on where she wanted to go. Well, if you're a smart black woman (and we believe you are) you don't take a trip without knowing where you're going. You map out how to get there. You know if you don't plan ahead, you may get lost, lose your direction, run out of gas or end up in a place you don't want to be. It's the same with your career. Even with the right road map, you can still go around in circles if you don't know yourself or your strengths. You also need goals, networking, a mentor, and visibility. Finally, you need a little bit of knowledge. If you don't, you may not know how to read the signs which are telling you to go, stop, or take a detour.

You could argue that you've heard this all before. You could also insist that no matter how well you plan your career, the "isms" (racism, sexism, favoritism, cronyism, nepotism and what a friend of ours refers to as neighborism) are going to get in your way. Success planning may not move all the mountains in your career, but it sure can help you move up and around them. Here's how:

1. Success planning gets you to understand what you really want.
2. Success planning reduces the frustration associated with assuming unclear and unfocused career paths.
3. Success planning motivates you to "work smarter" toward achieving career goals.
4. Success planning helps you discover the best places to use your skills and talents, and to find keys to opportunities.
5. Success planning increases your income potential and career mobility.
6. Success planning helps you to look down the road, not to just see and accept, but to shape the future that's ahead of you.

You can be successful. And we want **you** to be successful. So, let's examine some success planning strategies.

Success Strategy 1: Take Charge of Your Own Career

We'll understand if you're now asking, "How can I take charge of my own career when someone else makes the final decisions?" The point we're making is that you also have a fair amount of control over what happens in your career. If you, for example, want to become a doctor but refuse to go to medical school, you can't say someone else is the reason that you're not a doctor. While others, like your boss or a peer, can attempt to stonewall your career, you must try anyway and make every effort to guide your own career.

You begin taking charge by getting organized and making some plans. The drawback of not making plans for how you're going to get ahead is that later on you'll probably have to play catch-up. Every year that you delay is another year you'll eventually have to add on to your move to the top or a new career.

How long and why have you been waiting to get to where you want to go? Are you saying to yourself, "It will take forever." Forever is a long time, so the best thing to do is start planning the rest of your career today. Time, as you know, does move on with or without us.

Yes, by all means, if you're not sure about what to do or where to start, ask for help. It's an okay thing to do. Use your boss, colleagues, former teachers, a mentor and anyone else who can help you. Share your ideas with other people. Ask for their opinions, and be willing to listen to what they have to say. You might be quite surprised at how talking it out can steer you back on course. Keep in mind, too, that in this day and age it's hard to advance alone.

Remember, if you leave the driving to others there is no guarantee that you'll get to where you want to go. And if you're led down the wrong road, you'll have no one to blame but yourself.

All you have to do is take matters into your own hands. And the payoff will be better than if you had done nothing. It's such a simple choice (but maybe not an easy thing to do). You either take charge of your own career, or you take a back seat. You can also choose to cruise. If you do, be forewarned. Sooner or later you may be forced to make a decision because others are either passing you by, cautioning you to do something, or pushing you out of a job. Before you know it, you'll find yourself in a ditch unequipped to dig your career out of its hole, overcome roadblocks, or utilize the shortcuts to getting in the fast or passing lane to career success.

Success Planning Strategy 2: Get to Know Yourself

Black women have a lot of struggles with the question of, "Who am I?" If you also struggle with this issue, look closely at the real you. Get in tune with your inner self and find out your true needs. Write a statement of where you are now and where you want to be. Defining your true needs will help lead you to a career that is best suited to the woman you are. Before you can take on any career, it's important to know not only your personal likes and dislikes but your strengths and weaknesses. Only then can you figure out what's going to work in your career and how to overcome your limitations. The best way to do this is, again, to isolate your strengths and skills. You'll also save valuable time by getting to know yourself, first.

To begin, complete the skills identification exercise on the next few pages.

SKILLS IDENTIFICATION

A lot of black women aren't in the right careers because we don't know where our interests lie. We hear too many black women, at every age, say, "I don't know how to do anything," or, "I don't have any skills." But trust us. Everyone has skills that they have developed either at

work, at school, at home, as a volunteer, in a training situation, or by
pursuing hobbies and leisure activities. These skills, and accomplishments, tend to fall into groups or clusters. The following exercise will
give you an opportunity to identify your skills, especially those you
enjoy using and want to continue to use and develop.

Examine each cluster and check the column or columns that apply to
you for each of the skills listed. A skill may have a check in all three
columns if it's one that you both enjoy using and wish to develop
further. Pay particular attention to the clusters with a lost of marks in
the "enjoyed using" column. Then search for a career that taps those
skills.

IDENTIFYING YOUR SKILLS

Table 4.1

Communications/ Human Relations	Have Used	Enjoyed Using	Want To Develop Further
advocating			
clarifying			
debating			
discussing			
editing			
entertaining			
expressing feelings			
expressing ideas			
giving feedback			
informing			
interviewing			
listening			
organizing groups			
persuading			

promoting			
public speaking			
reading			
reporting			
selling			
speaking/signaling			
summarizing			
teamwork			
translating			
using humor			
using the telephone			
writing			

Table 4.2

Numerical/Organizational	Have Used	·Enjoyed Using	Want To Develop Further
accounting			
appraising			
attending to detail			
auditing			
bookkeeping			
budgeting			
calculating			
clerical			
coding			
comparing			

computing			
condensing			
copying			
estimating			
filing			
measuring			
problem solving			
programming			
processing			
purchasing			
recording			
scheduling			
surveying			
systematizing			
using statistics			

Table 4.3

Creative	Have Used	Enjoyed Using	Want To Develop Further
adapting ideas			
composing			
conceptualizing			
decorating			
designing			
developing ideas			
experimenting			

generating ideas			
imagining			
improvising			
innovating			
integrating			
inventing			
perceiving			
performing			
producing			
scheduling			
styling			
surveying			
systematizing			
three-dimensional design			
two-dimensional design			
using movement			
using statistics			
using voice			
writing			

Table 4.4

Mamangement/ Leadership	Have Used	Enjoyed Using	Want To Develop Further
administering policies			
articulating			
decision making			

	Have Used	Enjoyed Using	Want To Develop Further
developing			
evaluating			
expediting			
fund raising			
giving directions			
goal setting			
inspecting			
inspiring			
leading			
mediating			
motivating			
negotiating			
planning			
policy making			
problem solving			
recruiting			
supervising			
team building			
using tact			

Table 4.5

Physical/ Mechanical	Have Used	Enjoyed Using	Want To Develop Further
assembling			
athletic ability			
building			

cleansing			
disassembling			
driving			
food handling			
installing			
manipulating objects			
making repairs			
manual dexterity			
operating business machinery			
operating heavy equipment			
playing an instrument			
tending animals			
tending machines			
tending plants			
using hands			
using physical strength			
using tools			

Table 4.6

Instructional/ Helping	Have Used	Enjoyed Using	Want To Develop Further
advising			
communicating			
counseling			
demonstrating			
empathizing			

encouraging			
explaining			
expressing ideas			
guiding			
healing			
influencing			
information giving			
leading discussions			
lecturing			
listening			
mentoring			
monitoring			
motivating			
responding			
serving			
teaching			
training			
tutoring			
understanding			

Table 4.7

Research/Study	Have Used	Enjoyed Using	Want To Develop Further
abstracting			
analyzing			
checking			

classifying			
compiling data			
estimating			
evaluating			
examining			
experimenting			
formulating			
gathering			
graphing			
identifying			
inquiring			
learning			
observing			
record keeping			
remembering			
verifying			

EXPLORE YOUR STRENGTHS

If you made it through the last exercise, this next one shouldn't be too bad for you to handle. Remember, before you can plan your successes you must know yourself, from the inside out. To sharpen your focus on your abilities, work through this checklist of personal characteristics. First, read each word and underline the ones that describe you as you are now. Then, look back over the list and place a check to the left of the words that are highly descriptive of you.

Before you use this list, make several photocopies of it so that you can ask one or more friends and family members to rate you. This will give you an opportunity to see yourself as others see you and to compare their sense of you with your sense of yourself. However, keep in mind that they may perceive only limited parts of you, perhaps the qualities that fit in with their lives.

IDENTIFYING YOUR STRENGTHS

academic	dominant	meticulous	serious
accurate	eager	mild	sensitive
active	easygoing	moderate	sharp-witted
adaptable	efficient	natural	sincere
adventurous	emotional	obliging	sociable
affectionate	energetic	opportunistic	spontaneous
aggressive	fair-minded	optimistic	spunky
alert	farsighted	organized	stable
ambitious	firm	original	steady
artistic	flexible	outgoing	strong
attractive	forceful	painstaking	strong-minded
bold	frank	patient	sympathetic
broadminded	friendly	peaceable	tactful
businesslike	generous	persevering	teachable
calm	gentle	pleasant	tenacious
capable	good-natured	poised	thorough
careful	healthy	polite	thoughtful
cautious	helpful	practical	tolerant
charming	honest	precise	tough
cheerful	humorous	progressive	trusting
clear-thinking	idealistic	prudent	trustworthy
clever	imaginative	purposeful	unaffected
competent	independent	quick	unassuming
competitive	individualistic	quiet	understanding
confident	industrious	rational	unexcitable
conscientious	informal	realistic	uninhibited
conservative	intellectual	reflective	verbal
considerate	inventive	relaxed	versatile
cool	kind	reserved	warm
courageous	leisurely	resourceful	wholesome
curious	light-hearted	responsible	wise
daring	likable	retiring	witty
deliberate	logical	robust	zany
determined	loyal	self-confident	
dignified	mature	self-controlled	
discreet	methodical	sensible	

Review the previous list. Are there only a few checks on your list? If there are, check the list for any adjectives that you missed during your first evaluation. It's not uncommon to miss something during your first attempt. Go over the list, again, and think about each quality and whether it accurately describes you.

SUCCESS PLANNING STRATEGY 3: ANALYZE YOUR CAREER'S NET WORTH

What's your career really worth? Write down your salary on a piece of paper. Is it $15,000, $20,000, or $40,000? Now, consider if your company is getting that much service from you. Secondly, if you put a price tag on your career's net worth, is its value high or low? If it's low, or you think that your skills aren't of value to an employer, you may need to use the services of a professional to help you do a self-examination, and identify your achievements and capabilities.

CALCULATING YOUR CAREER'S NET WORTH

When you think of net worth, you probably think of assets minus liabilities. Translated into career terms, your net worth consists of anything about you that is a plus to your career minus anything that is weighing against it. Career assets include areas of expertise, education, experience, on the job accomplishments, one's professional image, etc. On the other hand, career liabilities can include the absence of these assets. For example, having a poor professional image can impact your career. Even people in your life can be a liability if they are detrimental to your success.

To help you calculate your career's net worth, form two separate lists of your career assets and liabilities. Career assets are everything that you have going for your career. That may mean a polished image, credentials, specialized skills, and anything else that is or has the potential to aid you up the corporate ladder. Liabilities are the things that are working against your career. Examples include the absence of education, low self-esteem, etc.

Once you're finished compiling your lists, make separate totals of your assets and liabilities. Then subtract your liabilities from your assets. If the sum is a negative amount, or if your liabilities are higher than your assets, your career is in serious trouble. Even if your assets are higher, you shouldn't assume that your career is not threatened. Having the best education or a variety of experiences won't guarantee success when your attitude is sabotaging your career. Always ask yourself if your assets are working for you, and identify the ways your liabilities are damaging your career.

Analyzing Your Career's Net Worth

The total of your assets and liabilities won't necessarily present an accurate picture of how well you're surviving or your chances of succeeding in the workplace. You have to learn how to analyze your net worth to determine if your survival potential is strong or weak. Age or length of time on your job can either strengthen or weaken your positioning in the workplace. So can continuing education. Youth can discourage the company from promoting you to management, while length of time on the job can encourage a company to let you go when it starts downsizing. The amount of education and training you have can move you forward or backward in the workplace. At the same time, the absence of certain kinds of education can steepen your career climb.

As a black woman, you can have it all; but the perceptions of blacks can pose a serious handicap. Again, you have to look at the effect that being black is impacting where you are in the workplace and how you're being groomed.

The major key to eliminating liabilities is to think about where you need to go and how a liability is holding you back. Once you do, you can begin to make decisions about who and what can help you to get to where you need to go. We'll give you an illustration. We have another friend who was experiencing problems on the job, because she was told she wasn't a team player. That perception became a liability to her advancement. As she thought about where she wanted to go in her organization, she made a decision to start attending happy hours and mingling with her peers.

It's in your best interest to find out what's hurting your career. Identify what you need to survive. Determine why it's important in order for you to get ahead.

Success Planning Strategy 4: Map Your Career Goals

Are you thinking, "I have tried setting career goals before, but nothing ever seems to work"? Or, "Somehow I never seem to achieve the results I intended to"? What really happens? Often, fear, procrastination, and indecision set in. We also keep our goals in our mind, and that's where they stay. As a result, nothing ever happens with them.

Goals will help guide you, especially when you can see them. Goals need to be:

WRITTEN DOWN
ACHIEVABLE
MEASURABLE
CONTROLLABLE

Here's how you should go about creating a positive and proactive program for developing and implementing your success goals:

1. Divide your goals into three categories:
Short-Range Goals—Those you want to achieve in one year or less
Medium-Range Goals—These you want to achieve within one to five years
Long-Range Goals—Those you want to achieve at least ten years into the future

2. Write goals for each category in specific and well-defined terms.
For example: "I want a position as a physical therapist paying 20 percent more than I am making now." The language of your goals must be positive.

3. Start with short-range goals.
These goals are more likely to be within your own control and are generally easily attainable.

4. Set target dates for accomplishing goals.
Assigning target dates provides constant reinforcement and a sense of accomplishment which subsequently helps to sustain your motivation. For example: In one week I will make ten networking contacts.

5. Use reward statements to motivate yourself.
Link the statements to what I want the outcomes to be:
I will obtain more fulfilling work
I will make more money
I will have a more flexible schedule
I will reduce my stress levels

6. State the steps you need to take.
Steps might include identifying companies that have physical therapists, revising/updating your résumé, practicing interviewing skills, or contacting your professional network.

7. List the obstacles that may arise.
What stands in the way of

achieving your goals? For example, "I'm unable to locate information for my résumé and I lost a copy of my license."

8. List the obstacles that arise that you can control. Which ones
can't you control? In our example, you might need to contact former
employers for information, or you can contact the state board of
licensing for a copy of the license.

Success Planning Strategy 5: Don't Climb Your Career the Hard Way!

Unfortunately, we have to add, that may be the only way you'll learn
how to plan it right. We've lost count of the number of black women
we've met who complicate their careers by making things harder for
themselves. You might be one of them. You don't know your assets
from your liabilities. You act as if it's too much trouble to put any effort
toward achieving your goals. Because you don't want to work at it, you
miss out on opportunities that end up being thrown to others.
Eventually, when you do get around to doing something, you find you
haven't made things easy for yourself. Then you start singing the "if
only I had" blues.

Let's be honest. We all have to pay our dues, in one way or another,
if we expect to succeed. You may have to pay your dues by making a
tradeoff, "the giving up of one thing in return for another considered
more desirable." And by the way, it's okay to make tradeoffs in the
name of your goals. Your tradeoffs can involve putting in time or
banking your money. Most black women struggle with giving up
something now in order to have something better later. That's because
we're living in a society of "she's gotta have it now."

Well, if you don't prepare now, you will pay later. Although it may
be a very worn-out cliché, nothing ventured, nothing gained. At least,
that's the story line behind the careers of most successful black women.
Take Patti Labelle, for instance. She didn't become a singer without
singing a note. Rosa Parks didn't serve as a catalyst to the civil rights
movement without refusing to give up her seat on a Montgomery,
Alabama, bus. Gwendolyn Brooks didn't win a Pulitzer Prize for
poetry by not writing a word. Wilma Rudolph, first American woman
to win three gold medals in track and field, didn't become an Olympic
achiever without sweat and determination.

These four women not only paid a price to obtain success, but they
had a strong commitment toward their goals. They didn't succeed by

standing on the same spot or waiting for someone else to do it. They planned their own careers, and they worked hard. They had plans. They had drive, they sacrificed, they made it through their journey.

Great careers don't come without sacrifice. Something in your life will probably have to go. Decide, now, what you're willing to forfeit to get what you want. Make sacrifices to reach your goals. A sacrifice doesn't mean that you have to give up something forever. However, it may require you to rethink your priorities, delay a major purchase, cut up your credit cards, or pay off your bills so that you'll have money to return to school. Tradeoffs come with the territory. If you're striving to develop professionally, you can't expect everything to happen at the same time. There are some things that you'll have to work for harder than others. But whatever you do, don't hold onto something at the expense of your career.

Success Planning Strategy 6: Gain the Upper Hand, With Knowledge

Knowledge is power! And power is having that knowledge. What do you know about the field you are in now? What do you know about the field you may want to transition to? Your knowledge base should include the following:

- Nature of the Work
- Working conditions
- Traning, other qualifications, and advancement
- Job Outlook
- Related Occupations
- Earning Potential
- Buzz words (terminology and lingo)
- Latest and future technology

You can fill in the voids of your career knowledge base by:

- Reading the trade publications of your field
- Upgrading your skills. Enroll in training courses or attend a seminar.
- Maintaining files on your field or proposed field. What's hot? What's not?
- Sharing your new-found knowledge at staff meetings or through the company newsletter.

Success Planning Strategy 7: Find a Mentor

What a friend you can have in a mentor. Mentors are the workplace's cheerleaders. They rally behind you, and give you reassurance. They guide, and they listen (that alone is enough of a reason for finding one). They're not just for the eager junior executive attempting the tumultuous climb up the career ladder. They are most valuable for those who need support, feedback, and advice related to career and business advancement. Specifically, a mentor can offer knowledge of an organization, unspoken rules, politics, and nuances; introductions to important people; perspectives on errors caused by inexperience, anxiety or naïveté; solutions to problems caused by errors and exposure to new career possibilities.

It's also possible to have a mentor who does not give advice. You can obtain one who helps you gain valuable information by simply following his/her example. In case you weren't aware, there's no rule that says a mentor must be chosen from the ranks of the business world.

The search for a mentor may not come easy. So, try to make a list of a number of sources. Not everyone on your list may have the time or inclination to offer their support. The intended mentor may want to serve as a best friend instead of a mentor. While the two are not mutually exclusive, your options are broader if things are kept strictly business.

Success Planning Strategy 8: Get in the Spotlight

It's truly not always what you know but who knows you that opens doors of opportunity. Exposure is another key to getting you from where you are to where you want to go. So, look around your company and search for opportunities. Also, check out organizations to which you belong. Identify positions or projects that will give you an audience. Every chance you get, direct your efforts at marketing yourself as a winner. Work hard and show off your good side. Become an asset to your company. Go the extra mile. Act like a good politician, but never make promises that you can't keep.

Who knows you? If you went blank, you are probably a candidate for raising your visibility. If you feel that a number of people know you, that's great. But what do they know about you? If you can't answer affirmative, you too may be a candidate for raising your visibility. All of us can use a little more of the spotlight on us. Why? To expand our network, to be in the know, to shine for career advancement.

HOW VISIBLE ARE YOU?

Answer yes or no to the following items:
1. In the last year, were you highlighted in the company newsletter?

   yes _____   no _____
2. Are people aware of your talents, <u>outside</u> your organization?

   yes _____   no _____
3. Do more than half of your company know you well enough to recognize you by name?

   yes _____   no _____
4. Have one or more individuals asked you to be their mentor?

   yes _____   no _____
5. Does your boss know the activities in which you participate <u>outside</u> your organization?

   yes _____   no _____
6. Do you belong to a number of professional or community organizations?

   yes _____   no _____
7. Have you been asked to speak at a conference or staff meeting?

   yes _____   no _____
8. Are you perceived in a favorable light within your organization?

   yes _____   no _____

Scoring

Total the number of yes and no responses.
More than six yes responses indicates people do "**see**" you.
Less than six yes responses mean you might need to increase your visibility.

WAYS TO RAISE YOUR VISIBILITY

1. Become active in professional and community organizations. Chair committees. Steer your involvement to hospitality, membership and public relations committees. Run for office.

2. Volunteer to chair the company's annual fund-raising drive or community activity, such as the United Way.
3. Write articles for the company newsletter or magazine. Share information about workshops or seminars you have attended.
4. If your company has one, join its speakers' bureau. Better yet, join Toastmasters International to perfect your communication skills.
5. Volunteer for high visibility assignments and do an outstanding job.
6. Set a goal to meet one new contact at each meeting that you attend. Stay in touch.
7. Forward articles of noteworthy information to key players in your organization. Don't forget to send a brief note.
8. Make friends with media contacts. Keep them informed of your activities. Also, have your friends notify the media of your activities.

Success Planning Strategy 9: Navigate Through the Networking Maze

Networking! Networking! Networking! It's the word that has become synonymous with locating jobs, promoting career advancement or expanding business opportunities. The concept is not new. Its popularity is due largely to the fact that it's not what you know but who knows you that creates opportunities. You can network more effectively if you follow these simple guidelines:

1. **Locate all the business cards you have collected.** Take out your address book, Rolodex, Christmas lists and any other material that have names of people you know or have met. Separate the names from these sources into two categories. Label one category **Support contacts**. This group should consist of people in the fields and positions that parallel yours or are similar to yours, as well as people who have extensive knowledge of your field. Label the second category **Career boosters**. This category will consist of people who seem interested in your career mobility; people you may want to emulate; and people who can give you visibility (media contacts, for example).
2. **Establish networking goals**. Determine what you want from your contacts. What do you need? Job leads, technical assistance, industry visibility, additional clients? Be sure your goals are realistic.

3. **Develop a script**. Before you make a phone call or initiate a meeting, know what you are going to say. Keep your calls short and to the point.
4. **Identify organizations to expand your network**. Professional organizations can provide both support contacts and career booster contacts. Use newspapers, trade publications, directories and personal contacts to develop a list of organizations. Determine if the organization has the resources to meet your networking goals by calling the contact person. Attend at least one meeting.
5. **Treat the system as a two-way process**. Be prepared to give as well as to receive. Send thank-you notes to contacts who have provided referrals. Share information. Project a "What can I do for you?" image.
6. **Keep your contacts current**. Maintain a network file. Make periodic phone calls, send short notes, arrange breakfast, luncheon, or dinner meetings.

SUCCESS PLANNING

Where you want to be in your career, and how you get there, has a lot to do with where you are. And where you are will tell you what you need to do to get there. So, before you get on the road to pursuing your goals, do a self-examination and set some goals. Have an organized plan that spells out who, what, where, when, and how. Remember, your climb doesn't have to be a journey to the unknown. What you don't know will most certainly hurt your chances of having a successful career.

On the way up, become aware of blind spots and roadblocks. And by the way, don't drive your career in the dark. Gather the tools that are going to get you to where you want to go. Build up your confidence level so that it doesn't cause you to put up barriers to your plans. Concentrate on overcoming your weaknesses or the obstacles that are in your way. Get training, and equip yourself with the skills that will move your career ahead. Keep learning, and don't be mediocre. Be the one who does more than just get by. Use the tools you have. Keep your eye on the road, even when it seems as if it has more bumps than road. And no matter how bumpy the road gets, don't lose sight of your goals. If the road becomes too difficult to follow, slow down or learn when to shift gears. If you do make a wrong turn, don't sweat. Just start again.

Consider your career as an important journey. Begin by deciding why you're taking it. Next, identify where you are. If you're not sure of your position, conduct a self-assessment, an inventory of your skills, or prepare an autobiographical sketch. Once you have an idea of what you want to do, write a one-sentence statement starting with the words, "I want...." Then decide the best route to getting there or the things you need to do to accomplish your goals.

This book will help you. Successfully plan your career, that is. We're going to guide you every step of the way.

Recommended Reading

Boe, Anne, and Bettie B. Younger. *Is Your "Net" Working: A Complete Guide to Building Contacts and Career Visibility*. New York: John Wiley, 1989.

Bolles, Richard. *What Color is Your Parachute*. Berkeley: Berkeley Ten Speed, 1992. Updated annually.

Campbell, David. *If You Don't Know Where You're Going, You'll Probably End Up Somewhere Else*. Allen, Texas: Argur Communications, 1974.

Davidson, Jeffrey. *Blow Your Own Horn*. New York: American Management Association, 1987.

Krannich, Ron and Carye. *Network Your Way to Job and Career Success*. Manassas, VA: Impact Publications, 1990.

Niven, Beatrice. *Black Women's Career Guide*. New York: Doubleday, 1987.

**Brigadier General Clara L. Adams-Ender
Deputy Commanding General,
Military District of Washington, DC, and
Commander (Fort Belvoir, Virginia)
Washington, DC**

How happy and proud I was to have been asked to share some thoughts with you about what it takes for black women to succeed in the world of work! To this point, I have had a successful career in the United States Army for the last thirty-three years, and I believe that my survival and progress qualify me to share these thoughts. I need to tell you that you have already taken the first step toward success just by having obtained gainful employment and entering the work world.

Your future success will continue to depend largely upon those actions which you choose to take.

Someone once stated, "Of all the people I know, I have had more problems with myself than anyone else." That was a really wise person who made that statement. I made that same discovery very early in my career. As a result, I decided that I had to learn how to manage and guide my behavior so that I did not work at cross purposes with myself in climbing the ladder of success. I discovered that if I did not manage or control certain ways of behaving, I could really limit myself from being all I could be. In essence, I was the one who was preventing me from being successful, and not anyone or anything else. There were three self-limiting behaviors that I found it very important to recognize and eliminate. They were being fearful, procrastination, and negative thought. I will comment on each of these behaviors and some actions that must be taken to overcome them.

Being afraid to act because of something within oneself is a self-limiting behavior. There are some things that should be feared; wild animals, leaping off tall buildings, and taking poisons, for examples. These things should be feared because they have the distinct possibility of wiping you out as a physical being! However, there are other things that are feared by people; success, failure, love, and rejection. These are illusory fears which means that they are not real and exist only in your mind. They are self-limiting, self-inhibiting, and self-defeating because they keep you from being successful in whatever you are trying to do.

How does one overcome being afraid to act because of illusory fear? First, it is important to acknowledge that you have the fear, then do the thing that you fear anyway. Always find yourself moving in the direction of the thing that you fear. Sometimes the fear will get worse for awhile, but just keep on moving. Over time, you will find that after you have done the thing you feared several times, the fear will gradually subside and eventually go away. Fear is something that must be moved *through*, not something to be *turned from*. You must do the thing that you fear you cannot do!

A second self-limiting behavior is procrastination. My definition of procrastination is putting off until tomorrow that which you could or should do today. It is getting into the habit of making statements like, "I'll do it when I have time," or "I'll do it when I'm older," or "I'll do it when I have enough money." Procrastination is simply the act of putting off life and merely existing. It is a self-limiting behavior because it prevents you from being able to act in the moment. No one else can limit you, but you limit yourself by putting off your own progress. As a result, your own inaction becomes self-limiting and self-defeating. Often it is tough to admit it to yourself, but you limit your own success through procrastination.

How does one overcome procrastination? Initially, it is important to ask yourself some soul-searching questions: "How come I do not believe that I deserve happiness now?" "How come I always look for reasons not to live fully?" After having explored these questions, and having found no good reason for postponing action, you must begin to live your life now. Learn to do the thing that you desire to do now. Make decisions about where you would like to go in your career and act upon them now. Look for the results of your efforts rather than reasons why you can't be successful at this moment. Procrastination is a self-limiting behavior which must be eliminated if you are to live your life to its fullest each moment!

The third self-limiting behavior is negative thought. It is the act of viewing all of life's experiences with a feeling of impending doom. Negative thought is a self-limiting behavior because it inhibits you from putting into motion those actions which will assist you in accomplishing your goals and objectives. Negative thoughts convey an "I can't do it" message to the person. As a result, all of your motion is then directed toward actions which support the message that "it cannot be done."

In essence, you stop yourself from moving forward just by what you decided in your head from the outset. John-Roger and Peter Mc-Williams wrote a book entitled, *You Can't Afford the Luxury of a Negative Thought*, in which the concept of negative thinking and its consequences are explained in detail. I would highly recommend this book to you. It is easy to fall into the habit of negative thinking, because we are often bombarded with negative messages in our society. Negative messages sell newspapers, ensure high television ratings, and contribute to successful political campaigns. Negative thought can limit progress in the work world because it limits positive action from being taken that will move you forward with deliberate speed. Negative thinking is a habit that must be broken if you are to realize your full potential in the work world.

Additionally, you must separate negative thinking from making a negative observation. For example, for someone to notice that you have a thread hanging from your coat is making a negative observation. If you are a negative thinker, you will think, "I must have something also wrong with my blouse. My other clothes must not be suitable. I must not be able to dress well at all. I must be a bad person." On the other hand a positive thinker will think, "I'd better get scissors and cut the thread. I must watch for such threads before I dress. It was so kind of Joan to tell me about the thread."

Giving up negative thinking may be the most important thing you will do to ensure your progress in the work world. You may start by simply noticing that you are thinking negatively and when it occurs. You may soon find that instead of saying, "It's no wonder I'm upset over what is happening," you begin to say, "I am really reacting negatively again." You will really begin to notice that it's not what is happening to you that is the real problem. Once you come to this realization, then begin to pause before thinking negatively by thinking about something else. For example, try to remember some uplifting thoughts or some pleasant thing that has happened in the past to get you through this period. John-Roger and McWilliams suggest that you declare periods during the day when you will not think negatively and pick out areas where you won't think negatively anymore, then gradually increase the periods and areas of your life until there is no more place for negative thinking.

There you have it, my Sisters of the work world—a brief lesson on how to eliminate self-limiting behaviors of fear, procrastination, and negative thinking. This lesson may be reviewed at your leisure and practiced repeatedly. My final words to you are to be positive, be kind, be persistent, and never, never, never, quit!

Sincerely,

Clara Adams-Ender

Cheryl Prejean Greaux
Director, Leadership 2000*
National Association of Negro Business
and Professional Women's Clubs
Washington, DC

*Ms. Greaux is an executive on loan from the U.S. Department of Agriculture

I am writing you on Dr. Martin Luther King's birthdate because as you know, he got it going for African American men and women. I know that you know that achieving workplace success is not an easy accomplishment. But survival in your chosen career is possible if you are forever vigilant about the **choices** that you make in life. I know that at every junction of my career, the **choices** that I made are what has made the difference.

Let's journey back to my high school days. I watched children for extra money while in high school. One night, while I was babysitting, my boyfriend pleaded with me to come over to allow us to have some time alone. I made a *choice* not to allow my boyfriend to come to my house. I studied instead. Now, you may say that was not an important decision; however, you do not know the persuasive powers of my boyfriend. Please believe me, my life might have been different if I had yielded to that temptation.

Another pivotal point in my career occurred when I made the **choice** to return to graduate school. I was in an environment where my Magna Cum Laude B.A. degree from Texas Southern University was constantly being devalued. I therefore decided to accept a coworker's challenge and applied for and received a teaching fellowship to the University of Texas at Austin. That **choice** has clearly made the difference in many selection arenas, as a master's degree sets you apart from the many who hold the bachelor's degree.

The next critical juncture occurred when I had gone as far in my career as I could in Houston, Texas. I knew that subsequent growth and development would have to happen in another environment. I began networking because clearly I could not make it by myself. You will never know which of the persons you will meet in life will one day have the power to open the next door for you. I, therefore, always make the **choice** to treat everybody as I would like to be treated.

My networking activity led me to my former boss who had an opening on his staff. I applied and was selected as a result of my superior performance and positive attitude while working for him. Always make the **choice** to give your best effort in each assignment.

After relocating to Washington, DC, I got the "grass is greener" bug and decided to leave the federal government and work in private industry. That was a **choice** that has made all the difference in my career. Girlfriend, I strongly suggest that you try both the public and the private sectors and determine which supports your upward mobility best.

Of course, I could go on and on about the numerous **choices** during my career following my marriage eleven years ago, most of my **choices** hinged on my desire to bolster my husband's career. Given that he is a senior executive in the federal government, and I am but two levels from that exalted point in my own career, I am totally pleased with the **choices** that I have made.

Regards,

Cheryl Prejean Greaux

Chapter 5

OUT OF THE GATE, AND OFF TO A RUNNING START

Career runners, like long distance runners, recognize that in order to stay in the race they need to set a proper pace. They know how far they can run, when to pass the baton, and where to keep their eye. They also recognize the importance of not only training well, but training consistently.

Runners say it takes patience and tenacity to cross the finish line. They know you can't panic at the starting line or think that just because you take an early lead you're guaranteed to be the first to cross the finish line. They say to win you have to keep your goals clearly in mind, know where you are at all times and not to worry about anyone else.

If you want to run your career to win, you have to do more than go the distance. First steps on a new job are important, but so are the right moves.

THE FIRST MOVE YOU MAKE
IS THE ONE YOU SHOULDN'T TAKE

No one in their right mind starts a new job or position with the intention of failing. That would be crazy. Everyone wants to remain in that honeymoon period when an employer seems loveswept. In the beginning, few people experience new job anxieties. It's not uncommon to hear a job newcomer say, "I want to start off on the right foot." Later, that same person may cry, "I struggled to be noticed but was overshadowed by others." As a black woman, it may not only be the newness of a position which will make you feel nervous but the problem of your color.

The first move black women tend to make is the one we shouldn't take—we try too hard. It makes sense, but your employer already knows that you want to leave a good impression. Unfortunately, it doesn't always work out in our best interest. You may think that agreeing to every assignment and emphasizing that you can handle anything will put you in the starting lineup. That, however, is not necessarily so. Save yourself some trouble. Don't try to do it all too soon. Often, a wonder woman attitude leads to early career cuts.

If you're going to be a super black working woman, don't be the one who loses her power by making the wrong first moves. To get off to a good start in a new position, set the stage for moving ahead by making the following moves.

Learn From the Past

Your new boss shouldn't be the only one concerned about your job history. Before you start your new position, pinpoint the attitudes and behaviors that helped or hindered your past performance. Try to narrow down the obstacles which were in your way. As you do, think about how you left previous jobs.

Act like a private investigator. Do a background check on you. Uncover the source of any interrupted career activity. Analyze your past. Find out if you tend to fall into the same old habits and patterns. Determine if your problems were due to your attitude, a person or an action. These may give you clues in what to avoid and mistakes you don't want to repeat.

Make a list of all your past problems. Be specific and describe what happened. What was going on at the time? Try to narrow the reasons behind each problem. Then review your list a second time. Think about what you would change if the same problems occurred again. While you're looking back, don't dwell on past mistakes. A new job means a new chance and an opportunity to start again. Leave your old jobs behind, and begin your new one knowing what you want for your professional future.

Take a Self-Inventory

The interviewer was probably the last person you wanted to tell about your real weaknesses. To get the job, you gave prepackaged responses.

You turned what could be viewed as a weakness into a strength. For example, "I'm detail oriented." That was a smart move. An interviewer doesn't need to know everything about you. But you do.

Once you're offered a new job, make sure your past problems are behind you. If you don't, they may get another hold of you. Whether or not your weaknesses are lateness, a bad attitude, disorganization, or poor employee relationships, head off potential problems before your new boss does.

On day one of your new job, request a copy of a performance form. Review it to determine how the company evaluates its employees. Schedule a meeting with your new boss. Ask you boss to explain each category to you, as well as what is expected of you. After you've been on the job for a while, use the form to give your performance monthly checkups.

Be a Spectator

During the first few weeks on your new job, be an Indian and not a chief. Watch what others are doing. Look around the office and find out who's who. As you do, pay attention to who the company's movers and shakers are and where key decisions are made. Find out why some employees stand out while others are passed over for promotions, advancement, or other opportunities. Other ways you can learn the company's do's and don't's are by networking and lunching with others. If no one asks you, find a way to get yourself included. Keep your ears and your hands open to any information that will clue you in to the climate of the office. Listen when you shouldn't. Keep yourself open to every opportunity.

Assess the Organization's Culture

Study the culture as if your life depended on it. Getting to know the way things are done requires being an observer rather than a doer. Look, don't touch. Find out what the rules of conduct are and how things are run. Some companies follow a strict agenda while other companies are more flexible and open to new ideas.

Your observations should give you a picture of how management operates and enable you to answer such questions as: Should you call everyone by their last name, or is everyone on a first name basis? Is there a dress code? Does everyone go out together, or do exempts go at one time and nonexempts at another? In which social activities are you expected to participate? Who has the power and how are they perceived by others? Does your boss have any power? Is he or she in a position to help you with your career and likely to support you and your ideas?

Slow It Down

As you're making your moves, don't try to do too much too soon. You want to slow dance your way through the first days, and avoid the fancy footwork. And get the unrealistic expectations out of your head. You can't rush career mobility. Unfortunately, it just doesn't happen that way. Take the initiative by asking for additional responsibility, but be patient. Know when to take the lead or when it's better to wait for someone to give you another project or task. Remember, no one knows you well. While your coworkers are still forming impressions of you, your superiors are still deciding if you have the right fit.

Give yourself time to learn the ropes and build positive working relationships. Be patient, and don't go overboard. You don't want to appear overly aggressive or turn others off.

Take the Fear Out of Saying No

Most new employees don't know when to just say no. Their second biggest fear is how to ask for help. Before you accept additional responsibilities, find out what it is you are being asked to do. Be clear about the reasons for which you were hired, and make a list of your job priorities. Decide if you can handle anything else.

As a rule of thumb, a newcomer should take on no more than one additional project or task. be selective about volunteering. Go after the extra task that's not going to take a lot of time, but will give you visibility. By all means accept a job, like United Way chairperson, which will offer you opportunities to get to know others throughout the company. Go that extra mile to get a job done in a quiet way without carrying a sign that reads, "I did; I did."

If you have to say no, you better make sure you have a list of good reasons. Say no when you don't have one more minute in your day to do another task or to do a job well. Say no if the task doesn't fit into your career plans, or if it doesn't offer exposure, advancement or development. Never sound like you're making excuses. Simply explain your reason for saying no. If you don't have the ability, resources or skills, say so. When you can't find an excuse, delay doing the task, or negotiate for a better assignment. Of course, if the big boss asks you, DO IT!, even if it means putting in extra hours. Taking on added responsibilities may put you in a position to bank a favor which you can trade down the line to get someone to do something for you.

Remember, you don't want to look like you'll do anything that you're asked. New employees are often tested to see how far they'll go before saying no or to determine if they have hidden talents or skills. So, be selfish, especially if it's going to help you in your career.

When all else fails, and you can't say no, don't be intimidated about asking for help.

Become an Expert

Do what it takes to put you in demand. Make yourself a high commodity in your company. There are any number of ways that you can become the company expert. Take a job no one wants and do it well. Specialize in an area of the firm's business in which few employees have experience. Volunteer for additional responsibilities. Put in the time to learn something that can help increase your worth to the company. Devote a minimum of one hour a day to reading information relating to the industry's or company's major product or service.

Be subtle, but don't be shy about sharing your areas of expertise with your colleagues.

START OFF ON THE RIGHT FOOT!

You'll get off to a good start on your new job if you take things slowly. Take time to let others get to know you. If you want to be welcomed, help your colleagues and coworkers to feel comfortable around you. On your first day, introduce yourself to everyone from the top down. View everyone you meet as a potential resource. Use them to aid your transition into your new job. Exclude no one. Even the janitor may be able to help you. To get things done, you have to get them done through people. While you're at it, make it a standard rule of thumb to never, ever begin a new job by criticizing the company or telling others what they are doing wrong.

Get a sense of your place and how to fit in. Create the right perceptions about you by making the right moves. Remember, you're an Indian, not a chief. So, walk softly and follow your organization's leaders.

Evelyn Bailey
Career Counselor
Independence Blue Cross
Philadelphia, Pennsylvania

Thank God for mothers. Mine forced me to pursue my first job after I dropped out of college. She put fire under my feet when she very politely gave me two weeks to find a job. Back then, you didn't just send off a resumé with a wing and a prayer, and sit back. You did a shuffle from door to door filling out applications.

One of my first stops was at the phone company, who turned me down flat. And it wasn't lack of talent that disqualified me. It was my weight. That was baggage I had carried with me through most of my life and hindered me as a child. I was the biggest in the class, and it seemed like I had the biggest feet. I didn't learn to ride a bike, because I thought my bike was too small. And I didn't learn to swim because I thought I would sink. I guess we all have a reason to be insecure. But I didn't let my weight hold me down forever.

My mother taught me that only when you're forced to get out there and stretch can you use what God has given you. She also said there's no such word as can't, and that you can do anything that you set your mind to do regardless of your deficits. Her words helped me realize that I should never give up on me and the things I wanted in life. Through her advice, I also learned to question and challenge the system to achieve my goals.

At one point in my worklife, a company scheduled an interview with me by telephone. When I arrived for the interview, the interviewer looked at me and told me there were no openings. When I questioned why I wasn't told this when I called, the interviewer suddenly remembered there was one opening and gave me a test. I passed and was immediately offered the job.

I can truly say that I put mileage in my career through persistence and hard work, beginning twenty years ago. My accomplishments also occurred while I struggled to raise my two children. While I am a veteran of Corporate America, I proudly received by bachelor's degree, in 1985, at the age of forty-six. Yes, I earned my undergraduate degree as an adult learner while holding down a job and juggling my work life with my family life. Then I pursued and obtained a master's degree.

I am delighted to share with you my thoughts and general philosophy for moving into key roles and surviving in any organization. I must also add that there is no perfect way to piece together a career. You must remember that all of us are unique. We each have special skills and talents that God has given us. Unfortunately, you can restrict yourself by not using your talents unless you are pressed to do so by your circumstances.

I cherish my ability to adapt to most situation, my quest for knowledge, my creativity, and my desire to help others. Most importantly, my faith in God and knowledge of who I am and where I began have sustained me throughout my career.

Do yourself a favor, will you? Rehabilitate your self-esteem. Always do self-assessments and determine the order of your priorities. Then be proactive, prepare and learn from your experiences. So many things that take place in the world of work were not taught to us by our parents or our teachers. This, alone, can be overwhelming if you are not firmly planted. But you can go far just by knowing who *you* are; not who someone else wants you to be, but the person you really are.

While getting to know myself helped me to get ahead, I also owe my career success to not letting anyone cast me for one role and one role only. That's how I made it beyond the clerical level. It's not easy to do, but it can be done. But you may have to give others a good reason why they should let you.

Show people in your organization that you are capable. Think about it. As a group, black women have been critically important to every aspect of life. We are the mothers, teachers, counselors, support people, homemakers, caretakers, lovers, seamstresses, breadwinners, etc. We can do anything. Therefore, we should learn how to use our abilities to promote us into higher level positions so that we can improve the quality of our lives.

We must pull together, and stop participating in backstabbing. We must support each other. We also must build a good reputation by establishing a sound performance record. It is very necessary to make sure your performance is not noticed for the wrong reasons. Market yourself. Don't brag! Make sure that you are known for the right reasons.

"Networking" is also very important. It's a form of building alliances and a coalition to support you. We have more people on our individual networks than we know. We have our families, old classmates, friends, coworkers, neighbors, former school teachers and so many, many other people we have forgotten. Stop and think about your personal, professional and business networks. They are resources to help you obtain information and people who can help support you as you move up the corporate ladder.

We hear a lot about mentoring today. What is it? What is its significance? I believe that we all need mentors and we can also be mentors. A mentor is that special someone, experienced in life, who can help you reach your life goals through their guidance, support, constructive criticisms, and willingness to listen. And they can be your personal cheerleader. Surely as you receive, you can give back the same to someone else.

There's so much to be said, so many things to remember. But, most importantly, remember to stay grounded in your religion, surround yourself with loving, positive friends and family, stay goal-oriented, and always give back something of yourself to your community. And read, read, read, and know that you are limited only by the limits of your mind.

Gain the power! Keep the faith! Respect yourself.

Sincerely,

Evelyn Bailey

Chapter 6

FATAL ACTIONS

In his book *The Magic of Believing*, Claude Bristol says: "At no time can you afford to rest on your laurels...because there are others who may have eyes on your coveted place and who would like nothing better than to push you out of it if they observe that you have a weak hold on it or are doing nothing to strengthen your position."

Some of us do have "weak holds" on our career: We have bad attitudes, keep bad company, make bad decisions, have bad timing, follow bad advice and bad-mouth the company, not to mention a lot of other bad habits. To make things worse, when someone tries to tell us about these habits, we become defensive.

WHO, ME?

Yes, you. We often look everywhere but within to uncover the source of our career problems. We don't know if our problems stem from motivation or ability. If by chance we do, we often overlook common threats to our success. We fail to understand how the most innocent acts can ruin careers. For instance, going to lunch with the wrong crow, innocent gossip, or even textured nails. Many of us find it unbelievable that some things so trivial can put a career on the line. At one time headed for the upper levels, we never moved past the first rung on the ladder to success. Little slips of the tongue, impulsiveness, and overreacting put us two steps behind when we should have been three steps ahead. As a result, we kissed our careers goodbye.

HOW TO AVOID FATAL ACTIONS

1 | **Operating from reckless abandonment.** Some of us don't pay attention to what we're doing. We ain't even call some of our on-the-job behavior willful misconduct. Perhaps, we should call it willful negligence. You act as though you can do whatever you want to do without regard to the consequences. We're not sure what goes on in the mind of a black woman who drives her career this way. She's convinced herself she can do anything that she feels like doing. She comes to work when she feels like arriving to work. She thinks because she's the only black that no one can do anything to her. When she's fired, she doesn't realize she was a victim of her own undoing.

Sorry, sister, but you're not invincible. So, run your career as though you care about it. If not, you're going to have your boss thinking that you don't know what you're doing or that you're incompetent. While you're at it, pick and choose your battles. And think before you act, or you'll be not only sorry but fired.

2 | **"C.P." (Colored People) time management.** Get a watch! As a people, we joke that black people can't start or arrive anywhere unless it's on "C.P." time. And if a black person's holding a function, most of us don't bother to show up on time. We assume that whoever's giving it will probably be late. You may be right. But if your way of being on time is to be late all the time, think about the message it sends. Your company may think that you have no regard for your employer's time or schedule.

Recognize that timing is important, not just in terms of your arrival or departures. There's a clock for other events in your career: for example, when to ask for raises, when to approach your boss with good or bad news, or when to pick and choose your battles. Then there's the clock that management uses to measure activities, like how long a meeting should last or how long a task should take. Finally, there's a clock that is ticking away inside your career plans that should tell you how long it will take for you to complete your goals, complete your education, move to a certain position, etc.

To avoid this fatal action, make sure your clock is synchronized with your company's clock. And whatever you do, don't regularly run late. As a matter of fact, don't be late at all. Do everything timely. Get to work early. Arrive at meetings fifteen minutes early. Set time limits on meeting your goals, plan ahead, and don't procrastinate.

3 | **Dressing with unsuccess.** Most black women love dressing. We also enjoy things that are big, bold, and beautiful. The problem is that some of us don't make a distinction between business and casual attire. We don't always look the part. Our clothing doesn't match our company's environment. Take our earrings, for instance. As lovely as big hoops and six inches of dangling gold are, these kinds of earrings should not be a part of your corporate wardrobe.

And if looks could kill, some black women would have been unemployed a long time ago. We've got the Tammy Baker look alikes and women with hairdos that look as if they used a comb without teeth.

A few of us also think revealing is appealing. It's not. Neither is busting loose, tight-fitting clothes, or stockings with seams up the back. Image consultants emphasize that the professional woman should dress in her best and for where she's going. When you're looking to move into management, check out what the women upstairs are wearing. Dress as a fly girl after work. That's not to say that you should dress down either. Avoid wearing shoes and clothes that look as if they came off Goodwill Industries' rack or that make you look matronly.

Make sure that everything, from the way you wear your hair to the shoes on your feet, advertises that you're a professional. Get rid of any looks that draw more attention to you than to your performance.

Appearance No No's:

- No run-over heels
- No dandruff showing in the hair
- No unironed clothing
- No dirty laundry
- No sculptured or textured nails
- No unruly hair
- No sneakers in the office
- No fly girl wear
- No runs in the pantyhose
- No hems held by Scotch tape
- No hanging slips
- No outfits that look like leotards
- No noticeable missing buttons
- No nappy roots or split ends
- No shades in the office

- No overused makeup
- No splits or tears in outfits

4 **Having a "tude."** Poor work habits aren't the only reasons black women kill their careers. On companies' most unwanted list are employees who are arrogant, obstinate, critical, moody, apathetic, temperamental, whiners, or excessively impatient. Hostility won't win you any popularity contests either. Some of us let our lips hang so low you could almost step on them, or give you looks that say, "I dare you to speak to me." Other black women walk around the office as if they're mad at the world.

You might argue that, from time to time, everyone comes to work with a bad attitude. We agree. But every day? you're overdoing it when you feel compelled to react to your emotions all the time. Sometimes the problem may be what you say. Other times, it's how you say it. Or, you may be experienced at "copping special attitudes" by using the silent treatment or giving the cold shoulder. You know how some of you do it. You don't say anything, but your body language says, "Don't bother me; I'm in a bad mood."

How do you avoid this fatal action? By not wearing your feelings on your sleeve or being so touchy. Bad attitudes don't have a place in the workplace. The worst thing you can do when something bothers you is to make a scene, especially in front of the office. It's unnecessary to loud-talk a colleague or make public announcements like, "Excuse me! I have a bone to pick with you." Choose the time and place to air your grievances. While you're at it, treat your black and white coworkers with the same respect. No one wants to work with someone who's unapproachable. So, learn how to control your emotions.

5 **The company that you keep.** We know you've heard the expression, guilt by association. It happens in the workplace, too. People in your social clique may have reputations which are giving you bad press. Companies still judge employees by the company they keep. That's why you should think twice about what kind of feathers your coworkers have before you start flocking with them. Keep in mind that not everyone in your workplace may be a friend to your success. In fact, some of your colleagues and coworkers may want nothing better than to see you fail. They will try to sabotage your career by misguiding you or feeding you bad information.

How do you avoid this fatal action? Learn whom you should keep your distance from and when to part friendships. Be mindful, too, that blacks who regularly socialize with only blacks are sometimes stigmatized. A company won't choose your friendships, but they will make judgments about them. Be forewarned. Make sure all of your encounters are of the right kind.

6 **Listening to the wrong people.** Often, those who hang with the wrong crowd are also influenced by what the crowd does. Black women can get caught up in winning popularity among their peers, or become so intimidated, that we follow someone else's agenda. Unfortunately, that may cause us to take advice from the wrong people and follow those who will never be leaders. We also don't always listen to people who have legitimate careers or who know what they're talking about.

How do you avoid this fatal action? Consider the source. Look at the lives of your advisers, and determine if what they show you is worth imitating. And still be careful. People will pull you into situations, and before you know it, you're out of a job.

7 **Biting off more than you can chew.** While many black women make poor decisions about what they should wear and with whom we should associate, some of us make poor decisions about our workload. We tend to take on more than we can handle. We don't manage our job, it manages us. We allow ourselves to be stretched in so many directions that everything in our work life becomes unmanageable. We can't keep pace with what's happening, so we lose track of everything, including where our career is going.

How do you avoid this fatal action? "Look before you leap." Trouble will always follow your career when you don't make judgments about when you have enough on your table. Count the cost of any decision you make. You also have to determine when something is worth doing. Unfortunately, there are many black women who make a lot of wrong moves and poor choices because of their blind ambition. That's why it's critical to both plan and think through your decisions before you make them.

8 **Complacency.** When it comes to our careers, the baddest of habits is complacency. Remember the story of the tortoise and the hare? No one could tell that old rabbit that he wasn't going to win the race. He snoozed a little, rested too long, and thought the race was in the bag. He was overconfident and complacent; he procrastinated. Naturally, he had a short-lived career. The tortoise, on the other hand, showed initiative. He wasn't content with laying back or letting anyone else run his race. He kept on going and didn't take unnecessary breaks. You already know who first crossed the finish line.

There are black women who don't get in the race because they don't care, or they're too lazy. A job to them is a paycheck. They feel trying to get ahead is not worth the effort. they also have lots of excuses for their lack of initiative. They claim they don't feel like struggling or they can't deal with the racial barriers. Some are laid back because it doesn't translate into money. Their philosophy of additional responsibility is "It's not in my job description." That's because their career development is a permanent rest stop.

9 | **Business immaturity.** A few of us will never be considered "Miss Business Manners." We misread the politics, and we don't know the first thing about acting civilized at work. We behave unprofessionally and lack business savvy. We don't recognize the appropriate setting for speaking up or addressing issues that concern us. In meetings, we rattle on and on, unmindful that others want a chance to speak. We don't understand the social graces that come with being a professional. We also don't know the difference between a bread plate and a salad plate. We keep our dinner napkins on the table. We attend meetings without pads and paper. We pop gum; we don't just chew it. We yell across rooms when we want to get a point across or the attention of others.

How do you avoid this fatal action? Simply, fine tune your business and social etiquette. Watch what others are doing.

10 | **Having loose lips.** Talking too much to the wrong person or about things you have no business talking about—things that would put your career in serious jeopardy if anyone in management knew—is a bad idea. Add to the list repeating everything you hear, breaking corporate confidences, and not knowing when to shut up. Companies hate gossips. They frown on employees who gather around water fountains to trade their latest secrets.

A common perception of black women is that we talk too much. Sadly, some of us are worse than others. They're the ones you hear say, "Child, I've got something to tell you, and I can't keep it in any longer." They are also the women who often ask, "Did you hear...? Have you heard...? or Girl, guess who just got fired...?"

Loose lips will sink your career. The best thing you can do with loose lips is to seal them. Resist the urge to join the corporate grapevine if you'll be linked to it. But take advantage of it when it provides you beneficial information. At the same time, stay away from individuals caught up in who's doing what and with whom. Think about your integrity. Don't be the one caught doing the talking. Rumor mongers have no credibility. They are recognized as nothing more than a corporate "enquirer."

To avoid this fatal action, make sure you career is the only current affair to which you stay tuned. The next time someone comes to you with malicious gossip, don't repeat it. Tell the person that you don't want to hear it. Change the conversation. If that doesn't work, walk away. Steer clear of anyone who is quick to share the secrets of others. Soon, they'll be talking about you.

11 **Being a busybody.** "Be quiet, here comes the church bulletin!" Does this sound like someone in your office? She's the one who sees all and tells all. She butts into every conversation, and always has an opinion. She doesn't wait for an invitation to join in a conversation, and always has an opinion. She doesn't wait for an invitation to join in a conversation. She gets in it anyway. She loves to pry into everything and anything. She's worse than "Curious George." When she's not seeking information to pass on to others, she's meddling in other people's affairs. Her only concern is everyone else's business. We hope we're not talking about you.

Busybodies. There's always one in the office. They come in all varieties. They're obsessed with everything but what they should be. If you're guilty of being busy, we suggest that you settle down if you don't want to lose professional respect and a good reputation. In addition, no one will trust you. Not your colleagues. Not your boss. Not anyone.

How do you avoid this fatal action? Learn to bite your tongue if this is a habit you don't know how to break. Try to stay out of anything that doesn't concern you. Mind your business, and don't stick your nose where it doesn't belong (unless, of course, you're invited).

12 **Being a cutthroat or a backstabber.** Another problem with black women in the workplace is the "crab syndrome." The reason? There's a feeling that black women pull each other down, like crabs in a barrel. Part of this is the way race issues make black women feel defensive. Of the women we interviewed about this subject, a large majority shared that this is a result of blacks being pitted against each other. They also feel that competition and jealousy also play a role.

These jealousies, they say, make some black women feel threatened and insecure.

How can you avoid this fatal action? Contrary to popular belief, keep in mind there's enough pie for everyone. if you're spending most of your time worrying about the person running against you, you'll never win the race. While we all compete in one way or another, companies want team players, not gunners. You can't expect to get ahead by stepping on or doing in others. You need to stop such behavior. Realize that we're all going in the same direction. Pull together for your black sisters. Share the ride. Make it comfortable for each other. Don't allow your insecurities to make you feel threatened. We're all going the same way.

13 Company bashing. Would you want someone who talked about you on your team? Neither do companies. To them it smells of disloyalty. You can't expect a successful career climb if you never have anything good to say about the company. Critics of company policies and practices are viewed as negative, disloyal, and nonsupportive.

When something about your place of employment bothers you, button your lips. Think twice before joining the chorus of bashers. Wait until you're at home to say it. Don't be like a friend of ours who got caught at the wrong time and in the wrong place confessing her dislike for her boss and company. The day she did it, she was in a public restaurant unaware that her boss's husband was at the opposite table.

How can you avoid this fatal action? The safest route to avoid an embarrassing moment is to avoid off-color remarks about management or the company. When you have nothing good to say, be cognizant of your surroundings. Learn to use your peripheral vision. You never know who's listening or watching.

14 Poor interpersonal skills. As children, we were always told if we couldn't get along with our sisters, not to play together. Companies feel the same way, only they'll suggest that you work elsewhere. To remain employed and move ahead, you have to show you're a team player and can get along with others. There's no other way to get ahead in the workplace. You can't do it alone. Companies want harmony, not rivalry. They expect cooperation and a team spirit, at every level.

Yes, there will always be people in the workplace that you don't like. But keep your personality clashes from affecting your performance. Work on the way you communicate with your coworkers. Try to be congenial, and remain professional. Pinch-hit for others. Do what you have to do. If it means compromising or just being civil, do it. The one you don't get along with could one day be your boss.

15 **Bringing personal problems to work.** We're going to be very direct about this one. Don't be a "kiss and tell" person and let everyone in your office know your life's story. The office doesn't need to know that your husband is seeing another woman or that your son was recently admitted to a juvenile detention center. And no one needs to know your health or financial situation, either.

You'd be surprised at the view corporations have about employees who constantly tell everyone their problems. Situations like arguing all day on the phone with your mate or other revealing circumstances can suggest that you can't handle problems or that you're unstable.

How can you avoid this fatal action? Guard your personal life. Be discreet.

16 **Giving lip service.** Now, you know some of us need to put our tongues to rest.

We talk a bunch of hype and out of the sides of our mouth claim we're going to do things we have no intention of getting done. And it's frustrating to the person who gives ear to it and knows we're "all talk." From an employer's standpoint, we leave the impression that we're not straightforward, and we don't have a willingness to work.

How do you avoid this fatal action? Live up to your words. If you can't do something, say so. Don't paint yourself into corners by making false promises. Show you can do what you claim.

If you want to get ahead, but feel like an outsider, look at what's keeping you from being on the inside. It's not enough to stay in the game if you're not playing by the established rules. Don't get into the habit of thinking that your problems have nothing to do with you. Remove your illusions, and look at reality. Do the right thing and be committed, even when the opportunities don't seem to be there.

Barbara Brandon
Self-Employed Cartoonist
Brooklyn, New York

If I could coin one phrase to label my career climb, I'd have to call it "the great hustle." Now, I'm not talking about being a shyster or a two-bit con artist. I'm talking about nerve, savvy and saleswomanship. I don't have a cease-and-desist nature. Instead, my makeup has always been one of tenacity. I just don't accept rejection easily. Determination puts muscle into my pursuits. When I dropped out of college, six credits short of my degree, I remained committed to pursuing a career in art. And it didn't matter what it took.

My career took a little longer to shape up without that final piece of paper. Nevertheless, I strutted toward J.C. Penney with my eye on working in their art department. I didn't care that I was required to work in other areas of the company. So, off I went to the record department. Every time I came into contact with higher-ups, I informed them that I wanted to work in the art department. Eventually, I was tasked with creating displays and dressing mannequins.

An inability to pay my rent and a low salary forced me to try something different. So, I packed up my gear, moved back to New York and obtained a job as a fashion reporter for a trade publication. Once, again, I saw an opportunity. The ad stated that trainees would be considered, so I decided I had nothing to lose by applying. I carried my portfolio to the interview, and as it turned out, they also needed an illustrator.

Before I could call the job my own, I was asked if I had previous writing experience. Quick on my feet, I informed the interviewer that I regularly wrote to friends and had prepared several papers while in school. The job was mine. My, what big eyes I had. At the same time that I became a fashion reporter, a magazine called *Elan* was published. Again, I picked up my trusty portfolio and scheduled a meeting with the editor. I told her that I liked the magazine and would do anything. She challenged me to create a comic strip and that's how I developed my own cartoon, "Where I'm Coming From."

The magazine folded with a life of less than three issues, leaving behind a very devastated new cartoonist. Well, I was devastated for no more than a minute. With *Elan* no longer in the picture, I turned to other options. I sent the strip to *Essence*. The response was favorable, but I kept being put off (the editor-in-chief felt it didn't fit into their format).

Fortunately, another editor felt that I had something going for me. And the powers that be offered me an editorial test to see if I could make it as a fashion and beauty writer. I passed and was given a four-month assignment while an employee was on maternity leave. She didn't return to *Essence*, and I remained there for five and a half years.

Being my usual insistent self, I continued proposing the idea of the cartoon to *Essence*, but it lay dormant. Little did I know then that another opportunity was about the knock at my door. In 1988, my father received an award for being one of the pioneer black cartoonists. The *Detroit Free Press* sent him a letter of congratulations and indicated that they were looking for black cartoonists. I sent samples of my work, and they soon began publishing my cartoon.

With one established newspaper carrying my cartoon, I decided to broaden my horizons and attempt syndication. Knowing something more about the business because of my father, I put together a press kit with samples of my work and mailed several to various syndicates. I ambitiously wrote letters to editors, providing them with all the reasons why they should look at my work. The responses came in the form of rejections charged with suggestions that I change my strip. But I decided if it was something that I was going to dedicate my life to, I wasn't going to do the cartoon differently. Persistence paid off, because eventually a syndicate offered me a development contract for one year.

Since the strip debuted, I'm up to sixty papers. Ironically, one of the original syndicates I approached told me they wouldn't be able to sell it to ten papers. They also indicated that it was not worth their while to syndicate me. How I gloated when at a party of cartoonists, they reversed their rejection and tried to offer me a contract. Without hesitation, I turned them down.

My advice, for what's it's worth, is to keep your mind open to possibilities. Take opportunities when they arise even if they don't seem to make a lot of sense at the time. I can't spell, and I never thought I'd write. But I never say no to something because I can't do it or it isn't in my plan. I also don't make plans that can't change. I feel everyone should try new things. When *Elan's* editor asked me to do the comic strip, I never thought about saying no. I was willing to give it a try.

Recently, a well-known television producer approached me about working with him. I didn't know anything about some of the projects he wanted me to try, but I decided to lean on my intuition and God. So far, it seems to be working.

I hope you, too, will do whatever works for you to succeed. Improvise, recreate, do again, change your course, or hustle. Along the way, don't compare yourself to other people. I believe everyone has their own path. So, don't worry about making what worked for me work for you. Find your own road. And should we share some similarities, that's okay, too.

Sincerely,

Barbara Brandon

Cathy Hughes
Owner and Chairperson
Almic Broadcasting, Inc.
WMMJ-FM and WMMJ-AM
Washington, DC

In my left hand is an article that describes my twenty-year career in the radio industry, followed by a long list of awards. In my right hand is one from a Detroit paper that describes me as a "voice of the black community and a firebrand." Another says I helped pioneer "The Quiet Storm" which took off across the country and revolutionized radio programming. I have these articles in front of me trying to figure out how to tell you where it all began and how I, an African American woman, came not only to own four radio stations but to have the only African American mother and son broadcast ownership in the country. I'm not sure if you'd believe me if I told you that I didn't just walk into the radio industry but welcomed opportunities to build and learn from the ground up.

Well, here it goes. I didn't come into this business blind. I was a volunteer at a radio station in Omaha when I got my first taste and hands-on experience in broadcasting. That's how I met Tony Brown ("Tony Brown's Journal") who opened a door for me. I didn't jump at the opportunity that he was about to offer me, because I told him I never finished school. but he knew enough about my community work for the Ford Program and OIC to believe in my ability. Before I knew it, God had somehow cast me for a new role in life in the nation's capital.

Then I experienced what many African American women do, self-doubt and fear. I was in culture shock. To make things worse, I had recently lost my father and went through a very lonely period of my life. But as I looked around Washington, DC, I found hope in my African American sisters. I had never seen so many accomplished women and decided that I would aspire to become like that which I was seeing.

My earliest career stop was in the city of my new home, at Howard University, as a lecturer in the School of Communications. By working hard, being innovative and creative, I soon talked myself into a job for which I wasn't applying. I was appointed first as sales manager and then general manager of WHUR-FM, the university-owned radio station. While this marked the first time that a woman had ever been selected to manage a broadcasting facility in Washington, DC, I was met with resistance by the men, and mutiny and rebellion by some of the women. But you can learn something from me. if you're not challenged you're not going to grow.

Instead of retreating from those who wanted to see me fail, I became a revolutionary and an agent for change to move the world of radio to another level. I took a lot of people by surprise. Although I was persecuted because I didn't have the benefit of a college education, I became self-educated. I refused to become a statistic, in spite of the fact that I had been a single parent since I was sixteen. I made up my mind that things were going to change.

I was able to increase the station's sales revenue from $250,000 a year to three million dollars a year and took the station from the #28 position in the ratings to the top three in the city. I grabbed hold of my faith in God, stayed focused on my goals, and kept fortitude at my side.

With those three weapons, faith, focus, and fortitude, I took on new challenges and decided that I must own my own. My goal was to build a communication vehicle that would help African Americans to understand "information is power!" Though I knew I could build my dream, I also knew I couldn't do it alone.

That's the first secret of my success. A lot of us don't get ahead because we think we can make it on our own. In almost every situation that helped advance my career, there were people I needed to assist me. Sometimes, the only way you can go forward is to go with someone else helping you or leading the way.

My next secret is having the right attitude. You have to be unwilling to do anything other than that which you set out to do. So many times, I have had to tell myself, "Cathy, come hell or high water, you're going to go forward. I may die trying, but I will not give up." There will be times in your own life when everything you are faced with says give up. But don't.

I hail you as fellow sisters of the dream. And I wish that I could tell you that the path before you is easy. I realize that some of you may be the rare and fortunate individual for whom every door will open automatically, for whom every problem will vanish upon the wave of your hand. Praise God for you. But if your path seems uphill, and every route fraught with danger and despair, understand that what you face is what most of us have to contend with in life. No journey is ever easy or short, but in the end you will be glad you took it. Take that journey, and follow your dreams, and you will have created something of great value for you and for our people.

Sincerely

Cathy Hughes

Chapter 7

SHAPING UP YOUR IMAGE

"Now that sister has it together. Who is she?"
"I don't know, but she's a class act! Personality and all."
"Stop! Girlfriend makes a statement. Look at her. Those clothes aren't wearing her."
"You got that right. The lady is sassy."
"And she doesn't even have to talk."
"But when she does, notice how still the room becomes. Just give me half of what she has."
"Girl, you wouldn't know what to do with it. Your image is seriously missing something."
"You're one to talk. All bacon and no sizzle."
"Humph! Natalie Cole wouldn't exactly call you unforgettable."

When you have it, no one can take it away. You know it's true. Some sisters have images that are so together, you couldn't touch them if you tried. They are black women who are not only savvy, but also smart and sophisticated. They walk into a room, and they're noticed in such a way it's as if someone yelled, "Attention!"

Remember when a polished image meant one thing—dressing for success? Key ingredients, like creating the right impression and perception, were left off the list. To be taken seriously women were told to dress like a man. No one bothered to tell us to accentuate our total image. At the same time, a new type of company woman emerged. She took advantage of her beauty by using it as a weapon for success. Eventually being pretty caught up with her, and she was found out. That's because nothing existed between her lovely ears.

As time marched on, we heard clothes make the man. But today, with the right image, a sharp-looking black woman will always have the advantage. She recognizes that it's no longer enough to be pretty in the workplace and that a compelling image requires more than having "cover girl" looks. She also knows that a makeover involves more than just putting on makeup or sporting new clothes. When the corporate curtain calls, she receives more than a brief applause. her image gets her a standing ovation. Do you want to know why?

PERCEPTION: IT'S 9/10 OF A PERSON'S IMAGE

You have only one reputation to lose. And it's not what you wear that will cause you to lose it. It's how you're perceived. Every workday, people are sizing you up and deciding whether or not you fit in. It often becomes very political, because what people see and how they think they see you may determine how far you advance. Unfortunately, you can't ignore it. Everything you say, do, or wear conveys an impression of you. In the workplace, people are always going to sit in judgment of you.

So, how do you know where you stand? The best image indicator is how people respond to you. You can't take a poll, but you can look for hidden signs. Tip-offs to a poor image are bad chemistry between you and others. If you simply don't feel like you're fitting in, or that people are having trouble relating to you, your image may be missing the mark. Another clue is how people communicate with you. If they tend to brush you off, bypass, or go around you, that also may be a sign that your image needs revamping.

When you have some quiet time, make a list of your company's choice employees. Beside each name on your list, write down all the features that make them stand out. Note the characteristics which contribute to why they are where they are. What image do they project and what gives you that impression? Also, think about your initial encounters with them. Consider how and why they left you with a favorable impression.

Next, do just the opposite. Make a list of your company's black sheep or people who were fired. Include the names of employees who are skating by, getting over, or doing just enough to stay off the firing line. As you think about what distinguishes each person on your list, keep in mind that people are also noticed for doing the wrong things. You may recall, Jim Baker, Jimmy Swaggart, and Richard Nixon killed positive images because of mistakes they made.

Now, think about celebrities such as Oprah Winfrey, Magic Johnson, and Michael Jordan. Why do they have such dynamic images? What makes them so likeable? Are their personalities low-key or upbeat? How does that impact the way the public receives them? Then let's turn to Jesse Jackson. what about him turns the public off or on?

COMMON IMAGES OF BLACK WOMEN IN THE WORKPLACE

Certain black women capture the attention of corporations in the same way that celebrities do. They have a strong presence and striking features. Others gain corporate attention for doing the wrong thing. That wrong thing often causes them to be overlooked or sidestepped. As a result, they are often dead-ended in their careers.

To help you see how certain behaviors influence perception (which ultimately influences how far you'll advance) we'd like to introduce you to a sampler of some of the working world's most common images of black women. Here they are:

Corporate Diamonds:

She's on the company's honor roll and has it all—smarts, savvy, sophistication, and a striking presence. She doesn't blend in. She stands out. She knows what she wants and how to get it. She operates with vision and is goal-oriented. Management is sold on her because she's bright, knows what's politically right, knows how to make things happen.

Perception: Professional and extremely polished.

The Bench Warmer:

She's a wanna-be. Only she will never be, because she says, "I only work nine to five." She's also an "I don't do . . . " lady. She'll tell you, "I don't do phones; I don't do copying; and I especially don't do anything that's not in my job description." She's also the one who says, "I don't have time to go to school. I can't be bothered with playing the game. I'm too tired to think about planning out my life."

As you can tell, she puts no effort into having a career. Yet, she frets when opportunities don't come her way. A lot has to do with her attitude and work ethic. She just doesn't see that she's what's keeping her from getting ahead. She's passed over for positions and opportunities and given only routine tasks. Every day to her is a casual day.

Perception: Nonassertive, complacent, and lacks initiative.

Miss Vogue On The Outside, Vague On The Inside:

She's one of the workplace's "fly girls." She gives more attention to her dress than she does to her career. She does just enough to get by and panics when given extra responsibility. If you ask her about trends, don't expect to hear anything about her industry. Fashion is her answer to everything in life. Working hard doesn't make her feel good but looking the part does. She hasn't caught on that her dynamic appearance isn't enough to get her ahead.

Perception: No substance; underneath her exterior, people think there's nothing there.

Sister Christian:

She owes an apology to legitimate Christians. She's a bible-toting fraud. She uses Christianity to justify her intrusion in people's lives. Her approach is to appear "innocent as a dove" and convince you that her intentions are sincere acts of God. When she hears you have a problem, she won't hesitate to come to your side. An hour later, she's not praying but gossiping. And she wonders why people try to avoid her.

You can usually spot "Sister Christian," because she is extremely self-righteous. She quotes scriptures and does exactly the opposite. She is quick to tell you what is wrong with your life, but if you peek inside hers, you'll be surprised at what you find.

Perception: Gossip and busybody.

The Queen B:

Ironically, she is one of Corporate America's success stories. She has a sapphire tongue, rules with an iron fist, and has a direct, nononsense personality. Her "keep your distance" nature often makes it difficult to work for her and get to know her. She manages by fear and wants things done one way—hers. She's loyal to you until you cross her the wrong way. Her management style also limits employee creativity and lowers morale.

Perception: Poor interpersonal skills, unapproachable.

Unpolished Gems:

Although she has a lot on the ball, she needs to be under the wings of a corporate diamond. She has some of the pieces to making it to the top but needs nurturing and a mentor. She also sets goals but isn't sure how to put them in action. Her self-esteem is often her biggest obstacle, and as a result, she doesn't know her own capabilities. She tries to do the right thing, but one small setback turns the lion in her into a lamb.

Perception: Meek and lacks business maturity.

Soft and Lovely:

She's too sweet to sometimes compete. Everyone likes her. She's non-threatening. She's extremely dependable and leads a safe, by-the-book worklife. She thinks it's better to do as she's told than to rock the boat. In meetings, she says very little, is quiet, polite and very pleasant.

Perception: Pushover, nonassertive, passive.

The Whiner:

Complain is her middle name. She reminds you of the stereotypical "nagging wife." If you tell her to smile, she just frowns. She's extremely disagreeable and never satisfied. From her standpoint, there's never a good reason for doing anything. She's critical of everything and everyone, from the company to management to her job. You often want to turn deaf ears to her, and tell her if she's so unhappy to leave the company.

Perception: Disloyal, uncooperative, and not a team player.

Evilene:

She's the sister with the "tude." Like the "Queen B," she has a serious attitude problem. She walks around as if she's mad with the world and has an abrasive personality. Some days she's approachable and other days she's not. On the days she is approachable, she's usually very argumentative. To hold a decent conversation with her, you have to catch her in the right mood. As a result, she alienates everyone around her.

Perception: Hostile and defensive.

Loud As She Wants To Be:

You can usually hear her before you see her. She's outspoken and holds nothing back. She also lacks tact and business manners. She's quick to speak her mind and doesn't hesitate to insult you or come on stronger when she embarrasses you. That's what keeps her going. To get attention, she strives to be the life of the party, even when there isn't one going on.

Perception: Unprofessional, no discretion or diplomacy, lacks tact.

The Unfashion Bug:

You look at what she wears, and you say, "She's got to be kidding." When everyone shows up in dresses, she wears shorts. You also think to yourself, how could someone with so much brains and talent not see that her outfits don't get it. Her clothes look as if she's been hoarding them for years. She doesn't realize that what was acceptable in the seventies has now become passé. When people look at her they see everything wrong. Her clothing is an ultimate distraction, and her hair is another story. Management relies on her skills, but they're hesitant to put her in front of a client.

Perception: Uncomfortable with herself, unpolished.

HOW TO SHAPE UP YOUR IMAGE

You can get your image together. But first find what's out of place and set it straight. You may know something's wrong but not know how to fix it. Sometimes, though, the image you present may be your way of compensating for things you think you don't have. And what you project, people expect.

Most black women would have better images if we felt more self-confident. Because we don't, some of us project the wrong things, and people perceive us in the wrong way.

Give Your Image A Lift

So, what do you do with an anemic image, and how do you pump blood back into it? Redeem it with good works. Look for ways to increase your self-esteem, change your attitude, improve your demeanor, and enhance your appearance. Show the company that you are a changed person. If you do it right, you can change perceptions and get people to notice you for the right reasons.

STEPS TO TURNING YOUR IMAGE AROUND

Step 1: Develop An Objective Eye.

First, be honest. Ask yourself if there are gaps between the way you look and how you want to look. To help you find your gaps, make a list starting with words, "This is what I look like now." Make a second list beginning with the words, "This is what I want to look like after..." Decide which of your gaps are the widest. Then look for the ones which are the most narrow, and try to first work on something easy.

Karen Kaufman and her husband are principals and founders of Kaufman and Associates, a Philadelphia-based image consulting firm specializing in image development for corporate executives and professionals. Karen says that each of us has certain self-perceptions that, coupled with societal expectations, impact our image. She adds, "Our gaps contribute to what I consider are four critical perceptions in business: trustworthiness, authority, reliability, and professionalism/ promotability. Most people don't realize that people make certain assessments in the first few seconds of meeting them. What's often overlooked is that it takes seven to eight different impressions to alter that first bad impression." To help her clients determine their gaps, here are ten factors that Kaufman uses as a measure:

Proportion: Height and weight are proportional

Carriage: Posture and gait exhibit refinement

Grooming: Hair, skin, teeth, nails and body are clean and attractive

Dress: Clothing, shoes, and accessories are role appropriate

Speech: Vocalizations are distinct and modulated

Diction: Words, phrases, and sentences are well chosen

Gestures: Expressive movements are used skillfully

Etiquette: Proper manner and protocol are followed

Habits: Personal idiosyncrasies are not offensive

Style: Projected image matches identity and purpose.

Step 2: Determine If Your Image Has a Clean Bill of Health.

There are any number of signs of a poor image. To find yours, develop an objective eye. Ask yourself questions like:

- Are there areas of my image that I should play up? Play down?
- What does my outward appearance say about me (e.g., party time, strictly business, the slob, etc.)?
- Does my personality have luster or is it dull?
- How do others perceive me?
- What comes to mind when I think about my total image (e.g., beyond repair, needs major fixing, requires a tuneup, minor rebuilding, etc.)?
- When I walk into a room, do people look at me twice, or do they glance quickly and then look away?

Use the image inventory in this chapter and conduct a self-check. Which categories do you fit in? Is you image exceptional or below average?

Step 3: Get An Objective Critique.

Before you seek another opinion, find out what you can do. For starters, look at yourself. Begin with your hair. Does it look like you did it, and if so, is it styled in a way that makes you look attractive? Does it complement your features, or does your hair hide your face? And when you look at your hair style, is it flattering? Does your hair shine? Is it full, or limp and dull and in need of a good cut? if your hair is dyed, can others tell by looking at your roots? Now let's move to your face. Look at your skin. Are you still breaking out? In addition, do you have hairs growing on your chin, or do your eyebrows look like a bush garden? Do you wear your makeup naturally, or do you wear too little or too much? Remember, with makeup you should use the right blend of colors for your skin tone.

Now, march to your closet. How much of your wardrobe consists of items of clothing that you bought off a rack and wore them instantly?

While affordability may be a factor, black women don't always have their new clothes tailored when the clothes don't fit. We wear clothes that are too long, for example, coats that are too long for our height. A lot of us also wear outdated clothing. And in spite of what they tell you, clothing styles may make a comeback, but they never come back the same. For those of us who are petite, we need to shop in departments or stores that cater to the smaller frame. The same holds true for the larger-framed women. Size is no longer an excuse for not dressing well.

If your assessment is leaving you with doubts about your image, ask a friend or your boss to sit down with you for a heart-to-heart talk about your image. You'll be surprised by the insights you can gain through another pair of eyes. You may think that you can't handle it. But don't ever be afraid to ask for feedback concerning how others perceive you. Someone else may be able to offer you sound advice concerning the messages that your attitude and appearance are sending to others.

If you can't find someone, consider contacting an image consultant. Image consultants can assist you by identifying specific things that you can do to make a difference in your image. Shop around. When you come close to finding one, ask about her qualifications and credentials. Experts suggest that you find out who taught her, how long she's been in the business, and specifics on the kind of training she has received. Also, request names of her clients, and ask for references. If you can't afford an image consultant, then find out if similar services are provided at your favorite stores. One of the stores that does provide these services is Casual Corner.

Step 4: Learn What is Acceptable Dress and Behavior For Where You Work.

If your image is not the one that your company wants representing it, then find out **what is** the right image. If you think that as long as you work hard that's the only thing that should matter, you're right. It is the only thing that should matter, but it isn't the only thing that does matter. We know it seems unfair, but image experts caution that people's perception is a reality. So, go back to your goal. The only reason that you want to fit in or adapt is because it is a part of your goal to succeed. If it's not your goal, then don't play the game. Play some other game.

We're always amazed at how people will gather the right credentials to obtain a job but not bother to ask what's politically correct to hold on to it. Look around. Make sure you're in tune with the "look" and

TABLE 7.1
IMAGE INVENTORY

Category	Below Average	Average	Above Average	Exceptional
Attitude	Constant complainer especially in front of an audience	Occasional complainer but with more legitimacy	Rarely complains and usually only to superior	Never complains
Appearance	Sometimes untidy	Makes a passable impression	Always neat and appropriately dressed	Extremely professional; obviously spends time and effort on appearance
Communications	Says whatever's on mind. Lacks tact. Poor writing skills.	Writing and thoughts are usually clear with minor errors	Writing and thoughts are to point	Excellent verbal and written skills. Diplomatic
Reputation	I don't care attitude	Does enough to get by	Takes pride in work	Goes the extra mile
Reliability	Needs constant supervision	Requires normal supervision	Needs to be checked on occasionally	Needs no supervision; can be trusted to do any job on own

TABLE 7.1 (CONTINUED)

Job Interest	Shows no enthusiasm for job	Shows enthusiasm but it's not sustained	Shows sustained enthusiasm for job and other related areas	Takes an unusually strong interest in job and work
Thoroughness	Requires supervision to make sure everything gets done right	Usually reliable	Rarely leaves a job unfinished	Very meticulous
Job Knowledge	Limited technical skills and lacks willingness to learn	Meets basic skill and procedure requirements	Quick grasp of procedures, policies and techniques	Always seeks to learn more than what's required.
Initiative	Never volunteers	Usually laid-back attitude	Often makes suggestions	Take-charge attitude; leads rather than follows
Adaptability	Somewhat resentful of change	Makes normal adjustment to change	Adjusts willingly and readily to change	Helps to put change over
People Skills	Resentful of criticism. Sometimes tactless or inconsiderate	Gets along well with others	Open to suggestions, friendly and cooperative	Welcomes constructive criticism; always helpful and cooperative

"conduct" of your organization. Consider the role that you want to play. What costume does that role call for?

Step 5: Maintain An Ongoing Personal Image Development Program.

Notice, we said ongoing. Work at it, constantly, much like a politician or a celebrity. Read women's magazines to learn fashion tricks. Stay tuned to how people perceive you. But a full-length mirror, and look at yourself every day. Again, if you continue to shop but you keep ending up with the wrong things; you experiment, but your makeup or hair doesn't seem right; you're spending money but not maximizing it; you have questions and you know something isn't right—enlist the help of an image consultant.

Step 6: Become An Image Copycat.

Imitate your company's "corporate diamonds." If you expect to join the ranks of the best, start looking and acting like its top brass. That doesn't mean you need to change who you are. You just have to do what's necessary to play the part. And learn from others, too. Do the opposite of what you observe others doing wrong.

Step 7: Learn How To Be Liked.

But don't be phony. Treat others in the same manner that you would like to be treated. Recognize and respect differences in people. Performance and personality will always get you over. if you're liked, someone will probably take care of you. And if you play your cards right, you'll get ahead and ride the wave of success for a long, long time.

Step 8: Stop Doing The Wrong Things.

Image consultants say that black women have a tendency to wear too little or too much makeup. More often, they say, we lean on the side of wearing no makeup. We spend more time dressing up our bodies, but we don't dress up our face. We also use accessories that don't go with our outfits or that are not in good shape, for example, cracked purses and run-down heels. So, rid your wardrobe of those things. JoAnn Nicholson, President and Founder of Color One Associates, Inc., an international image and style consulting firm, says that women, in general, also wear hair styles, clothing, and makeup that dates them. She cautions, "If you don't look contemporary, it's hard for people to perceive that you know what you're talking about today."

Color is also another image issue and should be a basis for anyone wanting a coordinated look, emphasizes Nicholson. "It's an issue because some colors overpower you or give you a washed-out look," she adds. "Wrong colors make your skin look muddy, gray, or sallow instead of fresh and alive. As a result, someone may look at you and ask if you're sick when you actually feel fine."

CREATING THE RIGHT IMAGE

One wrong thing said, or one wrong thing put on (like worn-down shoes), can take a look or image away. When it's gone, we have to work much harder to make a comeback. Image involves many things and not just finding a style and sticking with it. To have an image that makes a statement, you have to overcome your image problems. Common problems (some we've already mentioned) include inappropriate attire, inexpensive-looking clothing (image experts emphasize that expensive-looking doesn't have to have a price tag), wearing evening attire in the daytime, or wearing the right clothing in the wrong season.

Creating the right image is a learned thing. In addition, you can shape it up on pennies and on minimal budget. When we went to the experts, they made these suggestions:

- Buy full-length and lighted makeup mirrors.
- Experiment with separate pieces and try matching them together for that right look. Avoid color and fabric clashes.
- Find a designer who makes you look good. Keep in mind that not everything fashion designers create is complimentary to every woman.
- Don't let trends dictate your style (**HINT**: Just because the fashion pages suggest that everyone should wear pleated skirts, that may not mean you look good in them).
- Choose a look and stay with it.
- Shop at the end of the season.
- Look for quality pieces that you can mix and match.
- Train your eye to pick out something that has a good line.
- Read magazines, if you are a bad dresser.

- Buy simple things like solid colors which are easy to combine.
- Instead of getting into quantity, get into quality. (Color One's JoAnne Nicholson says that two suits, five blouses and two neck accessories can make thirty outfits).
- Dress in all one color. It's elegant. Try off-white with bone stockings and bone shoes.
- Find the right shades of color for you.
- Choose a hair style that you don't have to fuss over every morning and that goes along with what you are wearing.
- Use accessories to vary your outfits. Don't be afraid to wear clips if your ears are pierced, and make sure your earrings are not too small or too large.
- Carry a handbag that coordinates with your outfit.
- Choose glasses that are updated and complement your face.
- Buy good-looking costume jewelry, for example, Monet and Napier.
- Don't mix summer and winter attire in the same outfit. At the same time, don't wear evening wear during the daytime.
- Avoid 3-inch heels and higher.
- Be careful about changing your hair color, especially when you came into the company another way. Second, dye your eyebrows the same color as your hair, and pay attention to when your roots start showing.
- There's nothing wrong with washing out that grey. Rinses are in and a good way to highlight your hair.
- If you don't polish your nails, at least keep them manicured and at a reasonable length.
- Use no more than three lipsticks and one blush.

Every woman, the experts say, should have a look that makes people want to follow her around and ask who she is, how she did her hair, and where she shops. It's not that hard to make changes to your image. But it is hard to make them if you're not objective about yourself. That's because we're so used to acting a certain way, putting ourselves in one thing, and seeing ourselves in one way.

Go back to basics. Don't separate the interior from your exterior. Evaluate your wardrobe and go through your closets to see what you should throw away. Take a class with an image consultant. There are all kinds of ways to obtain information on enhancing your image without having it cost you an arm and a leg. Just remember, shaping up your image starts with you and your goal. Ultimately, you must be yourself. Improvement is important—but don't sacrifice your identity.

Recommended Reading

Bixler, Susan. *The Professional Image.* New York: Perigee Books, 1990

Nicholson, JoAnne and Judy Lewis-Crum. *Color Wonderful.* New York: Bantam, 1990.

Patton, Jean. *Color to Color: The Black Woman's Guide to a Rainbow of Fashion and Beauty,* New York: Simon & Schuster, 1992.

Summers, Sandy. *Sizing Up: Fashion, Fitness, and Self-Esteem for Full-Figured Women.* New Jersey: Simon & Schuster, 1990.

See also "Image Source List," Appendix A, p. 265.

Xernona Clayton
Assistant Corporate Vice President
CNN
Atlanta, Georgia

My beginning was a little different from the normal. I entered communications by happenstance. It was not a path I chose nor a direction that I was charting. I always felt that each of us should do something to bridge gaps of understanding wherever they exist. I had a gift for bringing people together of varying persuasions and life-styles. I worked closely with Dr. Martin Luther King, Jr., and often heard him discuss the value of the media.

I took off on some of the things that Dr. King said. With the help of a supportive mentor, I was given numerous opportunities to address different audiences. One of those audiences included a group of broadcasters during a time when there were no blacks on television in Atlanta. My opening remarks included the statement that Dr. King had made about their value and help in dramatizing the plight of black people. While all eyes were upon me, I admonished the media that the shutouts that they depicted during the sixties' riots also existed in their industry. I further reproached them for being just as guilty as the people in the places they chose to document. Needless to say, the speech received a lot of attention and a number of calls poured in from various television stations.

One of the first stations to contact me was a CBS affiliate whose executives asked to have lunch with me. Not sure if I was to be rebuked or reproached, I didn't run away from it. I accepted, because I knew I could back up what I said. I was surprised, however, that they weren't there to chastise me but to talk about how my speech embarrassed them. They wanted my help in breaking the on-camera color barrier. I assumed that they were getting ready to ask me to identify someone. It never occurred to me that I was the one under consideration. Although I was without a television background, they were still interested. That's how the *Xernona Clayton Show* came to life.

While I was living my life I didn't plan to make a mark. I also didn't make reservations. But I was building a reputation along the way. My thread of continuity has always been to do a task better than average. Most of us fit into the category called the norm. I never felt comfortable with just being average. I don't know where that yen to go beyond the realm of average came from. I've always been an individualist and not pulled into the category of the crowd.

As I look at all the wonderful things that have happened to me, none of them was planned. I read articles that said chart your course and define where you should be at certain ages. But I didn't know how to do that. My career really wasn't about planning. I've just been fearless in accepting new assignments and challenges. I don't mind going into uncharted waters or testing new ground.

I'll give you an illustration. Early in my career while here, and prior to working at Turner Broadcasting, I had never heard of takeovers. I was also totally ignorant about the process. At the time, I was reading press clippings and knew we were trying to take over CBS. But I had no relationship to it, and Ted turner literally threw me onto the task force. I soon found myself in Washington attending a meeting among all men. Somewhat bewildered, I sat around a table listening to very high-powered discussions that sounded more akin to Greek than English. The men, on one hand, assumed I was there to make a contribution to the decision-making process. On the other hand, I felt I was in deep water. But I kept my insecurities under lid. I recalled my father saying, "if you are totally ignorant of something, don't walk in a place and start talking."

When the time was right, I made a contribution. One meaningful recommendation, and a little insight, gave the impression that I might be the smartest person at the table. Unknowingly, I raised an issue that was extremely important, but no one had planned its inclusion. I left the meeting that day thinking, "Xernona, whatever those men learned they learned it from somewhere." I figured they either read it in a book or talked to someone. I told myself that whatever someone else knows is learnable. So, I researched takeovers and became versed in the lingo. I was rewarded with an elevation in position, more respect, and self-assurance, because I had added to my own intellect. I had credibility in a new area and added a new dimension to my overall learning process.

If there's something you can learn from me, it's don't ever pass up a challenging opportunity. It may not fit with what you thought was your course, but don't deny yourself the opportunity to participate in something different. Take advantage of opportunities, and don't be afraid to do something from a back seat. If I had ever told myself I don't know how; I can't do television; or I don't know what I'm doing, I'd never be where I am today.

Sincerely,

Xernona Clayton

Pat Thomas
Director of Human Resources
National Alliance of Business
Washington, DC

No organization owes you opportunities and not every situation has appropriate positions to which you can move when you're ready for new challenges. However, you can move—but you must learn how to play the game. I'm still learning the rules even though I've been working for more than twenty years. In fact, the games will always be there, but your strategies for mastering the game should change.

I started my career as a secretary, where I learned very quickly that there would be no real room for advancement. I had been introduced to the personnel area and knew this was where I wanted to go. So I started job hunting. I was fortunate to meet a vice president of personnel who was a former secretary and very receptive to helping secretaries to advance. She was instrumental in getting me hired as an employment manager. Over the next several years, I held several other positions in personnel including assistant personnel manager, compensation and classification analyst, personnel manager, to my current position as director of human resources.

Don't think my career moves were as simple as stated here. In fact, I was put in my place on numerous occasions—shot down by words and actions! I didn't really understand the game of moving ahead. But I knew I needed to do something. I knew I could not continue crawling;

sooner or later I had to get off my knees. I started watching the players on the job and learned from their mistakes and successes. For example, I learned that it was a good idea to let supervisors know you're willing to take on additional projects or responsibilities. I also learned to choose your battles carefully and to be careful of whom you socialize with both on and off the job site.

"If you wanna play the game, you gotta know the rules!!"

OK. So where's the list of rules? Who makes up rules? Can I change the ones I don't like? Are the rules for women different than the ones for men? Are the rules for women of color harder to recognize than those for other women? the brothers? Do the rules "really" apply to me? After all, I just got my Ph.D! And I do dress well! What's the game called anyway? Is it on cable?

You hear about "Games" people play all the time. What's different about this one is that it must be understood thoroughly by all of us who are striving to succeed and survive in the work world. Particularly by women of color. "The Game" is called *Office/Workplace Politics.* Office/Workplace Politics is defined as:

> The unavoidable games organizations and companies
> play that can propel, stall, or destroy a career.

Destroy a career! Umm! Sounds serious, you say. So what about these "Rules?" Sounds like you'd better learn to follow the rules. At least for as long as you plan to work. Worse yet, the rules change without advance notice. Each new job, supervisor or assignment can often bring its own set of new rules. But what's so important about learning these Game rules? Well, decide for yourself. The following are the basic ones:

Rule 1   Identify and classify the organizational players. The power players aren't always the ones with important titles and big offices.

Rule 2   Get to know the people with power. Take every opportunity for them to get to know you, especially your work.

Rule 3   Seek a reliable, trustworthy source (mentor) for information, advice, feedback, and moral support.

Rule 4   Don't wait for recognition. Plan strategically to reach your goals. Don't leave promotional opportunities and success to chance!!

Rule 5 Common pitfalls of office/workplace politics can be avoided by relying on common sense and your own ethical and moral instinct.

Rule 6 Be as objective as possible...don't personalize.

Rule 7 Be open to how your own beliefs and fantasies may stand in the way of reality.

Rule 8 Bail out of a hopeless job and retain your dignity.

In theory this all sounds like reasonable advice. But if you reflect back on any unpleasant experience you might have had in your own workplace, it's likely that you either didn't know or didn't follow one or more of the above rules. So if you haven't learned the rules of "The Games" yet, here they are. And if you discover a new one, pass it on to another sister!!!

Sincerely,

Pat Thomas

Chapter 8

CORPORATE STREET
SMARTS

It's not whether you win or lose,
it's how you control the game.
—Unknown

You know the drill of the workplace. "Work smarter, not harder. Think about it, before you talk about it. Attitude accelerates mobility. Likability enhances your promotability. Watch your back and who's behind your back. 'C.Y.A.' (Cover your a——!) When in business, always put it in writing. Never bite the hand that signs your paycheck. Don't burn your bridges. You have to get along if you want to belong."

Black people call it playing the game (a.k.a. office politics). And if there's one rule that "street smart" black women follow, it's the rules of "office politics." But doesn't it just burn you up that most of the time you don't learn the rules until after you break them? And when you do, you hear that little voice inside you ask, "Why didn't anyone just tell me?"

Well, you can retire that question. You're probably having problems because you're going to work trying to satisfy yourself, and you can't. We're all political figures in the workplace. Even if you're doing all the right things (like arriving to work on time or meeting your deadlines) you have to satisfy others in order to get ahead. And they may not be satisfied until you stop lunching with anyone they don't like. The only reason you want to satisfy others is because they may have influence over the future of your career. And you know what happens when you don't play by the person in power's rules.

THE ROAD TO SUCCESS IS PAVED WITH POLITICS

When management get together in their oval offices, they don't just look at evaluations and time sheets to decide who gets ahead. They poll each other with questions like, "What do you think about Stacy? Do you like her?" Someone could lobby for her and say, "I think she'll fit in, after all, she is a good worker." Someone else might respond differently. "I don't know about that, she's not a team player." Or, they could throw up something they heard or know about a person's personal life that has nothing to do with the job they're being considered for.

If you don't recognize that politics are the way to becoming a favored daughter of the workplace, you may stumble forward. It may seem unfair, but politics are the reasons why you have to play the game. Coming to work, doing a good job, and leaving on time aren't enough to move you ahead. Again, you have to play office politics, which essentially is understanding the culture, the written and unwritten rules of your workplace and who has power. You also have to play the game, which means you have to fulfill a certain role to show you understand what is politically taboo.

We must add that not everyone has to play office politics. If you plan to stay in a particular position, and have no desire to move up, you probably won't have to carry this burden. however, at some levels of an organization, you're going to have to play the game whether you want to or not.

To move ahead, you also need to know who is in the game and whose team you're on. You need, no, you *must have* a political base from which to work and constituents (supporters and people who have influence). And you have to be not only credible, but likable and visible.

Just as important, you need a strategy to assist you in playing the game and stationing you politically. You also have to make sure that no one catches on to what you're doing. This is the key element of playing the game. If not, you'll fall and tumble, never to be resurrected again.

HOW STREET SMART ARE YOU?

Corporate Street Smarts Inventory

Answer yes or no to the following:

1. In my current work environment, several people "owe" me favors.

   yes _____   no _____

2. My advancement may mean kissing up or kissing people's rear ends.

   yes _____   no _____

3. I know who has the power in my organization.

   yes _____   no _____

4. I keep abreast of all the rumors in the grapevine.

   yes _____   no _____

5. I have volunteered for undesirable assignments or committees.

   yes _____   no _____

6. I know what makes my boss "tick."

   yes _____   no _____

7. I don't speak my mind without regard to the consequences.

   yes _____   no _____

8. I "toot" my own horn whenever I can.

   yes _____   no _____

9. I have a mentor.

   yes _____   no _____

10. I know the "key" players in my organization.

    yes _____   no _____

11. I go out of my way to be nice to people who may help me now or in the future.

    yes _____   no _____

12. I attend social activities in my organization.

    yes _____   no _____

13. I always "dress for success."

    yes _____   no _____

14. I know how my organization views me and my work performance.

    yes _____   no _____

15. I would use influence to gain a promotion.

    yes _____   no _____

Now total the number of "yes" responses:

Scoring

Below 10 Don't stop reading!!!!
10–12   Grab some political favors.
13–15   You've got our vote of confidence.

THE GAME

In her book, *Games Mother Never Taught You*, Betty Lehan Harragan says, "To become a successful and proficient player you must be popular at the gaming table; you must be someone whom others like to play with." You must understand (and never forget) that your workplace isn't just a workplace, but an organization in which, to succeed, you need to gain membership. It doesn't make a difference that you were hired. To get ahead you have to belong. And to belong, you have to get along.

When Doug Wilder, Governor of Virginia, ran for President he made a political move. While he followed the formalities of getting into the race and setting up his political base, he didn't play the game of running very well. He understood the politics of Virginia, but in running he left out the forty-nine other states. He forgot that they were also a part of that base he needed to get where he wanted to go, the White House. His ratings in the polls weren't very impressive, and he was forced out of the race. In a newspaper article, he was quoted as saying something like, "The politics at this level are different. I didn't know that."

With all his experiences, the Governor lost sight of the game and didn't recognize that it wasn't enough to assess himself, he needed to assess the power and politics outside of the environment he was familiar with. Doug Wilder knew the rules, but he forgot about the players he needed to both win and compete.

While getting ahead in organizations is easy for certain black women, staying there is a whole different ball game. No wonder so many black women lose at office politics. We make the mistake of thinking that because someone hired us, we're automatically in. But having great skills or a good education doesn't put or keep you in the game. So, don't go around building a false sense of job security because you're employed or "the only one."

We already mentioned that the politics are different at every level. In the workplace, the politics for a manager are not going to be the same as the politics for a secretary. If you don't play the game according to where you are or recognize that your career is also dependent on how well you follow the rules and your access to people, you will always lose.

IF YOU CAN'T CHANGE THEM, CHANGE YOU

There's a sign in a black bookstore that reads, "To survive we must adapt..." But this side of office politics, and playing the game, often proves to be too much for some of us. this is due to our insecurity, uneasiness, or fear of losing our job. We're also hung up on the idea that to play the game we have to commit cultural genocide or lose our black identity. Others are so caught up into this issue of "I gotta be me" that we can't figure out how to adapt, much less fit in.

Sometimes, what you should do politically may be morally wrong. We suggest you always make a moral choice. Even if it means taking a stand on an unpopular issue. Of course, don't waver either. That's how George Bush got himself into trouble. During the 1988 election, he promised no more taxes, as he told all of America to read his lips. Then he contradicted himself, and fell out of grace with the people who supported him. As a result, Bill Clinton stands to benefit in the November 1992 election. Clinton and Bush are a good political example of how what someone else does before you can help you later, politically.

Politics vs. Your Morals

When politics go up against your morals, you need to decide what is most important to you. You may lose, but at the same time you can have victory in your defeat. As crazy as it may sound, at least you'll be able to go home and sleep better than the black woman who chose politics over her morals.

Morals or no morals, it should come as no surprise to you that your company expects you to live by its rules. Isn't that what your mother or father expected? What parent hasn't told their child, "This is my house, and either you live by my rules or get out." Even those joining the military have to play politics and live by the letter of the law. They have to shave their heads, wear uniforms, and do what their told. The workplace is no different. But if you're uptight at the thought of office games, it's probably because you think you can't win. And you may be right. Or you think you'll have to pay a price by losing part of yourself.

Then, of course, there's the fear of dealing with dirty politics or paybacks.

How to Get In The Game

To play the game and become an active player, you need the same things as a good pair of shoes: comfort and fit. Not friction, but comfort and fit. And if no one is comfortable with you, you're not going to fit in no matter how well you know the rules. You learn to fit in by becoming a trusted member of your corporation's team. Second, you can't be invisible, but you must become invaluable. Or to put it another way, "don't become disposable, become indispensable."

Face it, some people will try to squeeze you out of the game. Keep in mind, too, that you'll always have to cope with people's egos. Others will let you in but won't let you play. You've got to do what you can to earn the trust of the key players so that you can get into the game and play to win.

If the people ahead of you are pulling up the ladder that is in front of you, it may be because you don't have power, or because you're on the outside of the game and don't know who has the power and how they hold on to it. One of the best ways to get power is to link yourself to someone powerful in your workplace who knows the political ropes.

But where does your skill in the game come from? You could ask ten different black women this question and hear ten different answers from "just stay in your place" or "go with the flow." Players with the best skill usually know when the stakes are too high to move and when and where to position themselves. They also know how far they can go and where their boundaries lie.

CORPORATE STREET SMARTS

If you're street smart, you have the inside track to what no one else knows or what people forget to tell you. You know how to ask the right person the right questions at the right time. You're shrewd at moving around the workplace, uncovering every loophole or figuring out how to beat the system without doing anything unethical. You might call it getting over. But you also recognize that underneath every organization are informal rules that the organization plays by and uses to determine who will receive acceptance. You use those rules to find ways to slip through the cracks and outdo your opponents.

Playing the game is not about "kissing butt," but how to politically position yourself without changing who you are. To get you in the game, here are some rules to follow:

Pregame Rules:

You cannot control:

a. The tone of the office unless you are the boss.
b. The "good ole boy" network.
c. Subordinates, colleagues, or peers who do not like minorities.
d. The values of an organization.

You can control:

a. The pace of getting information to you.
b. Your battles—which ones to participate in and which ones to avoid.
c. The favor of your boss.
d. The expansion of your support base.

SIZE UP THE ENVIRONMENT

Watch everything and everyone! Why? Every office has a way the organization runs and its do's and don'ts, which spell out how employees are supposed to behave. These unwritten rules tell you if your are expected to call all managers by their first name or use Mr./ Ms./Miss. They also explain if the dress code is relaxed, allowing for jeans and slacks, or if dresses and suits are required.

Look for other signs, for example, of racism or sexism. Are blacks segregated in certain positions? What is the title and position of the highest ranking black woman? How far is she from the top? How are women treated? How are employees promoted, through informal means (supervisor recommendation for promotion) or formal means (application process)? Also, study the behavior of people who work above you and those at levels below you. Observe your peers. Who socializes with whom, and when? Record your observations. Determine any characteristics in the environment that can help you or hinder you. To help you assess your organization, use a form such as the one below.

ASSESSMENT OF ENVIRONMENT

Table 8.1

Observations		Plus	Minus
Dress Code	Informal	Will not need to spend a lot on wardrobe	
Blacks Employment	Concentrated in clerical positions		Need to network to determine strategies for moving up
Promotion Process	Application Process	Make friends with someone in personnel	

IDENTIFY THE PLAYERS

The players in an organization can act as boosters or blockers. Boosters are those who can help you advance, while blockers are those who can hurt your advancement. Boosters and blockers can be peers, subordinates, or superiors.

Let's take a look at some typical players in the workplace:

1. Lobbyists are supporters. They influence the decisions of a company's power brokers. They decide who gets hired and who should be fired. When on your side, they will campaign to put you on the team and make you an active player in the game. Favorite line: "Do you need an endorsement?"

2. Gunners are looking out for one person and one person only. They do not give up anything without getting something in return. If you have nothing to give, stay out of their way. Favorite line: "What have you done for me lately?"

3. Traders are always looking for reliable sources to exchange (trade) information. They look at the workplace as one where people give and people take. Favorite line: "You scratch my back; I'll scratch your back."

4. BWIAs are also known as Black Women with Attitudes. These players are always noticed (negatively). They seem to be angry with everyone and pose a very dangerous problem for those who they don't like. They can "forget" to send you crucial memos or to relay information, or stall your work. Make friends only if you need information or access to key players. Favorite line: "I got mine, and you can get yours."

4. The Set-Ups have negative views of black people, particularly women. They give you projects that you cannot complete within the deadline. Set you up in projects where you cannot deliver, or team you with impossible people. Your fate is sealed because you are tossed into situations where you cannot win. Favorite line: "Somebody has to do something about *these* people in the workplace."

5. Backstabbers, like gunners, are loyal only to themselves. Their expertise is planting false information about you. They may want your job, your desk, your friends, your projects. Or, they may just not like you. They thrive in seeing others uncomfortable and are known to be dishonest, cruel, and arrogant. Favorite line: "I know what you're thinking, but you can trust me, really..."

THE PEOPLE AT THE GAME BOARD

Companies usually give us one or two types of rule books, employee handbooks or procedures manuals. They don't, however, give you a board game that shows you how you'll move or lose your turn. But they do give you the next best thing, an organization chart.

In addition to assessing the territory and identifying the players, we need to know each player's standing in the organization—at least their "paper" standing. The best place to locate this information is by examining an organizational chart. Now we all know that organizational charts reveal how things are supposed to work. Often individuals who are high on the organizational rungs may not have any real power. The power base may rest at the lower rungs. As a result, you may need to focus on two areas—who reports to whom and who has the power.

In your spare time, pull out your company's organization chart, or create your own. Each box on the chart contains a position that you can possibly move to. Again, the boxes on an organization chart also suggest who has which responsibilities, or the most power, or how people rank.

While we are taught that all people should be treated equal, an organization chart shows us that we're not all in equal standing. Look at your chart. Does the mail clerk have the same power as the president? Are there managers who are no more than figureheads on paper? Study your chart to find out who has the real power and how people moved into their positions. Keep in mind, too, that just because there are people who've sat in the same box for years, doesn't mean that they have real power. They may have been deadened in their position.

ASSESSING THE PLAYERS

Identify the major players in your organization.
Part I – Complete the indicated information in each column.

ASSESSMENT OF PLAYERS

Table 8.2

Name of Player and Title	Level of Power High, Low, None	Booster or Blocker

Part II – If the players you identified can help you, what can they do for you? Also, ask yourself, can you trust them?

Name of individual	Potential Contribution to Your Career
1.	
2.	
3.	

At this point you need to take a closer look at the players in your organization.

Watch Your Back

Watch whom you talk to and what you say. Let's take a look at Brenda's story. For a year, Brenda attended Saturday meetings for her boss because he wanted to improve his golf game. His boss originally assigned him the task, but he passed it on to Brenda. When the committee succeeded, Brenda's boss took all the credit and didn't acknowledge Brenda's involvement.

Brenda got angry and confided to her coworker, Lisa, that she was tired of her boss's credit grabbing. You can probably guess what happened next. Lisa passed the information on to others, and sure enough, Brenda's boss learned of her criticism. Their relationship soured, and Brenda was forced to transfer to another department. The lesson to be learned: don't discuss organization business or personal business in detail with anyone in the workplace. You never know who has "ears."

You Can Draw More Bees With Honey

Years ago, one of our friends experienced a lot of difficulties with a boss who loved to provoke her (talk about a hassle-free workplace). She didn't know what to do. She tried to work with him, but he always gave her a hard way to go. He seemed to be troubled by her level of expertise and angry because other managers in the company recognized she had talent and potential. Every day was a struggle for her to go to work, because she felt she had to prepare for battle. Eventually, the personality clash between her and her boss started to affect her work. In meetings, he would get into verbal swapping matches with her. That was when she decided that enough was enough; she was going to quit.

She didn't quit but followed the advice of one of the vice presidents who observed what was happening. He told her to kill her boss with kindness and not to let him draw her into his insecurities. And you know what? It worked. After a while, she gained his respect. He still didn't like her but was surprised at how she was handling the situation.

Black women are so emotional. We allow ourselves to become everyone else's target. And we let the politics eat us up and cause us heartburn. But in the workplace, you need to learn how to tame your emotions. Don't make the mistake of showing your entire hand and letting everyone know when they're getting to you. That just gives them more ammunition to use against you. Think of it as giving bullets to a person pointing an empty gun at you.

Learn To Eat Crow

We have to admit that this isn't the most welcome advice on coping with office politics. But it's still good, sound advice. You can't win every time. Some situations are best to leave alone, because you may create more problems for yourself. Or, you may have to consider the source and ask if putting yourself in the political arena is really worth it.

The best time to eat crow is when your position may be seriously harmed or when you're dealing with someone else's ignorance. Not that ignorance is an excuse, but some people aren't worth giving the time of day to. They, too, may draw unnecessary attention to you.

When you take issue with the way things are done or with the culture of an organization, you also may have to ignore some situations. You'll have to set your own boundaries and decide how much you can personally take. Eating crow often involves a compromise from you and not the other person. Sometimes, too, it means doing what you can to cut your losses while you're still ahead. Your career may last longer as you learn when it's best to say and do nothing.

Use Back Alleys and Jump Fences

A common complaint of black women is that we don't always know what's going on in our organizations because someone is withholding information from us. Often, we hear, "The problem's my boss."

One of the political taboos that we feel is no longer taboo is going over your boss's head. It used to be that you were supposed to go up the chain of command. Then companies added the "open door" policy. That gave employees free rein to talk to any level of management to resolve a problem.

We think it's okay to go over bosses' heads, but not all bosses' heads. A lot depends on the situation and who the boss knows. But if, for instance, they're already headed for the corporate slaughterhouse, it may not really matter that you approached another manager for help in handling a situation. Second, you need to be careful about your approach. That's where the back alley comes in handy. You want to find someone who will be those objective eyes and ears to offer you a solution to handling your boss.

It really pays to be nice to people. They may become your ally (constituent) in a politically tight situation between you and someone who's trying to hurt your standing in the workplace. People in the back alley are those who are willing to go to bat for you or give you insights into how to handle a situation. All you have to do is approach them off the record. In doing, so, be careful. You need to find out who lunches with whom or which people socialize together outside of work. You don't want any information about you getting into the wrong hands.

Other back alleys to information and support are through mentors, and even by attending happy hours with colleagues. You can also use professional organizations to help you find your way through the political maze of your organization.

Find Out What Makes People Tick

Your purpose in succeeding at playing the game is to not push people's buttons the wrong way, but to understand where they're coming from. Half the time, though, we kill our career because we don't understand the culture of our workplace.

Your career can profit from your learning what rubs people the wrong way and the pet peeves of your organization. That takes a lot of observation, from watching body language to the way people respond to you or others in certain situations. You also may have to align yourself with an informant or someone who either has power, or is close to someone who has power, and can give you the inside scoop on the company's likes and dislikes. And remember, there's nothing wrong in taking the time and trouble to get people to help you understand the informal and formal power systems at play on your job.

CHOOSE YOUR BATTLES CAREFULLY

Before taking sides or involving yourself in conflicts consider the following:

1. Why should you get involved? Will your stance make enemies?
2. Is the battle worth making enemies?
3. How will this issue affect my job?
4. What are the odds of winning?

5. Who are the players involved?
6. What implications does this battle have on the players involved?

Learn when to let it go. Remember, you don't want to place yourself in a no-win situation. You cannot win all battles, so stop wasting your energies on small battles. Concentrate on the big ones—those that will make a difference in your career advancement. Watch these battles or they can be dangerous: your boss vs. another boss. Another rule of thumb to follow is to limit the number of enemies in an organization to none or one. Otherwise, others may view you as a black woman who can't get along with anyone.

MANAGE YOUR BOSS

First, determine your boss's political positioning. Second, keep in mind that you don't need to like your boss to do your job effectively. But you do need your boss's support to advance. in fact, make your boss your corporate campaign manager. That means you have to keep your boss on your side and in tune with your goals. It's in your best interest to also support your boss and do everything you can to make your boss look good.

Always let your bosses know what you're doing. And have them convinced that you both think alike. Your bosses will wonder if you can read their minds. They'll love you for it.

While we're throwing out tips, we'll tell you another little secret: Involve your boss in your decisions. In fact, if you make people feel they helped with a decision, you'll almost always keep them on your side and receive less resistance. It also helps to seal your acceptance and build a level of trust.

What's the best way to manage a difficult boss? That depends a lot on who the boss is and your boss's personality. Also, if you're not careful, your boss can be a roadblock to your career advancement. There are bosses who deliberately withhold information to keep their subordinates from getting ahead and bosses who believe that black women are cast for one role and one role only.

When there's a personality clash between you and your boss, it may be because your boss is insecure. If you're faced with an insecure boss, the best thing you can do is try to get other managers to rally behind you or to get a new boss. Also, do what you can to make sure your actions discredit your boss or that your boss isn't sabotaging your opportunities.

The following table should give you some help in dealing with difficult bosses. Locate the type of boss you have and follow the indicated strategies.

DIFFICULT BOSSES

Table 8.3

Type of Boss	Description	Strategies
Bully	Manages by terror. Abrasive, hostile, throws frequent temper tantrums, dictator, seems to have contempt for staff, crusty exterior	• Don't be intimidated, but don't start a battle • Ask for advice frequently • Provide assistance (try a little brown-nosing) • Stick up for your ideas. Move on if situation doesn't improve.
The Incompetent	Rose through the ranks not by skills, but by whom he/she knows. Depends largely on the skill of others for his/her success.	• Keep a work journal of your suggestions and ideas. You will need this information to request advancement, raises, etc. • Get all you can, then move on. Incompetents have tendencies to have "amnesia."
The Wimp	Quiet, unexpressive, does not make waves, little feedback, does not make demands, might be intimidated by superiors.	• To move ahead will need to bypass him/her. • Convince him/her that your ideas/ projects should be directly channeled to upper levels.

		• Keep him/her informed but don't expect a lot of support.
Know-It-All	Opinionated, pompous, superior, perfectionist, show-off.	• Get it right the first time - no typos or mathematical errors. • Handle details he/she does not want to complete. • Object to suggestions by using questions. The know-it-all likes to show off his/her knowledge, plays mind games.

Other ways of handling difficult bosses are to create paper trails to cover yourself. Follow up conversations with memos or keep a journal with the date, time, and details of conversations. If your boss is deadening or derailing your career, try to work around him or her. Get someone else on your side, for example, you boss's boss.

BE IN THE KNOW

Stop throwing away those annual reports, brochures, newsletters, speeches and other informational material distributed by your company. Why? Because all of these materials contain information (sometimes juicy, reliable information) that you need to identify players, size up the environment, or to develop career goals.

Here are some questions to clue you into the formal means of information:

a. What are the resources used to disseminate information?
b. How often is the information disseminated?
c. How is the information disseminated?
d. Who is involved with disseminating the information?
e. What individuals know about the information before its official dissemination?
f. Do you have any means to "tap" these individuals?

By the way, don't overlook the informal ways of getting information, especially the one commonly known as the grapevine. Don't turn your nose up or your ears down. The grapevine carries rumors and gossip which studies have proven can be as high as 70% to 80% accurate. Get all the information that you can so you're not left on the outside. To stay on the top you want to:

1. Identify the grapevines functioning in your organization.
2. Identify the individual people to go to for news.
3. Identify those who seem to know information before it is officially disseminated.

ASK FOR FEEDBACK

There are a lot of black women who aren't very street smart. Although they have brains and a lot of talent, their career is in a slump. They can't seem to pull ahead of the competition, and they're still trying to pull themselves out of jobs that aren't taking them anywhere.

If you still feel uncomfortable about your political savvy, find one or two people in your organization whom you trust. Tell them about your insecurities. Ask them if they feel you are playing out of your league or for suggestions on how to position yourself to get ahead. And don't be ignorant, stay informed!

Recommended Reading

Cuming, Pamela. *Turf and Other Corporate Power Plays.* New Jersey: Prentice-Hall, 1985.

Durbrin, Andrew. *Winning Office Politics.* New Jersey: Prentice Hall, 1990.

Grothe, Mardy, and Peter Wylie. *Problem Bosses.* New York: Feler Publications, 1987.

Harragan, Betty L. *Games Mother Never Taught Your.* New York: Warner Books, 1978.

Kennedy, Marilyn Moats. *Office Politics: Seizing Power, Wielding Clout.* New York: Warner Books, 1980.

Mary Hatwood Futrell
President
International Teachers Union
Washington, DC

To some degree, my career rise was purely by accident. I hadn't intended to be an activist in the union. I was a member of my local teachers' association and didn't like the fact that there were issues that weren't being addressed. This was during the time of desegregation. I thought the association should take a stronger stand about the fate of children and teachers. To advocate my concerns, I began attending forums which were held by the association.

My road to the top occurred because I stood up and was heard. I was willing to take risks and make a commitment of time and in myself. But I wasn't just willing to stand up and speak out about what should be done, I was willing to get in there and work to make sure my concerns were addressed. I recognized that it was going to take time and that it wasn't going to happen overnight. Buy my active involvement and participation in the union and association enabled me to acquire new skills that later benefited my career.

I started as a building representative. I volunteered to serve on various committees. I then was elected secretary of my local union. Subsequently, I became the first minority president of my local and state associations. These offices set the stage for me to be elected both secretary/treasurer and president of the National Education Association. Along the way, there were people who obviously didn't support me. I was even told by some that it wasn't my time; I hadn't paid my dues, and that I wasn't that active in the black teachers' association. But these thoughts never prevented me from going after what I wanted. I decided that no one else had the right to determine how long I had to wait and when I had paid enough dues. I felt that if I was defeated there were still opportunities for me within the organization. I told myself I am qualified and have proven myself in a number of arenas. If you are committed to pursuing your dreams, you too must expect that you will run against those who feel you can't do the job.

At the same time, it is important to keep the door open for others. I made it a point of making sure that I helped not only minorities but other members, especially women, who I felt would bring strong leadership to the organization. And I shared my leadership to make a more cohesive organization. I let people know that simply casting a vote is not enough. I also felt that a good leader is someone who can bring together people of different views and persuasions. Harry Truman said, "A good leader is someone who can persuade you to do something that you don't want to do and like it."

The most common mistake that I have observed in black women is that we don't realize that we can become strong leaders. We must learn to recognize that we do have something to contribute and get involved in the organizations of which we are apart. Further, we must be constantly aware that an organization is not one person but its entire membership. A true sign of a good leader is to get people involved, to get them to take risks.

Also, be willing to pay your dues. You can't go home and put your feet up and assume a position is going to be waiting for you. Do your homework and be prepared. And get involved. you can't complain about what's not happening if you're not there to bring about change.

Sincerely,

Mary Futrell

Julie Johnson
Supreme Court Correspondent
Time
Washington, DC

If you want to move up but have self-doubt, yet are trying to find your niche in the workplace, do what I did.

Option 1: Let a career pick you. Becoming a journalist came naturally, and in one sense the profession found me. Writing is something that always came easy to me. Of course I owe my direction to my parents, especially my mother who was an English teacher. But that's a story for another time and place.

You won't have to search high or low to find that talent you can turn into a profession. If you can sing, write, talk, laugh, count, use a computer, or do anything else well, you can turn your ability into a successful career.

Option 2: Be as educated as you can be. That used to be a deep-seated belief among African Americans. At some point that emphasis seems to have been pushed aside.

You must think about what education will do for you. It can situate you to be ready if you find you want to do something else. The more prepared and educated you are, the better able you are to make a move. You need also to be cognizant of what the markers are: background, experience, or education, that will determine how far and where you will advance. You also need to be committed to doing everything you can to reach the top of the yardstick by which you will be measured.

News organizations, these days, are increasingly wanting people to have more education. Right now, I'm pursuing a law degree to enhance what I can do and further specialize me as an expert. I believe in having a wide, over-arching umbrella. So, read and study to expand your knowledge in your field.

Option 3: Gain some experience. They call Missouri the "Show Me" state. Well, employers have the same attitude. They need to know you have what it takes to make it in their organization. They are not looking for bystanders. Be willing to start early and try diverse things to gain experience. Even in college, I worked on the college newspaper and became the first black editor. I also interned during the summer at newspapers and took advantage of the advice offered by my professors on which classes to take.

Option 4: Be flexible, even if it means leaving home. A lot of us have this attitude that if a career means leaving, we're not going. If that's how you feel, I say, stay. I've had to pull up stakes from one side of the United States to the other, to get the experience I needed. My willingness to travel landed me better jobs in various news bureaus, gave me more exposure, and put me in places I had never been. Traveling also positioned me to do national and political reporting. In 1984, I was assigned to the 1984 Democratic Convention. Eventually, I became a White House Correspondent and traveled overseas.

I've been a lone ranger in my profession. There aren't many women in my position, and not nearly enough black women. God has smiled favorably on me, and while I've had to make my share of tradeoffs, I've been blessed with a very supportive husband. During every period of my career, I've had to assess not only my situation but myself.

So, do us a favor. Let's stop limiting ourselves. And don't be the black woman who is overlooked because she was asleep at the switch. As the saying goes, "It is far better to be looked over than to be overlooked."

Sincerely,

Julie Johnson

Chapter 9

CHANGING THE ODDS

Only a handful of black women feel that they're up to the challenge of becoming one of those *baa-a-d* corporate sisters. But who says you're not up to it, or that you can't take on the challenge? In Marcus Garvey's book, *Message To The People*, he says, "There is nothing in the world that you cannot have so long as it is possible in nature and men have achieved it before."

As you flip through the pages of your favorite African American magazines, you shouldn't be surprised at what you read. "Former secretary finds a unique way to move into management." "Executive talked her way to the top." On and on, you read about black women who elevated their position by doing more with less and seizing opportunities at every juncture of their career.

Yes. Ordinary black women do make it to the top. And they don't have to sleep with a man to get there. Maybe you thought that making it to the top was reserved for none but the chosen. It does involve a choice, but it's yours.

ALL YOU HAVE TO DO IS ENTER

We understand how the low visibility and exposure to black women achievers may make you feel discouraged from trying to move to higher rungs on the corporate ladder. You don't compete because you feel the odds are weighted against you. But if you don't put your name in the ring, you can't expect to become a contender. A lot of what may prevent you from going for the brass ring, may go back to your self-defeating thinking patterns. You can convince yourself that you don't have what it takes or that you already have enough on your plate.

138

Perhaps you also think the bigger the organization, the harder it is to be noticed.

If you have your eye on rising, participate in your career in order to have a chance at winning. Look at it as a sweepstakes entry. You have nothing to lose by entering, but you have to enter to win.

So, How Do I Enter?

That depends on you. Creativity and risk taking are definite musts. And you need to be prepared to exploit opportunities. You also need the guts to give your career all that you've got. Believe it or not, you've been competing since you walked through your company's doors. Someone's been sizing you up from the minute your foot crossed the corporate threshold. That's right. Someone's watching you. You just may not have gotten significant attention. If no one notices you, don't expect to move up. And if you're doing just enough to get by, management scouts will surely pass you by when they conduct their corporate star search.

THE ABC'S OF MAKING IT TO THE TOP

A—Assume Nothing. Don't take it for granted that just because you're interested, everyone else knows it. Second, don't assume that the next available opening belongs to you because you've been standing in line. Keep working toward that next tier until you're made and given an offer.

B—Be Ready. Marcus Garvey called it "burning the midnight lamp." You have to be prepared. A position may already be earmarked for you. So, take yourself beyond what you think you can do. Otherwise, you may be passed by.

C—Cultivate a Positive Image. Be professional at all times, in your words, through your deeds, and by your appearance. In addition, become more serious but still show you have a sense of humor. Play down the attitude of "by my buddy," and play up the "I'm about business" side. Put respect ahead of likability.

D—Distinguish Yourself as Your Company's Limited Edition. Develop a niche. Become its leading expert. Companies are always in need of excellent writers, great organizers, dynamic speakers, computer wizards, analytical types, and number crunchers.

E—Expect to Work Your Rear End Off. Get into the habit of working smarter and harder if your aim is to get to the other side of the concrete ceilings. Double your effort. Managers and executives keep a more hectic pace. They arrive early, and they stay late. They often take the job home, or pass up lunches.

F—Focus on the Areas Where You Have the Best Chance of Success. Can you imagine how Romeo would have felt after climbing up to Juliet's window and finding his ladder was leaning against the wrong castle. You, too, want to make sure that you're headed in the right direction or else you'll miss out on hidden opportunities. In addition, draw a picture of your company's organization chart. Mark off the positions that have the most potential or doors of opportunity.

G—Gather the Right Credentials. Sometimes, the ladder we're on is too short. Our skills or our education may not extend far enough and, as a result, positions remain out of our reach. With certain companies, your only ticket through their doors may be to have an M.B.A. or knowledge of a particular skill, like programming. It's important to do your homework to make sure you can fit their needs. Check out the postings, read the classifieds, and look for areas where you come up short.

H—Hone Your Business Etiquette. Don't be a corporate hillbilly. Big cheeses usually are required to socialize, attend a variety of functions, regularly participate in meetings, and spend time with clients. So, make sure you know what is politically correct. Making it to the top means you have to look and behave like those already there. Learn how to meet and greet, as well as chat and chew. When you attend formal affairs, make sure your dress is suitable and that you know which bread plate is yours. If you don't know what to do, pick up an old-fashioned cookbook and learn about proper table settings. In addition, observe others.

I—Identify Splits in Your Company's Ranks. Exploit opportunities and make someone else's situation work to your advantage. Pull out that organization chart, again. Does someone appear to be falling out of favor or missing the mark? The only way you can get into a position is if there's a vacancy or one is created for you. So, wait in the shadows. A part of changing the odds is to be alert to new openings. That doesn't mean that you have to act like a cavalier opportunist, but the name of the game is to secure a place for you. The baton could next be passed to you.

J—Jump on Someone Else's Bandwagon. If you can lead your own, that's even better. If not, involve yourself with people who look as if they know what they're doing. Dovetail with your colleague's projects. Link yourself to those with great reputations. Single out people who are where you want to be. Make a list of the traits that distinguish them from the rest.

K—Keep Pace With Your Corporate Companions. A friend of ours always says that he doesn't believe in playing on a level field. He tries to stay one step ahead of everyone else. Now's the time for you to find out why your colleagues and others are standing where they are. Look at who's flunking and those who are making the corporate grade. Do the As have something that the Fs don't? If your coworkers only have A, B, and C qualities, make sure you have X, Y, and Z strengths. Keep the field unlevel, with you at the higher end. Be one up on the competition.

L—Look at What You Want in Relation to the Needs of Your Organization. Find out if they are compatible and if you can make a marriage of the two. Ask yourself if you have what it takes to make it to the top. Know your limitations, and don't play out of your league.

M—Maximize Your Contributions to the Company's Bottom Line. Become a costbuster. Look for ways to help increase profits and reduce costs. Add value to your worth to the company by looking for ways to become indispensable. Develop marketable skills. Expand your experience and contacts. Broaden your responsibilities.

N—Nurture Yourself. Take time out to develop yourself and respond to your own needs, for a change. Janet Jackson might have asked a different question, but what have you done for yourself lately? If you want to make your company a believer, you have to first believe in yourself. Your self-esteem will project either an "I Can" or "I Can't" attitude.

O—Operate Smart. Imitate your company's successful leaders. You don't have to become a clone, but while you're paving your way, become an executive look-alike. Practice the habits of your corporation's stars. Be what your company needs you to be without letting go of who you are or compromising your ethics. If you're not sure of what we're talking about, rent a copy of the movie *Working Girl*. Pop some popcorn, and jot down some ideas.

P—Put Your Name on Someone Else's Lips. Are you positioned where others can see you? If not, advertise. Do things to attract attention if you want to be seen. Build a coalition of support. Find someone upstairs who is on your side. Choose a mentor. Get the endorsement of others. When managers on your job offer to write you a letter of thanks for a job well done, tell them to write your boss, instead. Make your boss and the company look good.

Q—Question Your Boss. Send him or her a "Let's Discuss My Future" memo. Request a one-to-one meeting to talk about how you're doing. Be candid and straightforward. Come right out and say, "I'm looking to move ahead, and I wanted to know what I need to do to take advantage of opportunities here or in other areas of the company." if your boss says there are none, don't become discouraged. Move on, and keep searching. Talk to others within, and outside, your company.

R—Rethink Your Definition of Making It to the Top. What might not be a big deal to you might be something that matters to the company. Make sure that the things that are near and dear to your company are also close to your own heart. And be prepared to pay your dues and to put in time. Success has a price. Don't get carried away by an outsider's view of the top. Know what you're getting yourself into. Things might look a lot different once you're in.

S—Show the Company What You're Made Of. Let them see you're a team player. Give the company a taste of your loyalty. Be versatile and flexible. Don't give in to points of despair. Be persistent without being overbearing. Demonstrate that you have a thick skin and the ability to compromise.

T—Turn Your Attitude Around. Become good-natured. Throw a little humor, every now and then. Be a little friendlier, and extend yourself more. Reach out to others. Share your talents. Try to be nice. Smile. You're a candidate for success. Let others lean on you. Train the job newcomers. Let your actions send out the message that you were born to lead.

U—Uproot Yourself. Sometimes, you have to step outside or leave a company in order to get to the top. That may require making a transition, for instance, switching careers or relocating. Other times, you may need to look beyond your company's doors to build a chest of talents, and then come back in. That chest of talents can come from volunteerism, community service, participation in organizations, networking, etc.

V—Vary Your Vehicles. There's more than one way to get somewhere. If you keep on getting what you've always gotten, you're probably doing something wrong. Stop trying to get through the front door, and look for ways to sneak through the back door. Network. Take a lateral move. Go out on a limb, and do something gutsy.

W—Write Your Own Ticket. Toot your own horn. Look for ways to put more power in your hands or to put you next in line on the corporate ladder. You don't have to be nominated to get your name on the ballot. Lobby for positions that you want. Create a new job for yourself. Give a presentation. Initiate a project. Load up the suggestion boxes, and leave your name. Grab credit for yourself, by doing anything that will give you a claim to fame.

X—X-out Your Shortcomings. Get rid of some of the baggage that you've been carrying around with you. Break those habits that are working against you. You know what they are. And if bad work relations are hurting your career, mend some fences. Convert your stumbling blocks into stepping stones.

Y—Yield to High Visibility Opportunities. Forget about a "behind the scenes" career climb. It will never happen. So, set your humility aside. With every new opportunity, ask yourself what's in it for you. And look for ways to shine.

Z—Zero in on the Future. Avoid traditional roles. Have bigger eyes. Forget about positions that aren't showing the most growth potential. Bail out of dying fields and make a few new waves. Store up some bargaining chips. Build a record of performance that you can use as collateral for securing another position.

The meek seldom inherit corporate thrones. You have to be strong enough to overcome negative attitudes. You also have to have strong instincts, as well as desire, determination, and believability. In spite of what others think or say, have a fanatical commitment. Tell the skeptics, "I'm going to be a star. You can laugh at me, but one day you're going to see my name in lights."

Cater to your ambition. Get involved in your career plan, so that you can reach your goal. Also, recognize that women who succeed had a string of failures. What separates them is desire. They wanted it badly.

Dr. Lovetta L. Smith
Head Nurse, Substance Abuse Treatment Program
V.A. Medical Center
Gainesville, Florida

"Be prepared" is more than a scout motto—these are words to live by when you're a single black woman in the world of work.

Being a nurse was third on my career list—right after being a movie star and a ballerina. The first two choices fell to the side by the time I was ten; the third one stuck. Many people who knew me then might have thought my chances of becoming a nurse were about as great as my chances of becoming a movie star, particularly since at age twelve I developed severe juvenile rheumatoid arthritis, an illness that affects joints and muscles and by age eighteen put me in a wheelchair. But since I had a family who encouraged me, and teachers who supported me, I continued to act as if it was possible until it was accomplished.

My watchwords are (1) goals, (2) planning, and (3) risk taking. Set goals to find out what it takes to accomplish those goals and then be willing to do what it takes, including taking risks. I began to think of it as a "triple whammy" that I was black, female, and with a handicap, but also believed that even this combination could be overcome.

I was fortunate enough to understand that if I was going to be a nurse, I had to offer something "special" to offset the liabilities. And I set the goal to develop those special skills. I studied the ways by which one could become a nurse (there are several). I worked as a "candy striper," a hospital volunteer, and a nurse's aide. I talked to nurses and I had some good timing and good fortune. I was awarded a full scholarship for a baccalaureate degree in nursing. There were other routes that may have seemed less time-consuming in the short run (two- and three-year programs) but I intended to be a nurse for a long time and I knew that longevity in the profession would be better served by getting the college degree.

While in the program I got to know the professors and the dean, and they got to know me. That helped me when I had to start using crutches in my junior year and, they stood up for my going on clinical units in the hospital that way. It was that year that I discovered psychiatric nursing and knew that I had found my niche.

I also knew that to have the autonomy to practice in the way I wanted, a graduate degree was virtually a necessity, so I decided to work evenings, weekends, and holidays, and continued to study for a master's degree. When you're a "part-timer" (working less than forty hours per week) you get stuck with some of the less desirable time slots and assignments. That's the way it is, black or white, and it's good to recognize when race is an issue and when it's not.

My relationship with the dean led to my next piece of developing that "special" background. A former dean of the college became Executive Director of the American Nurses' Association, the national professional nursing organization, and through the connection between the two deans I became aware of a position at ANA for which I might be qualified.

With my master's degree newly in hand, I interviewed and got the position. I moved halfway across the country away from family and friends to take that job, but it was a once in a lifetime opportunity. I worked for ANA for four years and had contact with the leaders in my field. I was privy to the think and debate that forged the future directions of nursing practice in general and psychiatric nursing in particular. I began to develop a network of professional contacts that continues to be a support to my professional goals.

After ANA it was time to go back to school, this time for a doctorate. Again, it was time to search the issues and decide, a doctorate inside or outside of nursing? Once again, I decided that for the longevity of my career it needed to be a degree within nursing. One percent of nurses have earned doctorates, a fraction of a percent are people of color. It is important to build a support base: Doctoral study is difficult at the best of times—being black with a handicapping condition and using a wheelchair is not the best of times. Again, take support where you can find it—I have some black friends who are among the best and undoubtedly lifelong relationships, but I also have a white former roommate who brought library books back and forth to a hospital over an hour away from our shared apartment so I could continue to take one class and not lose my scholarship because of an unanticipated surgery. That's a true friend.

It took me six and a half years to finish that degree. Many a time I was on the verge of calling it quits, but I guess it was a combination of determination, perseverance, pride, and stubbornness that kept me at it. I even owe a debt of thanks to the one or two whom I watched graduate that caused me to think "I *know* if they can do it, *I* can do it."

I decided in the fourth year of my doctoral program that I needed a boost in morale, so I went back to work before the degree was completed, but it was also a risk to continue to suffer the doldrums that were siphoning off energy and motivation. I stayed at the university for nearly four years and then made a move to a position in a hospital. As a doctorally prepared nurse, I was involved in doing clinical research, doing individual, group, and couples therapy, teaching nurses and graduate students who use our facility, and doing consultation throughout the hospital. I did these things in the role of a psychiatric nurse clinical specialist for three years and recently assumed a head nurse position in the same hospital.

Many people ask why I took this position which "doesn't require a doctorate." My reason is that I want to learn about hospital administration and this is the portal—I also decided to work on a master's degree in nursing administration and am three-fourths of the way through that program. In approximately four years, our hospital is due to open a one hundred-bed free-standing psychiatric addition. My present goal, which I freely share, is to be a part of the management team of that facility. Goals, planning, and risk taking seem to be a formula that has worked for me before and I expect it to work again.

Sincerely,

Lovetta Smith

Enrica Morgan
President
Morgan Financial Services Corporation
Washington, DC

Ten years ago, I was mourning the death of my mother, who was also my very dear friend, and wondering if I had the strength to pursue my goal and begin anew in a second career. I was normally very determined and highly motivated (having been raised by two wonderful people who firmly anchored me in the belief that you can accomplish anything if you are willing to invest the time and effort required for mastery). But the loss of my mother, and the deep chasms that had developed between my siblings and me, had left me exhausted and empty.

My mother had fallen victim to Alzheimer's disease in 1976. In the six years that followed, all of our lives changed radically (mine, my brother, my sister, my two aunts, my three uncles). I was soon to learn that each of us reacts to illness and loss very differently and that being a caregiver would exert an ever-increasing demand upon me.

In the midst of all of this, I discovered that my position within the District of Columbia School System no longer challenged or fulfilled me. So, I began to formulate a plan to someday own my own company and provide for people many of the services involved in financial management (I had long been the caretaker of our family's assets—my mother having declared herself a nonparticipant shortly after my father's death). But I had to find the *right* time! Again, I was striving to balance my roles, for I was rapidly becoming mother to my *siblings*, financial manager, caregiver, stern mother, loving daughter, and strong niece.

It was then that I learned "Lesson No. 1"—There is no right time. Today is always the right day to do something—DO IT NOW! GET STARTED! Formulate a plan and act on it!

In 1980, I left the school system and totally immersed myself in the educational studies required of one who would serve the public in my field. This was a big step as schooling required money, and I had severed my connections to the school system. I had no money coming in. While I now tell my clients to always check their cash flow, at that time my cash had stopped flowing. Part of my plan had been to build an account which would fund my studies.

My mother's illness had progressed to the point that she could not longer remain at home. I had selected a nursing home, and I was visiting her two to three times a day. Truly I was being tested and just beginning to learn the value of persistence. I remember reading that "Life is a grindstone; whether it polishes you down or polishes you up depends on what you're made of." I decided I was made of *the right stuff* and traveling on the road to success.

The educational opportunities were very challenging, and I was tired, but stimulated. On the other hand, large chunks of my life were slipping away. My mother was no longer able to communicate. She had stopped eating (one of the true joys of her life) and was soon to be bedridden. My support system was comprised of my aunt who was then, as she is today, a beacon of strength in my life. A very strong woman, she always tended to her family and found time to help me.

Support is not a given—often our greatest resources lie within ourselves or those closest to us. My faith also has been a bedrock to me. Although it is not necessary that we ascribe to a particular theology or dogma, we must have a personal credo which provides the guiding principles of our lives.

As I continued on, three important things happened to me. I completed my studies, received a wonderful offer for employment and, early one morning, my mother slipped away.

I was exhilarated and devastated at the same time. I buried my mother knowing that I would have wanted her to stay with me always, yet accepting that the quality of her life had been so greatly diminished that God was indeed merciful. I accepted the position with a financial services company and, today, I am president of a company which I founded in 1988.

I learned much during those years and had many guideposts that I would like to share with you:

I used to think that everything was always either black or white. I now know that some shadings of gray are quite acceptable and that rigidity is not a virtue. *Persistence is.*

I have also learned that knowledge is the great equator of people. Growth in our skills and mastery in our chosen careers is what distinguishes professionals in what largely is a world of amateurs.

Something else I learned through the years is that very little is accomplished by bemoaning your failure to complete a task or allowing yourself to become overwhelmed by what lies ahead. A strong will coupled with a positive attitude will get you through the darkest times.

Faith and guidance are also my guidance. I recommend that you, too, develop a personal credo. Let it be reflective of your beliefs and the tenets by which you live your life.

Also, create a balance. Think of your life as a three-legged stool. One leg is your family and friends. Another represents your spiritual needs. The other consists of your professional goals and objectives.

Humility is another one of my guideposts. I have prayed for humility. It is wonderful to achieve goals and bask in the glow of our successes. The tragedy is to become so self-absorbed that we fail to appreciate and acknowledge the support and effort of others in our lives.

Everyone can use a guidepost for stress. I think the best one is to get physical. Exercise, participate in sports events, meditate, etc.

Finally, a special word of caution. We must be careful not to fall into the trap of racism. It can become an excuse for not pushing ahead. Be proud of who you are and what you stand for. As Colin Powell has said, "Don't let it become a problem. Let it be someone else's problem."

Sincerely,

Ricci Morgan

Chapter 10

I'M HAPPY
BUT SAD TO BE HERE

Who are you fooling by putting on that happy face? You're on a job that doesn't move you or shake you, but you pretend you're content. It's as if you'll settle for anything. Day after day, you grin and bear it, telling yourself, "This is the best that I can do." Too unmotivated to do anything, you simply find safety in staying with a corporation.

A number of black women aren't happy because we're dying in corporations or on government jobs. We can't stand our jobs, and we wish we could set our career on fire. Then we have the sisters who were already half-dead before they started working. The rest of us have no reason to worry about our career. It ran out of breath a long time ago.

No one has to tell you if you're unhappy, or if you're a career couch potato. As a matter of fact, the following song titles may come closest to describing your worklife as a black woman:

"I Can't Get No Satisfaction"
"Hey There, Lonely Girl"
"Stormy Weather"

You may insist that you feel exactly the opposite. Like being in a bad relationship, you know you're not where you should be. You're weak and feel the journey ahead is too long for you to endure. You're trying to get ahead, but you can't find your way through the workplace. And you're so reluctant to make a career move, others think you're content.

THE COMFORT NEST

Black women fall into the comfort nest for any number of reasons. Either you're tired of what you're doing, or you're too lazy to stretch your career. You also may have outgrown your job or have nothing to do. Your job is dull and boring with a capital B. You feel you've learned all that you can, and there's nothing more to get out of your job. So, you work in misery. While you may be unhappy, the golden handcuffs have locked you into your job. You want to leave, but the money's real good and your purse is tight. You really can't afford to take a pay cut and a lateral move is out of the question.

REASONS YOU MAY PERSONALLY BE UNHAPPY

Ask yourself why your career isn't moving. Seriously. Stop for a second, and pull out a sheet of paper. Write down all the reasons you're not improving professionally. After giving this exercise to most black women, we usually ask "If you could make your career happy, what would you have to change about you?"

Most black women have trouble answering the question. Aside from the concrete ceilings that prevent black women from getting ahead, our discontent keeps us content. So content that our reasons for not advancing often have a lot to do with indecision, procrastination, fear, and lack of planning.

Sometimes doing nothing costs more

We grew up in a house that sometimes needed fixing. One time there was a problem with a leaky roof. Another time, there was a problem with the plumbing. Our mother did her best to take care of the repairs as soon as possible. But sometimes, finances forced her to put off the repairs until later. She used the experience to teach us that the longer you let things go, the worse things can get. Her philosophy is that doing nothing doesn't fix a problem. She said it only makes it worse.

A lot of black women have remained in the sea of unhappiness for much too long. As time rolls on, we sink deeper and deeper into misery, eventually costing us a career. The job holds us hostage, and our career becomes lifeless.

If this sounds like you, it's time to take inventory and make some decisions, today, to overcome your discontentment.

Find Some Skyhooks

Use skyhooks to pull you up when your job makes you feel down. We also call them career pick-me-ups. They consist of creating diversions like:

- doing volunteer work in an area that interests you
- making the most of your off hours by taking classes, reading a good book, or taking up a new hobby
- doing lunches outside of work
- reading the business and community calendars of your local paper to take advantage of social events and activities
- indulging yourself in something new
- learning to relax by taking walks or meditating on the sunny sides of your job
- joining professional groups and networking
- making a conscious effort to get involved in what's going on around you
- learning something new about your company's line of business

Act Now, or Pay Later

First things first. Examine your career and determine why everything's not fine. Then center the changes on the things you need to do today. Don't put your happiness off until tomorrow. If you're not sure where to start, make a list of all the things that you know you need to do to get your career out of its rut. Work on your single biggest problem, first. Then go on to the next. Don't let your career go into cardiac arrest and force you out of a job.

Put time on your side instead of waiting until it's too late to look for ways to get out of the comfort nest. The longer you sit still, the worse things are going to get. You'll also limit your career.

Prepare for Bad Times While You're Having Good Times

Financial experts stress the importance of protecting yourself against emergencies. It also makes good career sense not to let boredom set in for too long a period. Protect yourself against unexpected situations that might interfere with your career plans.

Ways that you should prepare now for bad times are to:

✓ Keep your résumé updated. In fact, every six months revise it as necessary. Always have a spare on hand. At the same time, go fishing to see if it gets you any bites.

✓ Keep up with changing career trends. Even if you remain on the same job for years, knowledge may be your best form of protection against career casualties. Don't assume that what you don't know won't hurt you. It will.

✓ Keep an active career plan. If you're still working with an old blueprint for your career climb, throw it away. Create a new one. It should represent your vision of what you want and how you're going to get ahead.

✓ Keep contacts. Join organizations and network. Build a reliable support system and useful connections to get you through the bad times.

✓ Keep up with the competition. Remember, others—blacks, whites, Hispanics, Asians, etc.—are competing with you. They want what you want, too. Find out what's in their dog and pony show. Then make yours better.

✓ Keep your skills current. If you're going to talk, please walk the walk. Take advantage of on-the-job training. Go back to school. Become certified. Keep learning and don't stop learing.

✓ Keep you together. If your appearance or image reminds you of an old house, do some renovations. Freshen up your look and make needed repairs. If you don't know where to start, contact an image consultant. Work on both the interior and exterior you.

✓ Keep up with corporate forecasts. When trouble hits in the workplace, you don't' always get a second chance. Stay tuned to signs of trouble. They're usually there. Unfortunately, most people choose to ignore them.

MAKE EVERY MOVE COUNT TOWARD SOMETHING

To look for ways to give your career a lift, take inventory of your career. Start where you are. Track your career's progress from your first job until now. Take a large sheet of paper and draw a line from left to right. Draw small dots on the line to represent each job or position that you've held. Underneath each, record the position and any significant accomplishments you've achieved. Your chart should show you how well you have positioned yourself to reach your goals.

Career moves are like playing the game of chess. You have to plot your way to success. Every move should be a part of your strategy to win. When your career hasn't been a golden paradise, don't ask why, but look at how it got that way.

DON'T BURN BRIDGES, BUILD THEM

To get ahead in the workplace, you need supporters and a cheerleading section. But sometimes we lose that support because of our dissatisfaction with our jobs. So, we treat everyone as if they are the reason that our career's in a slump. Rallying the right kind of support can put you on your company's winners list and keep your job out of the doldrums. If you're not on the list of names to be given opportunities, do what you can to get on that list. Use others to help you. How? Make contacts, not enemies. Sell yourself to not only the people up top but those with whom you work. A good relationship with your coworkers will also give you the vote of confidence that management needs.

Whatever Is Gone, Let It Go

So what if things haven't gone well in your career? Stop depressing yourself about your job, and do something about it. Maybe you're upset because you don't have a career. Instead of navigating through the workplace, you feel like you're floating on a raft. As a friend of ours always says, you just have to catch the right wind. Just because you're career is knocked down doesn't mean you're knocked out. There are not always going to be perfect climbing conditions. Stay focused on your goal. Concentrate on where you want to go instead of looking backwards. What's important is you want better than you had.

If What You're Doing Isn't Getting You to Where You Want to Go, Do Something Different

If you don't like where you're going, steer your career in new directions. There are no rules that say you have to stay where you are. At every step of your climb, it's a wise move to have a "Plan B." Keep your options handy. Don't always travel the same route. Try new things so you can handle the unexpected. Some examples of the unexpected include:

- Losing your job after your company closes it's doors
- Having to take a pay cut
- Getting a new boss who doesn't like you
- Wanting a new position that requires skills you don't have

In every situation, always ask yourself the "what if's". Think about what reinforcements you may need should something go wrong in your career. Remember, if you do have to burn a bridge, be able to swim.

DETERMINE WHAT YOU NEED TO DO IN THE SHORT TERM TO HELP YOUR CAREER IN THE LONG RUN

Don't be a prisoner to job unhappiness. It's stifling and will interfere in your preparations for your future. Instead of retiring your career, make your future better. Tomorrow's opportunities may require you to vary your experiences, obtain new skills, make more money (to ask for more money), or expose yourself to new people.

You should always ask yourself if your version of survival needs to be upgraded. Maybe yesterday it was okay to have a high school diploma. However, tomorrow's jobs point to the need for a college degree. Now might be the time to get that education, before you're required. The same holds true for conducting a job hunt. If rumors suggest that your company is considering downsizing six months from now, why wait until you're forced to look for a new job?

In life, it's never too late to do anything, but it's better to start some things early.

SURROUND YOURSELF WITH THE RIGHT PEOPLE

Negative people won't want to see you get ahead. And keeping the wrong company can derail your career because organizations judge their employees by the company they keep, be careful about your associations, on and off the job. If someone you lunch with appears to be on the company's black list, distance yourself without looking obvious. You don't want to hurt your friend, but you also don't want to hurt your career.

You may feel that the right company is to not be in a black person's company. It's true that some companies do tend to become nervous when blacks gather together on the job. If this is happening to you and others, then collectively make a decision as to whether or not it is wise to limit your contacts to after work.

Keep good company, but also involve yourself in organizations and activities off the job that will put you in a professional limelight.

DEVELOP A "MY FREEDOM" PLAN

Don't stay with a company unless you're constantly growing. The wrong companies will stunt your career growth. If your job or career has you bored or hungering for more, ask for more responsibility or change jobs. If the field you're in is getting to you, than think about switching careers. Don't stay in any position or organization that is not giving you something back. In each job or position you accept, always go in with at least three things you want to get from that company. Your list could look like:

1. I want the company to pay for my schooling.
2. I want to increase my salary in one year by 20 percent.
3. I want to move into management in six months.

If your demands aren't being met, then think about moving on and putting together what we call a "my freedom" plan. Make a list of people and places who can help you make your move. Set goals for how you're going to make your break.

To STAY or GO?

Okay.

It's like this: You love your job. You love it not. You love your job. You love it not. You love your job. You love it not. You love your job. You love it not?

When the thrill of your job is gone, you may feel like you're in a bad relationship. You know you should leave. Yet, something keeps you there. Fear of the unknown? Maybe. It can't be the boredom. Money. That's it. It's the money. But after your paycheck's gone, there's still that nagging, aching, feeling. You look out your window and sing, "I shall overcome ..." Your work days are so blue.

On the other hand, you feel fine. All right, you feel sort of okay. The job doesn't pull you down, but something's seriously missing. You can't put your finger on it. The company's a great place to be. You can't beat the benefits. So, what is it that makes you want to make a getaway? You have a good position. Your boss likes you. But other people seem to be getting more and doing better. And you, too, want a piece of the pie. Then again, you're uncertain if anyone will give it to you. Maybe the simplest thing to do is to leave.... To stay or go? That is the question.

Our Staying Power

Black women know a lot about stability. It's a part of our history. We have held our families together, single-handedly, alone, day and night, through sickness and in health, nonstop, and seldom complained. Working continuously is one of those things that we especially do well. Our labor has always been one of love, even when it was filled with sorrow.

That staying power is a product of fear of change. It is one of the biggest obstacles to our success. We often feel it might be too traumatic to go. We can't help ourselves. When it comes to change, we expect a painful experience. We're convinced that it's not okay to change. While we do know about transitions, we don't handle job transitions well. The situations that life places us in also make us think twice about moving on.

Breaking from a job or branching into a new career is not an easy thing to do. But thousands of people are doing it. Quitting jobs. Starting their own businesses. Switching careers. Returning to learning. In fact, the Department of Labor cites that during our lifetime we will change careers three to five times. The days of jobs with longevity appear to be gone. What most of us need is career security.

Then Why Am I Sticking Around?

Did you ever think it could be a matter of indecision? Confusion? Uncertainty? The best way to get off the "stay or go" fence is to find out why you're still with a job, and ask yourself if it's worth keeping. Also, rethink your needs. You may be where you are because you don't know what else to do. A friend of ours once told us that when she started her job she just wanted a job. But then the money became good. And then the kids came. Then the company seemed like it might be growing. But when it didn't, her job became unfulfilling. And then she didn't know what to do. Then she felt stuck. And then she stayed.

SHOULD YOU CHANGE?

Let's take a look to see if your situation calls for a change or the need to stay where you are. In **Exercise 1,** check the items in Column I and Column II with which you agree and which apply to your current situation.

Exercise I

Column I

☐ You like what you are doing
☐ You are underpaid and overworked but the job provides flexibility, challenge and independence
☐ You are due a promotion shortly
☐ You have established a positive reputation as an outstanding and dependable worker
☐ You have received more than one promotion since joining the organization
☐ There is the potential for advancement
☐ The job is helping you meet established career goals
☐ You have a mentor within the organization
TOTAL ITEMS CHECKED _____

Column II

☐ You feel unchallenged
☐ You are at the top of salary range
☐ You hate your boss and he/she hates you
☐ You have been denied promotions
☐ You cannot be promoted because of downsizing or restructuring of the organization
☐ You are underpaid
☐ You do not have a mentor within the organization
☐ Your job is creating stress, fatigue, and anxiety for you
Total Items Checked _____

If you have checked more items in Column II than in Column I then it may be time to move on. More items checked in Column I than in Column II may mean you should consider staying where you are. But you also need to assess other factors. Have you checked your values lately? Values are important because they reflect what is important to us. Complete Exercise II below.

Exercise II

How Satisfied Are You?

The following list describes a number of personal satisfactions that people may value in their jobs. Review each and think about their level of importance to you by using the rating scale below:

4–Not important at all
3–Not very important
2–Important
1–Very important in my career

_____ Accomplishment (achievement, fame, recognition)
_____ Aesthetics (appreciation of beauty, arts, music)
_____ Appearance (physical attractiveness)
_____ Autonomy (independence, freedom, self-direction)
_____ Competition (winning, being #1)
_____ Contact with People (day-to-day interaction with public)
_____ Creativity (innovative)
_____ Emotional Well-being (peace of mind, adaptability)
_____ Health (physical well-being)
_____ Honesty (sincerity, openness, integrity)
_____ Justice (treating others fairly or impartially)
_____ Knowledge (seeking truth, information or principles)
_____ Loyalty (sense of duty, trustworthiness)
_____ Mental Challenge (thinking and analyzing)
_____ Money (getting rich)
_____ Physical Challenge (physical strength and stamina)
_____ Power (influence or control over others)
_____ Prestige (visible success, social recognition)
_____ Promotion (career advancement)
_____ Recognition (status, respect from others)
_____ Responsibility (accountability, reliability)
_____ Security (adequate salary, low possibility of getting fired or laid off)

_____ Skill (ability to use one's knowledge effectively)
_____ Stability (order, predictability, tranquillity)
_____ Working Alone (working independently)
_____ Working Under Pressure (pressures to meet deadlines)
_____ Working With Others (member of team)

Exercise III

Now choose ten of the work values which are presently most important to you and write them in the space below. Feel free to add any other work values that are not included in the list above and which are especially important to you.

1.
2.
3.
4.
5.
6.
7.
8.
9.
10.

From your list, circle those values which are not currently being satisfied in your present position. Underline those values which are being satisfied in your present position.

How are things looking? Are you leaning toward staying or leaving? Let's look at one final exercise.

Exercise IV

ITEM 1:

What are the benefits of staying in your present job situation?

ITEM 2:

What are the benefits of leaving your present job situation?

ITEM 3:

What do I enjoy about my present situation?

ITEM 4:

What do I like least about my present situation?

ITEM 5:

What skills or knowledge would I like to use that I am not currently using?

ITEM 6:

What is the status of your organization? Stable or unstable (consider finances, rumors of layoffs or takeover, on the verge of being sold, etc.)?

ITEM 7:

What external factors are likely to affect your organization (technological changes, governmental regulations, environmental consumer trends, demographic shifts)?

ITEM 8:

How important is your department to the overall organization?

ITEM 9:

How are minorities treated? How are black women treated?

Transfer your responses to the chart below. For each item indicate a +, − or unsure.

	+	−	Unsure
Enjoyment of Position			
Use of Skills and Knowledge			
Security of Position			

Meeting Career or Personal Goals
Company Stability
Value of Department to Organization
Treatment of Minorities
Treatment of Black Women

Scoring

Total your responses in each column. If most of your responses were in the + column, you may want to stay where you are. If most of your responses were in the − column, it's time to take that road to freedom. If you indicated you were unsure in most of your responses, stay where you are until you do some additional homework.

HOW MUCH RISK ARE YOU WILLING TO TAKE TO MAKE A CHANGE?

If you have a high level of doubt, uncertainty, or insecurity about yourself, this might be the time to work on you FIRST. What's creating your doubts, uncertainties and insecurities? Are there ways you can decrease the factors which may be immobilizing you?

Before taking any actions determine where that next job will take you and what it will give you that you don't already have. In other words, what kind of return will you receive in terms of benefits, money, skills, experience, security, satisfaction, or contacts? Remember change is risky—if you do not have what it takes to assume whatever comes your way, STAY WHERE YOU ARE! On the other hand, if you're waiting for that push to get you going, then we offer you that push! Don't spend another day wishing that things will get better!

If You Decide to Stay ...

1. Look for new challenges. Consider a different job or take on additional responsibilities. Try something new.
2. Keep informed about the status of your company. Read all company communications concerning the company. Tap into the grapevine.
3. Prepare for the company's future. Upgrade your skills by enrolling in company training programs or in courses at a college or university.
4. Become a joiner. Participate in committees and join professional and community organizations.

If You Decide to Leave ...

1. Develop a "my freedom plan." Prepare an exit plan with specific target dates.
2. Think about the tradeoffs. Consider what you will be gaining or losing by leaving.
3. Do your homework. Look before you leap. Explore your options. Think about what you can get elsewhere.
4. Leave the right way, and check to see if your company has "gag" laws which may influence any reference checks done by prospective employers.

The results of the written exercises should not be taken as the absolute solution to your stay or leave issues. The ultimate decision is based on YOU!—the amount of risk you are willing to take, and the level of commitment you plan to invest in the effort. We offer the following guidelines to lead you to your path of freedom.

1. Identify the goals that will be met if you leave.
2. Identify potential roadblocks that might occur. Which of these roadblocks can you eliminate?
3. Be willing to take risks and to receive whatever comes your way.

GET MISERY OFF YOUR CAREER'S BACK

Don't let misery take hold of your career. If you do, it will cost you. And don't be content with just working or comfortable with just coming to work every day. If you have to be there, be genuinely happy. Keep in mind that companies are not all following the principle of last in, first out. Instead, the laid back often get laid off. If you're not contributing to the bottom line, you may end up on the firing line. Nine times out of ten if you're not making significant contributions to your company, you're not going to survive. Eventually, your sluggish career climb will catch up with you and put you in an unemployment line.

Further Reading

Judith Bardwick. *The Plateauing Trap.* New York: American Management Association, 1986.
Susan Colantuous. *Build Your Career: Getting Ahead Without Getting Out.* Amherst, Mass., Human Resource Development Press, 1982.

Emily Barnes
President
Barnes & Company
Washington, DC

The one consistency in my life is my need to be challenged. When I started out in the workplace, everything was new, exciting and inviting. But after a couple of years of doing the same thing, I grew restless. I felt I wasn't working up to my potential. As a result, I went on a search to find something, anything, that would challenge me.

To take you back in time, in 1982 I was working as an assistant to the general counsel for former President Nixon's son-in-law, Ed Cox, at a quasi-government organization. Not trying to name drop, but whom I worked for should tell you that the job was to be appealing. And it was, but only for three months. Then I became one of the young and the restless. The problem wasn't the job. It was me, or rather, my internal conflicts. I'd wake up in the morning and find myself saying, "I don't want to go to work." And I'm sure you understand how that is, don't you?

Anyway, I started looking for other options. The best thing I did for me, outside of talking with other people and networking, was playing hooky from work. I knew that something I was missing was education. While I didn't expect that it would give me a first-class ticket to my "dream" job, I knew it would put me in the seat of opportunity. I also knew my chances for having more job satisfaction had a lot to do with my marketability and the kinds of skills I could offer an employer. Think about it. If you have something to offer, an employer's always going to want you.

Playing hooky from work paid off. I spent all day letting my fingers walk through the Yellow Pages (of all places) to find anything that had the word "education" in it. I called all kinds of companies, "800" numbers, national education associations, etc. You name it, I called it. Eventually, as luck would have it, I reached a woman who advised me to contact a center where I could find the resources I needed for college. So, for the next three weeks, I spent my lunch hours at the center reading information on college scholarships and grants.

I hit the jackpot when I finally found a scholarship that fit my needs. However, the only catch was that it was intended for graduates of District of Columbia high schools only. I fitted every category but that one. It was as close as I could get, and I badly wanted an education. So, I took a chance, anyway, and approached the Dean of the

University. As a result, in one month I was enrolled in college, full-time.

Uh-oh, here came another obstacle. I had an admission ticket, but no money. My other dilemma was that I living alone and had the responsibilities of most adults. I needed a place to live, had to eat, as well as pay my bills. I decided that some things had to go. One was my car, so I sold it. I also parted with my credit cards, but figured out a way to get two lines of credit. I knew that if I could work, part-time, I could use the lines of credit to work for me and replenish each in cycles. During the school year, I used the lines of credit. During the summer, I paid them off.

Well, you never have enough money. I started a home-based business on the side just by talking with people about the different types of skills and talents that I could use to assist them. While holding down a job, I began to organize and plan other people's lives and businesses. I learned there are a lot of different ways you can earn money just by tapping into your own talents, instead of keeping them in reserve. Before I knew it, I was on a roll. My small business was booming.

For as long as I can remember, I had been looking for something to make me feel complete. I mean something that truly makes a difference. I was finally finding it through my part-time business.

After school, fate took over. Being one of those people who plan everything, I searched for great jobs and was made three offers. However, with the stock market crash of 1987, all my offers vanished as quickly as they appeared. I was left without a job, no money, nothing. I spent every single day wondering, "What did I do wrong?" But that was my turning point. For the first time in my life I realized that regardless of how well you plan your life, any change can come about and wipe out all of your plans. When that happens, the best thing you can do is to find something to sustain you.

Little did I know that my sustenance would come through being an entrepreneur. As I was job hunting, again, my list of clients was growing significantly. As the list grew, I was forced to turn down job offers and look beyond my home for an office. Luck struck again after I offered my consulting services as an independent contractor to an association in exchange for use of office space. I never dreamed as a secretary that I would eventually be heading my own company.

But enough about me. What about you? Are you stretching yourself as an individual? I feel that every black woman should do things to make herself feel proud. We shouldn't go to work wondering what kind of contribution we're making to ourself, much less to the rest of the world. And should you come up empty after asking yourself, "What am I doing for myself?" do some soul searching. You, too, may have to leave your job or change your environment. If you're restless, find out what it's based on. You may need mental peace or to overcome obstacles within yourself. When you understand them for what they are, you will be better equipped to deal with whatever comes your way.

Sincerely,

Emily Barnes

Trinette Chase
Entrepreneur
The Z Doll Collection
Germantown, Maryland

If you had a crystal ball and could glimpse into my past, you wouldn't necessarily see a string of successes. I've had my ups and had my downs. I also didn't plan every move or gather the perfect credentials. In fact, I had no credentials. Instead, you'd become acquainted with a black woman who spent a major part of her life as a "have not."

I was reared in the projects. My life, as depicted in Langston Hughes's poem, "Mother To Son," hasn't been a crystal stair. Four years ago, I left the state of Florida with my youngest daughter and nothing but the clothes on my back. The drug situation was at its peak, and my oldest daughter had become involved with a drug dealer. So, I shipped her off to the Job Corps in Atlanta. At the invitation of a girlfriend, I fled to Maryland with my youngest daughter.

Things went from pretty bad to significantly worse. In less than a week, my daughter had left the Job Corps. Within one month, she was reunited with her boyfriend, the drug dealer. At sixteen, she found herself pregnant, and then her boyfriend was murdered. At the same time, my finances were moving toward "E." I also became seriously ill, was hospitalized and drained of what little money I had left. I was released from the hospital, and without finances or support (my girlfriend had moved back to New York shortly after I moved to Maryland), I was forced onto the streets and became one of the nation's homeless. I moved my family into a shelter and, shortly thereafter, my sixteen-year-old daughter lost her baby, at full term.

When bad things happen, most of us feel that we can't turn our life around. But I never let the low points of my life turn me back or cause me to give up. In fact, when my life has taken a wrong turn, I tried a different angle. That attitude helped me set the stage for my business's beginning.

I actually started making dolls for three reasons. One was as a hobby. The second reason was that I couldn't find dolls for my daughter that symbolized her heritage. The third reason was living in the shelter with my children forced me to think about what I really wanted to do and how to save my family. Though I was still somewhat broken, frustrated, and devastated, believing that things would get better carried me through. I also recalled my mother's words during my childhood in the projects. She said, "Just because you live in the projects doesn't mean you have to stay in the projects." So, I called upon my faith and made up my mind that I didn't have to remain homeless.

I returned to something familiar, dollmaking. Within the walls of the shelter, I decided that I could turn it into a business, even though technically I didn't have an address. I also involved my children and used what I already knew how to do, which was sew and style hair.

I don't know what your story is, or what your endeavors are, but never turn your back on you. You see, when I came out of the hospital my landlord didn't care about the state of my health nor my finances. The system also helped put me on the streets. But in spite of the help I wasn't getting, I kept searching for other avenues to aid me. I approached government agencies and went any place where I thought someone might help me. I never stopped trying to get ahead. Yes, I had to accept public assistance and live under "Section 8" housing. But whatever it took, I did. I peddled my dolls at trade shows, associations, and to individuals. And it paid off.

You, too, can make it. I did, though homeless, penniless and husbandless, with three children. So, if I did it, why can't you? Well, I hope these few pages out of my life will help motivate you to get yours.

Sincerely,

Trinette Chase

Chapter 11

JOB SHOPPING
WITH EASE

*More power to the black woman who's able to get the job she wants
without her efforts going up in flames. Good for her. Unfortunately
for the rest of us, we've got to do more than put our career on
automatic pilot and wait for the jobs to come. In fact, most of us will
avoid the prospect of a job search. The market is crowded, and there
are almost six million black women competing in most of the same
aisles: service, technical, sales and administrative support occupations. We won't even mention the exact number of black women who,
according to the National Urban League, are trying to enter the
workplace but remain unemployed because they can't afford adequate
child care. Or, that over 50 percent of all African American working
mothers are living in poverty.*

*But one thing we know, we try anyway. Beating pavements. Wearing
our best. Knocking down doors. Giving our feet blisters. Cold calling.
Waiting and hoping for responses that may never come. In between the
rejection and frustration, our job shopping is boring, tedious, and
time-consuming. Half the battle is knowing what we're doing.*

NO TIME TO LOSE

It's a black woman's time to go job shopping! The future work force is
expected to make a lot more room for minorities and women. Two out
of three new entrants to the workplace will be women. Minorities will

make up 26 percent of the new work force. Not only will the number of black women in the labor force increase by over 2.5 million, but there will be more jobs available to us. The vacancy signs will go up, and it will become our turn to fill many of the openings. Should that give us something to shout about? Not unless we're prepared, having something to offer, and let go of the perceptions that someone else is going to bring the jobs to us. And yes, we can get the jobs in spite of invisible barriers and concrete ceilings, which hinder our ability to survive in the job hunting arena.

Before You Get on the Job Trail ...

1. Forget about making a wish, have something more definite in mind. Do your homework. Know why you want to go shopping and what you are looking for.
2. Start shopping before the eleventh hour. Most of us, unfortunately, shop too late or on an empty stomach. We're so hungry for a change that we accept the wrong jobs or take the first one that is offered.
3. Make it easy for yourself. Don't block your job path with doubts and anxieties. Be positive and patient. Getting a job takes time. Human resource experts say that it takes a person looking for a job under the $30,000 bracket an average of five months to secure a position. Individuals looking for salaries above that level, or in more executive positions, can expect a minimum of a year's search.
4. Return to learning. Go back to school and arm yourself with new skills or additional credentials to make yourself more marketable.
5. Get a handle on your job hunting strategies. Plan ahead. Shop around. Look for fresh and new approaches to penetrating the job market.
6. Put yourself on a job shopping budget. Think about how much you are willing to invest in finding a new position. Also, ask yourself what you will need in terms of new clothes, a résumé, stamps, or stationery.
7. Locate some helping hands. Black women truly struggle with knowing when to get help or how to rely on others. Seek out professionals, like career counselors, or take a career planning course at a local community college or university. Find out what's being offered by women's centers in your area.
8. Change with the times. Be in tune with not only your needs but

the needs of the marketplace. Learn which jobs are hot and which are not. Keep up with the fast growing as well as declining occupations. Sources for job trends are available in your local library, in the reference section.

9. Don't keep your job hunt a secret, but use discretion sparingly. Get the word out. Why hide the fact that you are looking for a job (except from your employer)? Other people may be your ticket into the hidden job market. Remember, someone has to know that you're looking before they can make you an offer.

10. Go for growth. Stay away from jobs that offer no future or a chance for you to climb. And before you leap, ask yourself where a job will take you.

11. Diversify. Don't be a one-dimensional career woman. Consider adding new experiences to your level of expertise. The more you have to offer a future employer, the better your options will be.

12. Stop being a career vagabond or a corporate gypsy! While staying put too long on a job will not always benefit you, too much movement can also hurt you.

13. Don't worry about shopping for a job without a job. It's no longer an issue, with more and more people than ever before being laid off.

14. Find companies that are receptive to minorities or that have placed cultural diversity programs at the top of their agenda. According to *Working Woman* magazine, among companies with such programs are Apple Computer, Avon, Corning, Digital, DuPont, Hewlett-Packard, Honeywell, Pacific Bell, Security Pacific, U.S. West, and Xerox Corporation.

15. Think about ways to get through the bad times when a prospective employer rejects you or doesn't respond. When you are rejected (and you will be, at least once), plan to get out more. Double the number of résumés you're mailing. Remember, one rejection doesn't stop the show.

16. The day you begin a new job, start looking for your next one. Approach each day as if it's your last one. We're not saying that you should never stay, but we are saying always be prepared to go. The days of the gold watch era are gone. In today's changing times, companies are treating their seasoned veterans as seasonal employees and letting them go with only a moment's notice. If you wait until you have to look for a job, you may end up in a workplace in which you don't want to be.

17. Shop alone. Your friends are your competition, too. If you do choose to partnership your job hunt, do it with someone who's in a different field and not seeking the same type of job that you are. Carpool to job fairs; swap information; share networking tips; pass on leads that you're not going to use.

YOUR BEST JOB BETS

If there's a theme for the future work force, it's "more of us and less of men." What this means is that companies are going to have to look beyond the "old boy networks" to find a new pool of talent. And who do you think will be waiting? Us—minorities and women. The down side for black women is that we may not be ready to take on those opportunities. We are at somewhat of a disadvantage, because we are employed in occupations that the Department of Labor says are projected "to grow more slowly or decline; or, regardless of the growth, that pay relatively lower wages."

Our Underrepresentation In More Highly Skilled Occupations

In addition, the future growth positions are those that will demand higher skills, which many of us lack because we tend to be less educated. The higher the educational requirements, especially at the college level, the less likely you are to find us. If you look at, for example, health treating and diagnosing occupations, few African Americans are physicians or dentists, but many of us are dietitians and physician's assistants. There are more of us who are licensed practical nurses than registered nurses. We dominate the clerical occupations, but not the professional specialties. Under managerial specialties, we tend to stay in what we refer to as the "female ghetto," Personnel. Even there, few of us are managers. Three times as many blacks are teaching at the prekindergarten and kindergarten level than at the university and college level. We are retail sales workers, but seldom retail buyers. We are behind the shoe and apparel counters but seldom behind desks to market real estate, insurance, or securities. We significantly hold down almost every type of clerical occupation, from mail clerks to secretaries.

Other Occupations Where Doors Remain Closed To Black Women

As we write, for the first time in history a black woman stands a good chance of becoming a U.S. Senator. Black women have a thin presence in not only the executive branch of our government, but less than 2 percent of all black women have careers as mayors, authors, judges, aerospace engineers, dental hygienists, airplane pilots or navigators, geologists, speech therapists, dentists, newsroom editors, television directors or general managers, etc.

WHERE THE JOBS WILL BE

When we hear black women talk about going in search of new careers, we tell them to make sure that they are on the right side of town and where the jobs will be (see illustrations). Over 23 percent of all black women are huddled together in service occupations. Although that is where a number of the projected jobs are expected to increase, unfortunately, that's not where the money is. The Department of Labor projects that above average growth rate for jobs that require relatively higher levels of education or training, for example, executive, administrative, and managerial workers; professional specialty occupations; technicians and related support occupations.

PROJECTED GROWTH OCCUPATIONS, BY LEVEL OF EDUCATION REQUIRED
Table 11.1

Group I: *Occupations generally requiring a bachelor's degree or more education*
Systems analysts and computer scientists
Physical therapists
Operations research analysts
Psychologists
Computer programmers
Occupational therapists
Management analysts
Marketing, advertising, and public relations managers

Teacher aides and educational assistants
Registered nurses
Legal secretaries
Medical secretaries

Group III: *Occupations generally requiring high school graduation or less education*
Home health aides
Human services workers
Personal and home care aides
Correction officers

General managers and top executives
Teachers, secondary school
Teachers, elementary school
Accountants and auditors
Lawyers

Group II: *Occupations generally requiring some post-secondary training or extensive employer training*
Paralegals
Radiologic technologists and technicians
Medical assistants
Physical and corrective therapy assistants and aides
Data processing equipment repairers
Medical records technicians
Surgical technicians
Cooks, restaurant
Respiratory therapists
Licensed practical nurses
Maintenance repairers, general utility

Travel agents
Flight attendants
Salespersons, retail
General office clerks
Cashiers
Food counter, fountain, and related workers
Truck drivers, light and heavy
Nursing aides, orderlies, and attendants
Janitors and cleaners, including maids and housekeeping cleaners
Waiters and waitresses
Food preparation workers
Receptionists and information clerks
Gardeners and groundskeepers, except farm
Guards
Child care workers
Secretaries, except legal and medical
Cooks, short order and fast food
Clerical supervisors and managers
Stock clerks, sales floor

SOURCE: Bureau of Labor Statistics

Occupations with the largest job growth, 1990–2005, moderate alternative projection
Table 11.2

[Numbers rounded in thousands]

Occupation	Employment		Numerical change	Percent change
	1990	2005		
Salespersons, retail	3,619	4,506	887	24.5
Registered nurses	1,727	2,494	767	44.4
Cashiers	2,633	3,318	685	26.0

General office clerks	2,737	3,407	670	24.5
Truck drivers, light and heavy......	2,362	2,979	617	26.1
General managers and top executives	3,086	3,684	598	19.4
Janitors and cleaners, including maids and housekeeping cleaners	3,007	3,562	555	18.5
Nursing aides, orderlies, and attendants	1,274	1,826	552	43.4
Food counter, fountain, and related workers	1,607	2,158	550	34.2
Waiters and waitresses	1,747	2,196	449	25.7
Teachers, secondary school	1,280	1,717	437	34.2
Receptionists and information clerks.......................	900	1,322	422	46.9
Systems analysts and computer scientists	463	829	366	78.9
Food preparation workers..........	1,156	1,521	365	31.6
Child care workers	725	1,078	353	48.8
Gardeners and groundskeepers, except farm...................	874	1,222	348	39.8
Accountants and auditors	985	1,325	340	34.5
Computer programmers	565	882	317	56.1
Teachers, elementary	1,362	1,675	313	23.0
Guards.......................	883	1,181	298	33.7
Teacher aides and educational assistants	808	1,080	278	34.4
Licensed practical nurses.........	644	913	269	41.9
Clerical supervisors and managers ..	1,218	1,481	263	21.6
Home health aides	287	550	263	91.7
Cooks, restaurant	615	872	257	41.8
Maintenance repairers, general utility	1,128	1,379	251	22.2
Secretaries, except legal and medical	3,064	3,312	248	8.1
Cooks, short order and fast food....	743	989	246	33.0
Stock clerks, sales floor	1,242	1,451	209	16.8
Lawyers.......................	587	793	206	35.1

SOURCE: Bureau of Labor Statistics

Fastest growing occupations, 1990–2005, moderate alternative projection
Table 11.3

[Numbers rounded in thousands]

Occupation	Employment		Numerical change	Percent change
	1990	2005		
Home health aides	287	550	263	91.7
Paralegals	90	167	77	85.2
Systems analysts and computer scientists	463	829	366	78.9
Personal and home care aides	103	183	79	76.7
Physical therapists...............	88	155	67	76.0
Medical assistants	165	287	122	73.9
Operations research analysts	57	100	42	73.2
Human services workers	145	249	103	71.2
Radiologic technologists and technicians	149	252	103	69.5
Medical secretaries	232	390	158	68.3
Physical and corrective therapy assistants and aides	45	74	29	64.0
Psychologists	125	204	79	63.6
Travel agents....................	132	214	82	62.3
Correction officers...............	230	372	142	61.4
Data processing equipment repairers	84	134	50	60.0
Flight attendants	101	159	59	58.5
Computer programmers	565	882	317	56.1
Occupational therapists	36	56	20	55.2
Surgical technologists	38	59	21	55.2
Medical records technicians	52	80	28	54.3
Management analysts	151	230	79	52.3
Respiratory therapists.............	60	91	31	52.1
Child care workers	725	1,078	353	48.8
Marketing, advertising, and public relations managers..............	427	630	203	47.4
Legal secretaries	281	413	133	47.4

Receptionists and information clerks	900	1,322	422	46.9
Registered nurses	1,727	2,494	767	44.4
Nursing aides, orderlies, and attendants	1,274	1,826	552	43.4
Licensed practical nurses..........	644	913	269	41.9
Cooks, restaurant	615	872	257	41.8

SOURCE: Bureau of Labor Statistics

THE HOW TO'S OF THE JOB TRAIL

How to determine what you want

Some of us are still struggling with the question of, "What do you want to be when you grow up?" We don't know what we're looking for or even why. That's why we recommend, outside of trying out every job you can get, that you take an interest inventory. Some of the more widely used inventories are:

1. Self-Directed Search (SDS)—This is a self-administered interest assessment that asserts most people can be categorized as one of six personality types: realistic, investigative, artistic, enterprising, social, or conventional.
2. Strong Interest Inventory—This is a computer-generated report that provides information about similarities between people's interests and a variety of careers.
3. Myers-Briggs Type Indicator—Identifies personality preferences of individuals relative to their work type and environment.

Information on these inventories is normally available at career centers or at local universities and colleges. You should also contact Psychological Assessment Resources, Inc., located in Odessa, Florida, by calling 1-(800-)331–Test or the National Career Development Association in Alexandria, Virginia, at 1-(703-)548–3400.

Once you have a better idea about your chosen career, you should set the stage for your shopping spree by making up a job shopping list. Your list should answer the following questions: Why do I want to go job shopping? What am I looking for? Am I job shopping for more money, challenges, because I am facing a layoff, lack career advancement, in need of a supportive work environment, or to switch careers? The list should also include information concerning expected salary, types of positions that interest you most, and specifics on how soon you want to be in your next position. Remember, it's equally important that you consider what you'd like to do versus what you don't want to do. If you don't like to type, for example, don't bother adding jobs to your list that require typing.

How to Research the Job Market

Okay. Now, you feel you're getting somewhere. You know what you want, and it's time to find the best places to shop. But, again, before you go anywhere ask yourself if your skills will be marketable elsewhere and if so, who might be interested in them. Second, locate sources of information on companies and positions at your local library. In fact, every year *Black Enterprise* publishes a list of the best places for blacks to work.

To go after the best job buys, don't lose sight of the available opportunities projected from now until the year 2000. There is no sense exploring dead-end or declining occupations. Consider the growth rate for occupations, the number of job openings, and differences in growth by level of education. Employment will continue to shift from the goods-producing to the service-producing sector of the economy. So, what should that mean for you? Your best bets for employment, according to the Department of Labor and other experts, will be in the areas of health services, computer technology, engineering, and business services. Workers with the most education and training will have the best opportunities for obtaining high-paying jobs in growing occupations.

Whoopee! Now what? For starters, identify companies that hire individuals with your talents and skills. Head for the library, particularly those on college campuses, which is a good source when seeking this kind of information. But what are you seeking? Look up information on the:

Location of companies
Products and services of the company
Company competitors
Type of employees hired
Hiring practices—job fairs, classified ads, personnel office

Number of employees
Names of key players in the company
Management style
Corporate culture

Complete this task before and during your job shopping will eliminate wasting time pursuing companies that may not be interested in the skills and experiences you possess. We have provided a detailed listing of major resources in the Appendix.

How To Strut Your Stuff In Writing

Every step you take in your job hunt, if planned right, will lead to job success. Keep in mind, too, that we have become a very results-oriented society. For this reason, employers are not only looking at the skills and experience of prospective employees but at their accomplishments achieved in prior positions. What is an accomplishment? It's an activity that you completed that had had some **positive** impact on your organization. For example, did you:

Increase productivity
Save time and/or money
Solve a problem
Simplify procedures
Develop a new idea
Complete a major project before the deadline
Receive a special award for performance
Achieve a goal for the first time

You must be able to convey, both in writing and verbally, that you are the greatest employee a company could hope to hire, otherwise your job shopping trip will be doomed. Companies want people who can deliver. Here are some examples of accomplishments:

Processed more than 30 orders daily, resulting in sales of $150,000.
Successfully recovered $3.1 million in past due accounts.
Initiated a company newsletter which improved morale.
Developed in-service training program for counseling staff which
    reduced staff turnover by 45 percent.
Selected for and served on United Way Committee. Received
    "Outstanding Service Award" for services rendered.

Increased telephone handling capacity for incoming calls by 50 percent.

Now it's your turn.

First, prepare a list of at least 20 work-related accomplishments. Your list of accomplishments should begin with an action word. Refer to the list below to help you write your accomplishments.

Examples of Action Words

Addressed	Created	Formulated	Proposed
Administered	Decreased	Generated	Recruited
Advised	Demonstrated	Guided	Reduced
Analyzed	Developed	Handled	Researched
Approved	Devised	Headed	Simplified
Arranged	Directed	Identified	Supervised
Audited	Distributed	Implemented	Supported
Automated	Drafted	Improved	Tracked
Budgeted	Eliminated	Increased	Trained
Catalogued	Established	Maintained	Translated
Compiled	Estimated	Managed	Utilized
Conducted	Evaluated	Moderated	Verified
Contracted	Examined	Negotiated	Won
Controlled	Expanded	Performed	Wrote
Coordinated	Facilitated	Planned	
Counseled	Filed	Produced	

Second, write a letter of recommendation to a prospective employer describing your strengths, skills, and accomplishments. Before you get bent out of shape, you will not be mailing this letter! Just have someone you trust review the letter to determine if the content emphasizes benefits to the employer. Are there any areas you need to strengthen? Parts of the letter can be used to prepare responses to interview questions such as "Why should we hire you?" or "Tell me about yourself." This information will enable you to renovate your résumé.

HOW TO RENOVATE YOUR RÉSUMÉ

We know very few black women who obtained jobs without having to document their qualifications. It definitely pays to advertise. Hint,

hint, you need a résumé. A résumé has two major purposes: to take you into the future and to "market" your skills to a prospective employer. If your current résumé does not meet these purposes, then it's time to renovate. If you do not have a résumé, then it's time for you to construct one.

Time and time again, black women come to us with résumés that look as if they came out of the Dark Ages. They are still back in the past when résumés read like job descriptions, or they think because it's printed on expensive bond paper that an employer is supposed to do somersaults. Some of us try to get fancy, by using a format that is unsuitable for the field we're in. For most business situations, you will use either a chronological or functional format. The choice of format will depend on where you are trying to go—your job target. Furthermore, you don't have to stick with one format. It's okay to experiment with more than one.

The Chronological Format

The chronological résumé is the most familiar and widely accepted format. This type of résumé reflects your most recent job and works backward. Emphasis is placed on duties and accomplishments within the job titles mentioned. Use this format if:

1. You have a steady work history, with no gaps.
2. Your most current job is related to your job target.
3. Your work history reflects continuity and career growth.

Do not use this format if:

1. You plan a transition to another career.
2. You have gaps in employment.

The Functional Format

The functional résumé differs significantly from the chronological résumé. Its emphasis is on areas of strengths and not on experience. Because it downplays experience, this format is not well received in some circles. Human resource professionals often feel the candidate is hiding something when using this format. Nonetheless, the functional résumé does have some merits. Use this résumé if:

1. You hare planning a career change or redirection.
2. You have limited work experience.
3. You want to emphasize particular strong areas.

Do not use this format if:

1. You are unable to identify 4 to 5 functional headings to highlight.
2. You want to stay in the same field.

Résumé Contents

Review the sample résumés (provided to us courtesy of the McKinley Group) on the following pages. Your résumé should include:

1. A summary of your background
2. Objective (optional) if you are firm about your job target
3. Dates of positions, given in years
4. Accomplishment statements that begin with action verbs
5. Location of positions—city and state only
6. No more than two pages of information

SAMPLE CHRONOLOGICAL RÉSUMÉ

Name
Address
Home Telephone
Objective

Position in Sales or Marketing Management

HIGHLIGHTS OF QUALIFICATIONS

- Over 20 years' experience in account management, marketing and business development.
- Extensive sales experience in Federal Government arena.
- Excellent record of achieving sales budgets. Exceeded sales goals the last ten (10) consecutive years.
- Principal strengths include resourcefulness, creativity, problem-solving, goal- and profit-oriented, working well with others.

PROFESSIONAL EXPERIENCE

Temporaries Unlimited Washington, DC   **1969–Present**

Government Sales Manager   **1986–Present**

- Developed government business in the Washington Metropolitan Area by increasing awareness of the temporary service industry in targeted local and federal government agencies.
- Initiated contacts and met with high-level government decision makers and end users.
- Increased federal government accounts by 150 percent. Generated over $2 million in new sales revenues.
- Represented firm at trade shows and job fairs.

Branch Manager   **1982–1986**

- Successfully managed a profit center with more than $1 million in annual sales.

- Monitored overall branch operations, sales, and profitability.
- Established and successfully met branch sales goals and objectives.
- Developed and instructed leadership and team work training sessions.
- Promoted to Government Sales Manager.

Territory Manager   **1979–1982**

- Developed marketing strategies, and generated sales that increased annual sales quota by 210 percent.
- Received President's Club Award for outstanding performance. Ranked in top 30 percent of entire sales force.
- Served as team member of Profit Center of the Year, which was awarded for exceeding all sales and quality service goals.
- Promoted to Branch Manager.

Office Manager   **1974–1979**

- Managed daily operations of a $4.5 million dollar profit center with a temporary work force of 300 employees.
- Recruited, selected, and trained operations associates and temporary employees.
- Supervised professional staff of 10 nonprofessional staff of 8.
- Received President's Club Award in 1976, 1977 and 1978 for outstanding performance.

Staff Supervisor   **1969–1974**

- Recruited, interviewed and selected temporary employees.
- Filled client requests for temporary employees.
- Accompanied associates on sales calls to conduct departmental profiles and to evaluate client needs.

EDUCATION AND TRAINING

Liberal Arts, Fayetteville State University
Dale Carnegie Sales and Management courses

Company-sponsored courses: Sales Forecasting, Strategic Market Planning, Sales Training, Customer Service, Train the Trainer

MEMBERSHIPS

National Association of Professional Saleswomen
Black Human Resources Network

SAMPLE CHRONOLOGICAL RÉSUMÉ

Name
Address
Home Telephone

SUMMARY OF QUALIFICATIONS

A seasoned professional with more than 10 years of successful human resource management and administrative experience. Major strengths in program design and evaluation; grant/contract proposal preparation; vocational counseling and job placement. Additional skills in marketing and sales. A results-oriented team player who communicates effectively.

PROFESSIONAL EXPERIENCE

Independent Consultant   **1990–Present**
Silver Spring, Maryland

- Senior Consultant to a large health maintenance organization, responsible for the design and implementation of a job classification program including: evaluation and revision of position descriptions; internal evaluation of positions using a point factor method; administration of a salary and benefits survey; development of compensable factors used to measure levels of job complexity; design of questionnaire for data collection; facilitation of focus groups; and analysis of data and preparation of final report.

- Lead Consultant in the preparation and delivery of a $5 million dollar proposal to provide training services to employees of the U.S. Office of Personnel Management including: preparation of technical and cost proposals; writing position descriptions for 6 labor categories; recruitment of Project Director; design of compensation package for project consultants; and coordinating national search for staff and consultants.

Coordinator, Cooperative Education,   **1985–1990**
Northern Virginia
Community College, Alexandria, Virginia

- Recruited and selected qualified applicants for a multidisciplinary Cooperative Education Program.

- Developed and implemented program marketing strategies that increased minority student participation 100 percent.
- Coordinated an annual Career Fair that attracted more than 120 employers.
- Wrote a successful grant proposal to develop a campus-wide Minority Awareness Program.
- Conducted employability skills training for a culturally diverse student population.
- Served on the Board of Directors for a national ad campaign for Cooperative Education.
- Served as Vice Chairman of the Minority Recruitment Team for Northern Virginia Community College.

Director, Fairfax County Youth   1983–1985
Employment Program
Fairfax County, Virginia

- Managed registration and job placement for 95 percent of program participants.
- Revised the program's transportation system, decreasing the cost by $20,000.
- Supervised and trained a staff of 18.

Coordinator, Fairfax County Word Processing   1982–1983
Placement Program
Fairfax County, Virginia

- Recruited, assessed, and placed graduates of the county-sponsored word processing training program.
- Designed and administered successful marketing strategies that increased graduates' placement rate more than 60 percent.
- Conducted employability skills training programs.

Coordinator, Job Seekers Club,   1980–1982
Northern Virginia Manpower Consortium
Fairfax County, Virginia

- Screened more than 1,000 clients for job placement.
- Contacted and maintained communications with potential employers.
- Trained clients in job search techniques.
- Assisted with the marketing of program to employers.

Employment Assessment Specialist   **1978–1980**
Northern Virginia Manpower Consortium
Fairfax County, Virginia

- Developed, monitored, and evaluated employment assessment activities.
- Revised Employment Assessment curriculum and materials.
- Identified clients' skills, interests, aptitudes, and work readiness.

EDUCATION

Master of Arts Degree, Human Resource Development   1991
Marymount University, Arlington, Virginia

Bachelor of Science Degree, Business Administration   1984
Strayer College, Washington, D.C.

Associate Degree, Business Management   1979
Northern Virginia Community College, Alexandria, Virginia

PROFESSIONAL AFFILIATIONS

Past Vice President, National Capital Association of Cooperative Education
Member, National Capital Association of Cooperative Education
Member, Virginia Association of Cooperative Education

SAMPLE FUNCTIONAL RÉSUMÉ

Name
Address
Home Telephone

SUMMARY

Extensive background in reporting, writing, editing and proofreading. Effective researcher with proficiency in interviewing. Possess keen ability to acquire and disseminate information, using diction and style appropriate for the specific audience.

ACCOMPLISHMENTS

Writing and Editing:

- Wrote over 50 bylined stories for the *Washington Post*, nation's third-ranked newspaper.
- One of 14 reporters who chronicled 42 hours of violence in Washington, D.C., as part of a *Washington Post* front page special.
- Generated content, conducted interviews, wrote and edited weekly "column," as editor of the High School Honors pages for the *Washington Post*. Also supervised layout and the work of five freelance writers.
- Researched and collaborated on feature article for French magazine, *Marie Claire*, highlighting various facets of Washington, D.C.
- Oversaw content development, assigned and edited copy, supervised production and distribution of 12-page community newspaper, the *Connections*.

Public Relations:

- Maintained working relationships with over 40 high school teachers and administrators as well as the public affairs offices in four school districts.
- Participated in annual career day workshops at area elementary, junior high, and high schools.

- Led workshop on interviewing techniques for over 20 high school journalism teachers.
- Created publicity strategies for 25 church and community activities including a 1990 mayoral forum which generated press from three local television stations. The *Washington Post* and the *Washington Times*.

Fund-raising Management:

- Maintained budget in excess of $5,000 as editor of the *Connections*, a community newspaper.
- Raised over $13,000 as chair of charity fashion show benefiting AIDS Research.
- Generated over $8,500 in sales and 65 percent repeat business as part owner of "Underwraps," an all-occasion gift basket business.

EMPLOYMENT HISTORY

Public Information Officer	**1991–Present**
National Medical Association	
Editor of High School Honors Section	**1989–1991**
The *Washington Post*	
Collaborator/Researcher	**1989**
Marie Claire	
Nightside Copy Aide	**1988–1989**
The *Washington Post*	
Associate Editor	**1987–1988**
Inside Washington Publishers	
Photo Library Intern	**1987**
USA Today	
Staff Writer	**1986–1987**
Flipside 87	
Columnist/Sports Editor	**1987**
The *Community News*	
Reporter	**1985–1986**
Neighbor Magazine	

Intern   **1983**
"ABC News Nightline"

EDUCATION

Pursuing Master of Arts Degree in Political Management
George Washington University, Washington, D.C.
Bachelor of Arts in Print Journalism, 1987
Howard University, Washington, D.C.

SAMPLE FUNCTIONAL RÉSUMÉ

Name
Address
Home Telephone

AREAS OF EXPERTISE

- Project Management and Evaluation
- Training and Development
- Human Resource Management
- Curriculum Development
- Organizational Development
- Association Management
- Strategic Planning
- Conference Management

SELECTED ACCOMPLISHMENTS

- Managed the development and marketing of a national demonstration project focused on the reform of public school systems and programs for at-risk youth; provided technical assistance to business executives, community leaders and school personnel in program design and implementation; prepared program budgets and fund-raising plans; assisted with the organization of project-related meetings and training institutes.
- Directed the development of a national employment and training program for disabled individuals; marketed the program to various businesses; facilitated the organization of partnerships between vocational rehabilitation agencies and private industry.
- Managed the Human Resource Department of a large trade association, including benefits administration; employee recruitment and selection; EEO and Affirmative Action; employee relations and employee orientation.
- Designed and facilitated workshops on leadership, strategic planning, recruitment and retention strategies and professional development for Fortune 500 companies, nonprofit organizations, government agencies and educational institutions.
- Conducted process and impact evaluations of federally funded demonstration projects; made recommendations for improvement and prepared final reports.
- Designed and coordinated membership surveys and opinion polls; compiled and analyzed the data; prepared reports of the findings.

- Planned and coordinated meetings and conferences including site selections; contract negotiations; speaker recruitment; registration; budget development and on-site management.

PROFESSIONAL EXPERIENCE

Senior Trainer, ABC Company Baltimore, Maryland	1991–Present
Internal Consultant, XYZ Company Washington, D.C.	1989–1991
Project Manager, DEF Company Washington, D.C.	1988–1989
Project Director, GHI Company Washington, D.C.	1985–1988
Personnel Manager, JKL Company Washington, D.C.	1981–1985
Personnel Administrator, MNO Company Washington, D.C.	1976–1981

EDUCATION

Master of Science, Personnel and Human Resource Management
American University, Washington, D.C.

Bachelor of Science, Business Administration
Virginia State College, Petersburg, Virginia

PROFESSIONAL AFFILIATIONS

American Society for Training and Development
Society for Human Resource Management
Washington Personnel Association
National Association for Female Executives

Sample List of Functional Headings

If you plan to use the functional format, identify at least four areas of your expertise. Select those from the listing below. Feel free to add any areas that may not be included. Start by checking off the functions below that describe your abilities and potential and that are in line with your job target.

Accounting	Finance	Production
Acquisition	Fund-Raising	Program Development
Administrative	Graphic Design	Programming
Advertising	Inspecting	Promotion
Architecture	Instruction	Publicity
Aviation	Interviewing	Public Relations
Boating	Investigation	Public Speaking
Career Development	Investment	Purchasing
Chemistry	Layout	Real Estate
Communication	Legal	Research
Community Affairs	Management	Retailing
Construction	Market Research	Scheduling
Counseling	Materials Handling	Secretarial
Culinary	Medicine	Selling
Data Processing	Navigation	Social Work
Design	Organization	Supervision
Drafting	Planning	Systems and Procedures
Electronics	Presentations	Teaching
Employment	Printing	Testing
Engineering	Product Development	Writing and Editing

HOW TO SHOP AROUND

If you are really serious about this business of finding a new job, then identify people who can give you leads. It may make the difference between keeping your old job or getting a new one. Black women typically don't ask for leads, but depend on what we call the "hit or miss" four: applying for positions at personnel offices; direct mail campaigns (mass résumé mailings); responding to the classifieds; and utilizing the services of government and private employment agencies. Sound familiar? How did you find out about your last job? Through the Sunday paper, maybe? Here's a little advice. The problem with the "hit or miss four" is that you are required to wait, sometimes indefinitely, for someone to do something for you. Sometimes you hit, more often than not you miss out on other job opportunities. In addition, the response rate to these methods ranges anywhere from 2 to 14 percent. Direct mail campaigns, in general, account for 2 to 5 percent, while answering want ads may give you return of 14 percent. Applying directly to personnel offices and government agencies are equally discouraging, reflecting only a 12 to 13 percent response rate.

Are You Saying that Black Women Should Abandon Traditional Job Shopping Methods?

No. Not at all. We just recommend that you use a combination of these methods to receive a better rate of return on your job shopping methods. In addition, look for more promising job avenues. Tap the hidden job market—positions not listed in the newspaper nor placed with employment agencies. The best place to tap these openings is by networking, through which, according to Human Resource experts, three-fourths of the better jobs are found. Remember, it's not what you know but who knows you.

How to Create, Make and Keep Contacts

In today's job market, your tools to success are not all based on degree, skill, or experience. Success also comes from who you know and:

WHO KNOWS WHO
WHO KNOWS WHERE
WHO KNOWS WHEN and
WHO KNOWS HOW to get you the right job.

In other words, you need to network. Networking involves creating contacts, making contacts, and keeping contacts. So, start talking and get to know a lot of people!

Creating contacts begins with who you know—Notice, not who's doing the hiring, but WHO YOU KNOW. Who are the people you want to recruit? Everyone and anyone starting with immediate family, friends, and neighbors. Pull out that phone book, that yearbook, the church directory, etc. Start building a list of contacts. Network building is driven on the same concepts that enable groups like Amway, Mary Kay, A. L. Williams and Avon to succeed. You begin by putting together a list of people closest to you. Consider them your direct contacts. From this inner circle, you add on others including organizations and associations of which you are a member. That outer circle or groups and people you don't know are known as indirect contacts.

Think of each person or group you add to your network as drawing you a step closer to your next job. The opportunities to expand your network are all around you—in your home, your community, the office, even at church.

**FAMILY
FRIENDS/NEIGHBORS
COWORKERS/EX-BOSSES/ACQUAINTANCES
MINISTERS/TEACHERS/FORMER CLASSMATES
DOCTORS/POLITICIANS/LAWYERS/BANKERS
INSURANCE AGENTS/SALES PERSONS AND MANY,
MANY, MORE YOU HAVEN'T BEGUN TO CONSIDER AS
CONTACTS**

The more names you compile, the greater access you have to employment opportunities. If you make the mistake of eliminating a prospect, you may be cutting off a link to someone who knows someone with a job for you.

INITIATING CONTACT

Having a prospect list is useless without a plan of contact. Contact is initiated when anyone in your network is willing to talk with you. Unless the entire world is not speaking to you, this should be easy to accomplish. Most of us have at least one or two family members we speak with regularly. In our conversations, we are often asked, "What have you been doing lately?" This is your moment to share that you are conducting a job search. Don't blow it. The smart job-seeker will respond that she is looking for a job and at the same time request assistance by asking any of the following questions:

1. I'm looking for a job in (field); Can you help me in any way?

2. Do you know of anyone who can help me with my job search?
3. I'm thinking about exploring job opportunities at Company X; do you know of anyone I can contact about opening or current requirements?

Note: Other ways of leading into requests for help are to mention success you had with previous job searches. Remind the contact of his/ her personal friends who are employed by a company, or in a field, of interest to you. Your network motto should be, WHERE THERE'S A CONTACT, THERE'S A CHANCE FOR JOB SUCCESS.

Indirect contacts (people you don't know well or have never met before) are more difficult to initiate. Most people feel uncomfortable about approaching strangers. Such encounters must be handled with tact and planning. First impressions of you will either close or open additional doors for you. Indirect contacts, therefore, should be handled with indirect methods (the most popular is the information search—in a roundabout way you explore job opportunities about the field, industry, training, or requirements connected to a potential job opening). Normally, you arrange a meeting with the contact to discuss your field of interest, not emphasizing that you're searching for a new job.

Some Do's:

1. Do your homework. Know why you're calling the contact and what your objectives are for making the contact. Keep calls short and to the point.
2. Try to have a name (referral) to use in your introduction.
3. Be warm, genuine, enthusiastic, and polite.
4. Plan ahead. Be prepared to have questions related to your interest.
5. When scheduling appointments, be on time, polished, equipped with résumés, a notebook, pen, and answers to questions which might be addressed.
6. Be thankful and show it. End calls or meetings with a networker's two most powerful words, "Thank You." Always follow up with a letter (within no later than twenty-four hours).
7. Make phone contacts early (before 8:00 A.M. or 8:30 A.M.) or after 5:00 P.M. to avoid secretaries and other measures which may screen you out.

8. End meetings or close calls with one or more referrals—they can be people, places, hotlines, or organizations which may assist you.
9. Maintain records of conversations or meetings with your contacts.
10. Include a network budget in your financial plans. It should include such costs as membership dues, luncheon/reception fees, and magazine/newspaper charges.

Some Don'ts

1. Don't tell indirect contacts that you're looking for a job during the initial call. State you are exploring employment opportunities or requirements for a specific field.
2. Don't expect too much or make the contact feel obligated to you. Be patient or you may give the contact networker's burnout. As with any relationship, it takes time to build.
3. Don't take up too much of the contact's time on the phone or in face-to-face meetings.
4. Don't overlook literary sources, like association or organization directories for potential resources.
5. Don't handwrite follow-up or thank-you letters. And NEVER use your employer's stationery for your communications.
6. Don't forget to ask for a business card or the correct name, title, position, and address of your contact. And if you don't have a business card, invest in one.
7. Don't be rude to secretaries or clerical support persons who may connect you to your contact.
8. Don't be afraid to call your contact more than once. Be patient and persistent without being pushy.
9. Don't turn down invitations. These can lead to other networking opportunities.
10. Don't overlook magazines, like *Essence, New Woman, Savvy, Working Woman, Executive Female,* and others with subject matter which may make good networking conversation.

KEEPING CONTACTS

Once you become a success at initiating contacts, "keeping contacts" should be fun. A network will stay alive as long as there is activity. That means staying in touch with those who have aided you in the past.

Your keys to keeping contacts include:
1. Maintain a network file. This file should consist of 3 × 5 cards with the name, title (if applicable), address, phone number, and the referral source of the contact. You should also indicate the outcome of any calls or meetings).
2. Hold on to any notes taken during meetings or calls. Preferably, you should record such notes in a small spiral-bound notebook.
3. Keep an updated phone book, current calendar, and a box for business cards.
4. Be generous with your time when a networker calls.
5. Pass on what you've learned once networking has worked for you.
6. Join organizations and associations in your field and remain active.
7. Stay abreast of current trends and happenings in your industry or with your contact. Send articles of interest, birthday cards, etc.
8. Be the rare exception who returns to a contact to say "Thank you for your help." Networking let's you know there is no "me," "my," nor "I," only "we."

HOW TO BE A CREATIVE JOB SHOPPER

Be bold and willing to do something different. A number of our clients have indicated that the following methods helped them to obtain interviews and to land positions:
1. Contact directly individuals mentioned for achievements in *Ebony, Black Enterprise, Jet* magazines as well as *Fortune, Forbes* and *Business Week*. Remember there must be a fit between you and your prospective employer.
2. Get closer to key players in organizations. Attend meetings where they "network." How do you find them? Follow the business meeting calendars of the daily newspapers, which regularly post meeting dates of professional and other networking organizations. Then let the organization know that you will be a guest.
3. Send a congratulatory letter to those who have been recently promoted or hired. It is not uncommon for those who assume new positions to reorganize their offices with new personnel. Your letter, therefore, should not only say congratulations but also mention your skills and talents.
4. Station yourself outside where you want to work and distribute your résumé to everyone leaving. We once advised one of our clients to stand outside the stock market building in another city

and to introduce herself to corporate women who looked interested.

5. Try creative gimmicks for conveying information in your résumé. Turn it into a brochure, video, or slide show. Remember these ideas will work only in organizations that are creative.
6. Become a volunteer, or obtain part-time work in a field that interests you.
7. Practice small talk. Strike up conversations on planes, at functions and other gatherings to expand your network of contacts.
8. Target smaller companies. That's where a significant number of the new jobs are expected to come from over the next few years.
9. Avoid the rush. Let others beat you to the punch. Delay mailing out résumés until a week after the date of the ad. In the first few days after an ad is placed, normally companies are inundated with résumés. By waiting, you won't be a part of a company's paper chase and are more likely to have your résumé reviewed.
10. Consider nontraditional career fields where few women or minorities hold jobs.
11. Join an association or organization tied to your field of interest and become a local and eventually national officer to give you more exposure.
12. Take up a hobby, like golf, that key managers in your company also show an avid interest in.

NON-TRADITIONAL WAYS TO BE CREATIVE

1. Send your résumé to the hiring authority via a courier or express mail service.
2. Locate the car of the hiring authority and put your résumé on the windshield.
3. Print a business card with your name, telephone number, and address along with a summary of your qualifications.
4. Place a "position wanted" ad in the local newspapers.
5. Identify the organizations where key managers from the prospective employer are members. Attend the meetings of the group and introduce yourself.
6. Create a sandwich board with your qualifications, and walk in front of the place where you would like to work.
7. Send balloons or flowers with your résumé attached.
8. Send a singing telegram detailing your qualifications.

9. Make your résumé different. Make it larger or smaller than normal.
10. Rent an airplane or helicopter to display a banner about you.
11. Rent a billboard describing your qualifications.

Special Note None of these recommendations comes with a guarantee that you will succeed. A lot will depend on the employer. So, do your homework.

HOW TO WORK YOUR JOB SHOPPING PLAN

Job shopping is not for the lazy. Most of us say that we don't want to be rejected—yet we don't treat it like a full-time job. The unemployed should spend at least forty hours a week on job shopping. You can't get a job using only part of your free time. If you are currently employed, your search for a new job should take at least twenty hours per week. Use your lunch hour and annual leave for scheduling interviews. Arrive earlier, or leave later, and use the extra time for making phone calls or planning daily job shop tasks.

Establish a system for implementing your job shopping goals and tracking your progress. Your system should include a daily or weekly plan that spells out what you're going to do, when you're going to do it, how you'll do it, what you'll need (resources) and the results. Use a similar table to track your progress.

JOB SHOPPING ACTION PLAN

Table 11.4

	TASK	INFO. NEEDED	TARGET DATE	OUTCOME	DATE COMPLETED
1.					
2.					
3.					
4.					
5.					

6.				
7.				

How to Get Noticed

You're ready. You know what you want. You know where to get it. You have the résumé to do it. You even have a plan and a number of leads. You received the long-awaited call. So, how do you prepare for the interview and get noticed for the right things? After all this, could plans go up in smoke?

Sure they can, without you opening up your mouth (although that will do it, too). We can look good for that 10:00 P.M. night on the town and have *all* heads turn. However, we need to understand that when it's time to get an employer's attention, it's best to leave our fashion statements at home and work with the business basics. Of course, the rules change if you are attempting to enter the entertainment world or trying to meeting Denzel Washington.

When you go to your closet looking for that Perfect 10 interview outfit, stick to dark suits, preferably navy blue or black, with a white or cream blouse. Also, wear a plain pump and a mid-size heel. Limit your accessories to conservative jewelry, and wear no more than one ring, one watch, and one bracelet.

On your list of "interview don'ts," include dangling earrings, large hoops with or without your name on them, open-toed shoes, sling-backs, or five-inch heels, heavy perfume or makeup, sheer or lowcut blouses, miniskirts or skirts with slits, Mrs. T starter kits (two or more chains around the neck), Spandex or Lycra dresses.

How to Do a Job Fair

In the past five years, the number of job fairs have risen significantly. But it never fails, when we have our booth for **Black Women Can Win!** we observe certain habits that are characteristic of black women. Most of our observations concern what we don't do.

One, we tend not to come the day before to check out what's available or which company's are going to be there. Yet we hear black women complain that there are too many people to know which line to stand in first.

Two, we don't pick up information. We breeze past tables and act as if we're window shopping. However, we miss out on a lot of information that may be of assistance to us in our job search.

Three, if workshops are offered we don't attend them. Often, job fair sponsors hold forums, like recruiters' round tables that can provide you with useful insights on what employers expect of potential candidates. It also provides you an opportunity to meet people who are doing the hiring.

Four, we don't talk to anyone. We walk around as if we're lost. Over the years, we have observed that even in other types of gatherings black women don't know how to mingle. We seem to be at a loss for words or the right things to say.

Five, we don't prepare for the job fair. We forget that we are standing in line to be interviewed. We walk up and hand a recruiter our résumé and then stand there and look dumb.

Six, we don't dress for the occasion. Recruiters at job fairs are doing more than passing out company information. They're looking for people to add to their organization. If you are not in your best business attire, you may very well be overlooked.

Seven, we don't arrive early. By the time we do arrive at the job fair, we're frustrated because the lines are too long or a specific company's recruiter has gone for the day.

Eight, when the sponsor provides a list of positions that a firm is targeting, we avoid standing in the line even if that employer is on our list. While a particular company may have certain positions that it wants to fill, you never know what's in a company's future plans.

How to Use An Employment Agency

If you don't remember anything else, keep in mind that employment agencies and search firms are in business to make a profit. Second, because money is the bottom line their emphasis is on helping the employer, not the prospective employee. So, here are some rules of thumb to follow:

1. Choose with care. Several employment agencies have been sued for failing to locate positions for minority candidates. These agencies, for example, used techniques such as coding applications according to race and then forwarding only white candidates on to their clients.

2. Ask for referrals. Contact friends who have used employment

agencies for referrals. Also, consult magazines, like **Black Enterprise,** that list minority search firms.
3. Use a tester. Ask a trusted white colleague to use the same agency, and compare the climate and treatment. Of course, make sure your credentials are fairly similar.
4. Contact the agency directly. Do some prescreening. Ask questions about what types of people they have placed and with which companies.
5. Use agencies that recruit for your field of interest. If you want to be an accountant, don't go to an agency that specializes in word processing.
6. Stay away from agencies that charge fees. We know of one case where the agency put together a listing of vacant positions that was drawn from newspaper ads, yet charged applicants $40 for the list.
7. Check with the Better Business Bureau to see if the firm has a history of complaints.

Let's face it, employment agencies are not for everyone. In fact, if you are searching for a managerial or executive position you may want to consider a professional recruiter, particularly if your salary exceeds $40,000. By the way, executive recruiters also go by other names, like headhunter or executive search consultants. They are similar to an employment agency, except that your résumé will not move unless a job order calls for your specific qualifications. There are also two types of recruiters you should know about. One is a contingency recruiter. He or she is paid by an employer only after a candidate is hired. A retainer recruiter is paid by the employer regardless of whether or not a candidate is hired.

How to Prepare for the Interview

While we genuinely don't want to fail in the interview, most of us really don't know what an employer looks for when sizing up a potential candidate. We're careful about how we look and what's in our résumé, but we don't convey the answers to questions that an employer has: Can you do the job? Will you do the job? Is there a fit? Once you shake the hand of the interviewer, he or she sees two things: race and gender. To overcome biases associated with these you need to be well prepared for the kinds of questions you may be asked.

Typical interview questions

1. Tell me about yourself.
2. What are your strengths?
3. What are your weaknesses?
4. Why are you interested in our organization?
5. What can you contribute to the organization?
6. Tell me about a problem that you resolved. Tell me about a project that you initiated.
7. Describe your leadership or management style.
8. Why are you interested in leaving your current position?
9. What are your career goals?
10. How long do you plan to stay with the company should you be offered a position?
11. How do you handle situations in which your way of handling a situation differs from your boss's?

When It's Your Turn To Ask The Questions

Once the interviewer has asked you enough questions, you may be asked if you have any of your own. Never every say no. Interviews are not one-sided. So, of course when you are asked if you have any questions you are going to say **yes**. Here are a few to consider using:
1. How long has the position been open?
2. Why is the position open?
3. What is the company's management style?
4. What are some of the future company goals?
5. What kind of training is available?
6. What weaknesses do you find in my background relative to this position?
7. What are the most important traits that you are looking for?
8. Will you need any further information about me?
9. What is the next step in the process?

Notice these questions do not mention salary. Money questions should never be raised by you in the first interview. Let the interviewer take the lead when it comes to the issue of money. And when it is raised, don't allow yourself to be cornered into naming a specific dollar amount. Before you offer any salary expectations, ask for the salary range of the position. This way if the bottom of the range is higher than you anticipated, you can ask for more. One of our friends recently interviewed for a position, but never mentioned money. Neither did the prospective employer. When she was finally offered the new position, the prospective employer offered her a salary which was double what she was making. As a rule of thumb, don't volunteer information that may put you at a disadvantage.

HOW TO KEEP YOUR EMPLOYER FROM FINDING OUT ABOUT YOUR JOB SEARCH

In short, what your employer knows about your job hunt may in fact hurt you. So, don't raise any flags to alert your current employer that you are ready to go. Here are some helpful hints on keeping your shopping a secret:

1. Interview during your vacation time.
2. If you have not been coming to work "dressed for success," don't start now. Bring your interview clothes with you and change in the ladies' room (hopefully in a more removed location from your office) prior to leaving.
3. Request that recruiters call you at home *only* or before or after your work hours.
4. Don't tell a soul on your job that you are job hunting. You don't know whom anyone talks to.
5. Limit your personal calls.
6. Don't leave any visible signs that you are conducting a search on your desk.
7. If you choose to use the company's computer, do not leave it unattended or lay diskettes in places where they are liable to be discovered by the wrong persons. If you can, don't use the company's time to look for your job.
8. Ask for information concerning your performance gradually. If you need copies of your performance evaluations, don't say, "I'd like a copy of my evaluations for the past three years." Instead, say, "I'd like a copy of my performance evaluations for the last three quarters in order to assess where I am."
9. Don't dramatically increase your use of sick time in order to schedule interviews.

You Can Do It, But ...

1. Don't do it alone! Talk to everyone you can—both direct and indirect contacts.

2. Market yourself as a results-oriented product. Develop accomplishment statements that support your Why Should You be Hired? Why are you great, wonderful, perfect, etc.
3. Don't be afraid to try nontraditional job hunting strategies. See Appendix A, **Image Source List**, p. 265.

Recommended Reading

Petras, Kathryn and Rose. *The Only Job Hunting Guide You'll Ever Need*. New York: Poseidon, 1989.
Parker, Yana. *The Résumé Catalog: 200 Damn Good Examples*. Berkeley Ten Speed, 1988.
Jackson, Tom. *The Perfect Résumé*. New York: Anchor Books, 1991.
Farr, Michael J. *Getting the Job You Really Want*. Indianapolis, IN: Jist Works Inc., 1988.
See also "Job Shopping Resources," Appendix B, p. 266.

Joyce Greene
Manager of Advertising and Sales Promotion
Amtrak
Washington, DC

I received a letter from a young woman who had read an article featuring me and other black women who had successfully "climbed the corporate ladder." The article relates how I started my career as a sales person at Montgomery Ward, as well as the career path leading to my current position. This young woman, like me, had opted to go straight to work from high school because she wasn't sure of the benefits of college or of what she wanted to do in life. Now after attending a trade school, the height of her day is to stand at a copy machine. This was obviously not her vision or dream.

Reading this letter brought back vivid memories because it is an accurate description of the dilemma I faced in high school. I made essentially the same decision, not to go to college. I didn't end up at a copy machine; I wanted to work and liked the challenge of proving that I could work smart and be the most productive employee. I guess this was a naive ideal of youth but it really worked for me. As a result of my productivity, on various jobs, I was promoted at the tender age of twenty-three to supervisor of the payroll department, handling five payrolls for Montgomery Ward. I felt really good about this accomplishment and decided that I should move on to other companies and challenges. While my productivity and enthusiasm continued to work for me, eventually I ran into the "if you had a degree" brick wall.

Hindsight is 20/20, and I would advise anyone to go to college as soon as you can. Delaying college resulted in over six years of attending college at night while holding down a full-time job during the day. This was a sometimes grueling experience as well as a fulfilling experience. I enjoyed college enormously, and I participated in every way possible that college life offered. I won awards (*Wall Street Journal* Award for Market Research, *Who's Who Among College Students*), was the yearbook editor and vice president of the student government, and even became a sorority girl. And I let everyone on my job share in my successes, which raised the level of how people viewed me.

While I worked on my degree, I never stopped looking for challenges and ways to improve my productivity. In my search for challenges at new companies, I eventually ended up at Amtrak in the finance department, supervising the payroll process. I knew that finance was not the place for me and sought to parlay my proven work ethic into a job in the marketing department. Once I discovered what I wanted to do, I took a chance. I asked for the chance and the challenge which landed me a job in advertising and sales promotion. Not the job that I have now, but close enough to the action to see, strive for, and decide in what direction my career should move.

I know that it sounds easy, but I must tell you that my rise to the job that I have today was hard work. It is not easy being a woman or a black woman with all of the situations you have to face. I decided early on that race and gender discrimination was the other person's problem because I was not going to let it get in the way of my goals. It is not an easy situation to ignore, but it can be dealt with in an appropriate manner. I worked in a basically male industry most of my life, and I have learned to handle it and am learning to handle it better each day.

To tell you a story, I started a new job working with a guy who wasn't pleased about working with me because of my race. I approached this situation head-on. I invited him to lunch, and I related to him that I knew that he had concerns about working with me. I just wanted to assure him that what we had to do were the tasks described in our job descriptions. This did not mean that we had to like each other, although it would be helpful. It did mean that we had to work together to achieve a common goal. I even told him that it was okay to dislike me as long as it did not interfere with our work.

Did he ever like me? I don't think so, but I do know that our department benefited from the work accomplished. I was able to handle super projects to my benefit with or without him. You see, it is a nice feeling to be liked. It is a tremendous feeling to be admired and respected for what you accomplish. Letting race and gender discrimination be your obstacle or your excuse will only block your progress. It's up to you to make things work and to not allow stumbling blocks to stand in your way. If I had allowed this—competition, criticism, or not being liked—stand in my way, I would not be able to tell you that I manage four agencies, assisted in the production of many of the Amtrak television commercials, newspaper and magazine ads that you see today, was the Amtrak manager for four television travel shows produced for BET, coordinator for the Amtrak involvement in the first Bryant Gumble Pro-Am Golf Tournament to benefit UNCF colleges and much, much more.

My advice to you is to challenge yourself, discover your capabilities and interests, pursue your dreams, get the best education you can, and don't let or put stumbling blocks in your way. I did it the hard way at first, but since then I have risen to the challenge and continue to believe in myself and my ability to contribute and succeed.

Yes, a black woman can be beautiful, bright, powerful, and successful. If we believe in ourselves, then do everything that we can, we can make our dreams come true.

Sincerely,

Joyce Greene

Chapter 12

FED UP AND
FIGHTING BACK!

Before Rodney King there was Pamela Mitchell....

In 1987, she was an unknown part-time reservationist at the Marriott following the same routine as she had for the past eight months. It was just another workday and a job to put extra money in her wallet and to pay off some bills.

Nothing in her wildest imagination prepared her for the events that would follow that day. There were little signs from the week before—but nothing that she took seriously. Her coworkers tried to warn her that her new hairdo was not going to fly with the corporation. In fact, they said it might just put her job on the line.

Pamela thought it was a joke and paid no attention to the warnings. "Why should I?" she thought to herself. It sounded like a bunch of nonsense. When the week passed without a word from management, and no mention that there were policies concerning an employee's hairdo, she assumed everyone was kidding.

During the weeks that followed ...

The week passed quietly, but the next Monday unfolded much differently. Pam recalls how the front office manager approached her and said, "You know you can't wear that." Puzzled, Pam asked, "What are you talking about?" The manager pointed to Pam's head and replied "Your hair." She then went on to explain that the style was referenced in the employee handbook.

Pam couldn't believe what she was hearing. All she could think about was the cost of her new "do" and that she was working a part-time job, from 5:30 P.M. to 10:30 P.M. To top it off, it didn't even require any face-to-face contact with the public. She couldn't figure out the problem. Just maybe, she was being filmed on "America's Hidden Video."

It wasn't a joke. The manager told her that the braids would have to go. She gave Pam a one-week ultimatum that either she comply or face the consequences.

Another week went by, but Pam didn't remove her braids. The same manager asked to meet with her and said, "I see you haven't complied." Pam nodded and then was directed to the manager's office where she was instructed, again, that the braids had to go. She was also shown a memo and directed to sign it. The memo explained that she would be given thirty days to take out the braids or be fired.

Thirty days later ...

Another meeting was scheduled between Pam and the manager. But Pam had a principled opposition. She looked directly into the eyes of the manager and told her with conviction that she would not be removing her braids. Again, she was reminded of the guidelines which referred to her hair style as a fad. That would be as close to an explanation that Pam would receive.

Pam would not bend. The manager then warned her that if she did not adhere to the rules she would be sent home. After three warnings, she was told, she would be subject to dismissal. She was also asked why she couldn't wear a wig.

PAM CONTACTS A LAWYER ...

Pam was sent home. Shocked and stunned, she made a decision. It was time to obtain legal assistance. She found Eric Steele, a Washington, D.C., attorney, and an expert in employment law. The prospect of taking on the Marriott did not shake him. He had the experience and he knew the law. So, he gave Pam some sound, but simple, advice. He told her to document everything that had happened and to refuse to discuss the situation with anyone but him. Pam knew her case was in trustworthy hands.

Everything was about to hit the fan, and the Marriott didn't know it. They also didn't know the man whom they were going to have to contend with, attorney Eric Steele, Pam's own "Perry Mason." He was not one to waste any time. Pam had a strong case, though her lawyer knew the case could not be won singlehandedly. He was well versed in the rules of the employment game, and he had faith. He used every avenue, and put the story on the UPI. Soon, the media became a champion of Pamela's cause.

At the same time, Eric had filed the complaint with the Equal Employment Opportunity Commission. Months later, and with one of the best employment lawyers, Pam found herself opposite the Marriott to defend her braids.

It took eight months from Pam's initial encounter with the front manager to bring the situation to an end. In June 1988, less than a year later, the Marriott Corporation decided to settle. Pam returned to her part-time job. She remained there for two more years until the Marriott laid her off in March of 1991.

CONFRONTATION OR COMPROMISE?

This is the dilemma you face when someone violates your rights in the workplace. You feel caught between letting it go or being a conscientious objector. You fear that if you air a battle cry for fairness, you chance retaliation or losing your job. Or, you can follow the basic law of the land, "employment at will," which gives you and your employer the right to end your relationship at any time.

Employers *can* fire you. But not for illegal reasons. Eric Steele, attorney-at-law, advises his clients to be well-read and resourceful in order to know when their rights are in violation.

HOW CAN I DETERMINE WHEN MY RIGHTS ARE IN VIOLATION?

A good starting point is knowing the definition of discrimination. Title VII of the Civil Rights Act of 1964 prohibits discrimination because of race, color, religion, sex, or national origin. Employment lawyers refer to discrimination as any situation in which you are being treated differently from anyone who is considered a protected group. It also must be factually based.

But the question still remains. How do you know if it is what you think it is? Legal experts recommend that you go by your gut instincts. They say if things don't feel right, you may be hitting the nail on the head. However, they also caution you to not be led by your emotions. Look for disparities in treatment, wages, assignment of jobs, etc., to give you clues.

It's There All Right, But Should I Be A Whistle Blower?

That's a decision only you can make. You may feel as if you're being an informant, but you also have to decide what is palatable. To make that determination, consider the following:

1. If you don't stop the situation, will it continue?
2. Do you feel strongly enough about it to try and change it?
3. Are you prepared for what taking on the corporation might involve?
4. What do you stand to lose should the outcome not work in your favor?
5. Are your allegations based on fact?
6. Have similar situations occurred, and has someone else had the same type of fight?

WAYS TO ARM YOURSELF

Okay. You tell yourself, "I'm ready and I can handle this." Now what do you do?

"Run," says Eric Steele. **Run like the wind to find some help.** You may have to stop in Personnel, but Steele says that you can't put your faith in every company. "Some EEO (Equal Employment Opportunity) officers are there to paper over the situation and to provide ammunition should the law come down on the company," he adds. Legal experts also emphasize that it's almost impossible for an EEO officer to serve you and the company at the same time.

Gather as much information as you can, without doing anything improper. Make copies of salary charts; keep records of memos, evaluations, and anything else that is relevant to your situation. Document everything, and create a paper trail.

Cross your t's and dot your i's. Make sure that you're playing it by the rules. You don't want to kill your claim. So, don't even take a pencil home. If you have a lateness problem, don't have it anymore. Be prepared that the company may try to come after you.

Maximize your ability to prevail, by doing the right things. "Take performance issues off the table," advises Eric Steele. Try to show that you have years of good performance evaluations and a strong track record. If you have excellent performance, you can remain in the game.

Have some money. A legal case involves many hours of time for lawyers. While in most instances you may be able to recover your back pay, some lawyers may require considerable "up front" money or a contingency fee.

Find a reputable lawyer. Approach finding an attorney as a smart consumer. Ask for referrals. Read the paper and see who's representing whom and winning. Contact the bar association, as well.

If you can, move on to another job. If not, brace yourself. When two once friendly parties are in opposition, the relationship can chill. At its extreme worst, a situation on your job can become unpleasant, stressful, or hateful. The uncomfortableness may make it difficult for you to stay until the bitter end.

NOW WHAT?

You did it. You thought the day would never come. But you object to the way you're being treated. So, what should you expect, and how long will the process take? You've heard all the gory stories concerning the effectiveness of the EEOC. You're not impressed. You watched the Clarence Thomas vs. Anita Hill controversy, and it still gives you the chills. Then, the thought of going one-to-one with your employer has you wondering if it's really worth it.

Those are all normal feelings. That's why a good lawyer and the EEOC will help walk you through everything that you need to do.

FILING THE CHARGE OF DISCRIMINATION

You, or anyone else, can file a charge of discrimination on your behalf. It takes a call, correspondence or a visit to an EEOC office to file what is known as a "Charge of Discrimination." You'll be asked a number of questions which all amount to **Who, What, Where, Why, When, and How.** There are also set time limits on filing charges. You should contact the EEOC and request their booklet, "The Charging Party," for more specifics on your rights and responsibilities, as well as procedures, litigation, relief for actual damages, and even what to do if you experience retaliation.

Why Is There Discrimination and Why Can't Some Blacks And Whites Get Along?

In December, 1991, the *Washington Post* featured an article concerning white perceptions of blacks, based on a poll which was conducted. One of the themes that emerged was best described by the president of the polling firm, Geoffrey Garin. Most of the whites felt, he said, that "Whatever prejudice whites feel to blacks is provoked by things that blacks do, and whatever prejudice blacks might feel to whites is provoked by something that happened a long time ago."

After the release of that article, a young black woman asked us, "Why can't blacks and whites get along?" Her question was filled with a lot of emotion and concern. But we couldn't come up with any simple answers. We knew that the ability of blacks and whites to relate to each other depends on a number of factors. One is individual awareness of one's own prejudices. Then recognition of the cultural and environmental differences where one is raised to believe that someone is more or less inferior. Finally, experiences shape our prejudices. What one person of a particular race does can shape our view of that race.

The Rodney King incident is a good example of how whites and blacks can view the same situation differently. There was more outrage in the black community about the handling of the incident, yet whites were more outraged by the riots that followed. Blacks felt that our history was enough justification for the riots.

Whites are also suspicious of blacks based on their own history. A friend of ours once had a unpleasant interaction with a white colleague who had a problem with blacks. When our friend confronted his colleague, he informed him that he had once been held up by a black man. Our friend responded, "If I was a white man who held you up, would you hate all white people, too?" Taken aback, his colleague couldn't respond but to say that our friend was the first black person that he really got to know.

Within the black community, we often are confronted with the cultural biases of other blacks. We face strong pressures from our peers to fall into the mainstream of our culture or the viewed way that blacks do things. As a result, we teach each other to not like certain things, for example, country/western music. Or, we think we're all supposed to have eaten chitlins or to be able to dance. We show the same prejudices toward each other that whites show toward us when we act or think different from the majority.

Is It Them Or You?

Blacks can be prejudiced, too. We don't always recognize our own biases. A few of us use emotions to respond to racism, and hurt our careers. We also are guilty of blaming racism for our faults, and using color as an excuse. Some of us also feel that white people are always out to get us and that they are our only problem. So, we rush to judgments about others, or we allow a few experiences with one set of white people to cloud our thinking.

The first step in coping with prejudice is to be aware of your own. Unfortunately, until something gets your antenna up, you may not consciously think about how you feel about white people. Most whites, too, may not consciously think about their feelings toward blacks until they are surrounded by a room full of black people.

Blacks see color too. When some of us see white, we automatically assume a person isn't going to be sensitive to our needs. A black person who knows the history of the treatment of blacks may see the police and think the person is a card-carrying member of the Ku Klux Klan.

Are there thoughts that you have left unsaid concerning whites that may have you on a self-destructive course? Do you cover up your deficiencies in the name of race?

Recognize that you have to be bicultural to not only survive in the workplace, but to attain. You have to know when to adapt and when assimilation is necessary. That doesn't mean that you have to have a Sambo complex and act out other people's expectations.

You already know what you need to do when confronted with racism. But what do you do about becoming aware of your own biases? Try this exercise by completing the following thoughts:

1. If there's one thing that I honestly could share with white people about black people, it's that they make us feel...
2. I wish that my white coworkers would recognize that black people...
3. My perceptions of white people are...
4. The situations that make me feel that I am being exposed to racism are...
5. I am most race-sensitive when...

IF YOU IGNORE IT, IT WON'T GO AWAY!

We feel that prejudice is a learned, yet often conscious, decision. No one's born a racist. Racism is based in fear, assumptions, experience or lack of experience, and yes, sometimes entirely on perception. These factors make it doubly important that you find out what kind of frame of mind you're in concerning race. If you ignore it, it won't go away.

Answering the previous questions should tell you whether or not there's a personal history that makes you believe that everything that happens to you is a result of race. You may be playing old tapes or having flashbacks of a time and place when a white person didn't treat you well. And it is hard to let go when you know "you've been done wrong." But don't always be suspicious. Watch for generalities. Judge whites, and blacks, on an individual basis. Build a case on **fact**, not **fiction**.

Anise Key Brown
Black Affairs Liaison Officer
Office of the County Executive, Montgomery County
Rockville, Maryland

I have been around. And how I got around was by being unique and innovative in every position I've held. Service to the community has also been the foundation upon which I have laid my career. Early in my career, I learned the value of participation in civic and community affairs.

For seven years, I taught at Johnson C. Smith University where I was awarded several grants for being instrumental in developing a number of college/community-oriented programs. One of these was a series of "Black on Black" crime seminars funded by the Sperry and Hutchinson Foundation, in New York. I also served as a Research Associate for the City of Charlotte, North Carolina, wherein I was involved in a model project designed to decrease criminal activities in several low-income housing projects. I also worked in Los Angeles, for the Department of Human Services, designing programs and activities for the Office of Elderly and supervising the "Meals on Wheels" program. As Assistant Program Director for Delta Sigma Theta Sorority, Inc., I also helped direct the implementation of the organization's first telethon to solicit funds for the establishment of the Delta Research Educational Foundation. While I have received numerous awards and recognition, such achievements came out of a desire to serve.

My advice to you is simple. If you follow this twofold message, you will not encounter many detours on the road to success. Oftentimes, the road to success is paved with obstacles because we have forgotten our heritage. If we do not know whence we came, it is most difficult to know where we're going. Knowing where we came from does not necessarily mean a street address or a specific hometown. It means our heritage, our roots and the need to give back to our own.

For black American women of African descent, knowing our heritage means strength, unity, grace, solidarity, commitment, dedication, sacrifice, and love. These attributes are but a few of the many ingredients that define us as unique and special women. In our everyday struggles and ambitions to succeed, we sometimes forget our special qualities and assume the habits of the large society. In doing so, we allow our success to be defined for us by others. We must remember that for centuries, we have succeeded in our own right and certainly against all odds. The reason for our survival and success is based upon the foundation of knowing who we are and using that knowledge to empower our communities.

This strength to sustain and the dedication to respond to a higher calling by sharing and giving back to our community is a responsibility which cannot be forsaken. By using this premise as a framework, we as a people will never be destroyed or denied because of the deep-rooted ebony soil in which the seeds of our heritage were planted. It is this genuine effort to share and give back to our community that continues to empower and sustain us as a people. Taking out without putting back soon leaves nothing. Yet if we continue to replenish, we soon will overflow and this generosity multiplies.

As a little girl living in a segregated environment, one of the things that I always wanted to do was to be able to enter the dominant society so that I could discover what "they were doing" and bring it back to my community to help my people grow. There is no greater feeling of satisfaction than one in which you feel that you have made a positive impact in someone's life. Take the time, the resources and the money to outreach in your community and to do your part.

My roots gave me a strong self-image. My self-image gave me the desire to give back. Success is defined by me. As long as I know whence I came, and employ myself to give back some of that which has been given to me, then I know I will be all right. As long as you remember these two things, my sisters, then success will be yours no matter what you do.

Sincerely,

Anise Key Brown

Yetta Galiber
Executive Director
Information, Protection, and Advocacy Center
for Handicapped Individuals, Inc.
Washington, DC

As a black working woman, you've probably told yourself, "I have never had it so tough!" We have so much to carry but don't always have someone to carry us. As a young woman sitting on the front row of the Supreme Court, I listened to the arguments for school desegregation and made up my mind that my career would and must involve a commitment to people, especially my own. I tried to understand why my father could chauffeur a supreme court justice but wasn't allowed to enter front doors because he was a black man. So, I dreamed a world where there would be equality for all people.

I was blessed to marry a responsible black man who is also a dentist. Together, we were able to substitute things for our children that racism didn't allow them to have. While I loved my children with all my heart and soul, I began a quest for creating that world I dreamed of. My quest led me to a home for homeless children where I spent a wonderful day doing nothing but washing, pressing and curling the heads of about 100 lovely little black girls. That one experience, and similar ones, helped lead me to such appointments as Director of the Friends of Juvenile Court and eventually to the position of Executive Director of IPACHI (above), from which after twenty-one years I am now retired. Through these positions, I learned that it is not hard to succeed when you are doing for others.

My career didn't unfold because of my résumé. I found something that I really wanted to do and a cause I believed in. I started it as a volunteer at Junior Village, a home for homeless children where I chaired the Volunteer Advisory Council. On one side of the system I saw all white volunteers, and on the other side I saw all black children being programmed to fail by society. I knew I had to help such children dream their world, too. That's when I also learned that success isn't a matter of being black or white, moving up or making money, but about helping others. You see, we are all temporarily able-bodied. At any moment something can put you in the same shoes that someone else is now wearing. My success formula is all about making things better for my fellow man or woman.

I once developed a program to train inmates at Washington's Lorton Reformatory as teachers' aides so that they could help the profoundly mentally retarded learn self-help and language skills. I witnessed the impact of how rejecting someone else's labels and the failure diseases that society places on its castaways can change lives. This same group of inmates gave me my greatest award. It read, "The Black Madonna— She said yes when others said no." You, too, must say yes to yourself when others are trying to tell you no.

Most African American Women have gone about their careers in the wrong way and for the wrong reasons. We haven't put people first. But when you know you've made a difference in the life of another human being it will do something inside of you that nothing else can, not even your paycheck. I've received many awards, applause, and writeups in major magazines, not for what I received but for what I gave.

One little step in the right direction, for the right reasons, can take you where you need to go. But don't take your eye off your goal. Get rid of your excuses. They are one of those failure diseases, along with self-doubt and negative advice. And never, ever allow people to get in your way, no matter who they are. Above all else, don't look for someone to do something for you that you can do for yourself. And when you have to work for someone, find someone who looks at life the same way that you do.

There are two things that bother me. One is that excellence is not something that people seem to be concerned about anymore. We must realize that if one of us shirks our responsibilities, it makes all of us look bad. Keep in mind that you will always be beautiful to others when you act beautiful. Be sure that you do everything with integrity.

Second, I'm troubled by the way we keep accepting the worst things for ourselves. We must be steadfast and believe in what we're doing. We should have a self-determination that makes people back down when they try to get in our way. Oh yes, I have learned when it is appropriate to make a loud noise and to tell someone trying to hold me down, "I refuse to let you." You must do everything that you can to make people deal upright with you. That means you don't have to tolerate other people's racism nor their jokes.

You must be true to yourself and informed. Many black people haven't moved ahead because they haven't had the right information. So, get the right kind of information and whatever else you need to help you get ahead.

Finally, when your career isn't a "crystal stair," keep climbing until you reach your goal. Once you get there, help other people for their own improvement and not to lord over them. A few of us have the idea that we can treat others as if nothing is important except what we are about. You must remember, the more you know, the more your obligation is to give.

Sincerely,

Yetta Galiber

Chapter 13

FACING A LAYOFF?

HOW TO HAVE A SOFT LANDING

Oh, what pain, the grief, the stress! When the economic forecast looks grim, you may wonder how to protect yourself from industries suffering from recession flu. The headlines of the times usually include, "Unemployment Claims At Their Highest Level," "The Misery Continues," "Experts See Recession As Unfinished," "Area Firms Lighten Their Cost Loads," or "Angry Words Fill Unemployment Offices."

These are the kinds of headlines which would make anyone want to face a layoff lying down. Others choose to swallow a strong dose of denial, thinking it can't happen to them. Maybe it won't. But it could.

Recessions can be the best of times, or the worst of times. Stock prices rise, stock prices fall. Housing markets accelerate, housing markets slow down. Car sales boom, car sales lag. Unemployment high, unemployment low. If it doesn't hit your home, you'll probably know at least one person who is a casualty of a recession.

During the 1991 recession, companies suddenly had new buzz words, from "downsizing" to "right sizing" to "voluntary separation." Nice words to sum up their wave of employment cuts, typically known as a layoff or RIF (reduction in force if you are a government employee).

According to a July 1991 report by the Bureau of Labor Statistics, there were almost 8.6 million persons unemployed. The same report also indicated that the jobless level was 1.6 million higher than in July 1990, when the recession began. In addition, the number of persons considered partially unemployed for economic reasons was 940,000 higher than the previous year. If such gloomy statistics didn't convince you to have reason for concern, then you must have been happy. Hopefully, you didn't have to find a way to be happily unemployed.

One wonders how you face a layoff with a soft landing, especially when you're a black woman and studies like one done by the National Urban League report that African American women fare the worst when it comes to unemployment. The Urban League report went on to say that during the 1991 recession, we "experienced higher unemployment and lower wages than our male counterparts." We already told you that black women are twice as likely as white women to be unemployed.

With one in five black women facing unemployment, do you lie down and play dead when the notices come or, do you prepare for the worst? The following are some useful tips and anti-layoff measures:

MINIMIZE YOUR ANXIETY: HAVE A PLAN

There's no time like the present to develop a course of action to help you survive a layoff. According to Paul Fitzgerald, a vice president for Drake Beam Morin, an international career transition firm, a well-thought-out plan does not guarantee success, but it will greatly increase your probability of survival. Also, determine if your position contributes to the company's bottom line. If it doesn't, learn skills your company can't afford to do without. For starters, determine who's most vulnerable at your workplace and when and where you could face a direct hit. Start keeping your ear to the ground. More than likely what you hear from the grapevine is true. If it is, it will give you a chance to put out feelers. Second, identify those areas of your personal and professional life where there is the potential for pain. If your money's tight, start saving. If your list of skills is short, acquire some new ones.

Locate the Nearest Exit

In some instances, the best thing you can do when you get that notice is to not stick around. The minute you suspect that your company or firm is having hard times, on the verge of a merger, about to reorganize or reduce its workforce, decide if you should stay or go. Be on the alert for news about industries facing hard times. Evaluate your position's worth to the company. Think about what sets you apart from others who are under the company's axe. If you want to stay, try fighting for your position. Go to the chief decision maker and put up a good argument about why they should keep you.

Keep Your Emotions at High Altitudes

Denial forces many to have difficulty coping with the thought of unemployment. Even when firms send employees advance warnings of pending downsizing, it is not uncommon for some to feel it won't happen to them. Those who eventually find themselves in unemployment lines often experience periods of depression and stress. "Unemployment is often experienced as a highly stressful life change," writes H.G. Kaufman in his study of unemployment among professionals. According to a number of career counselors, people who are unemployed should try to stay positive. If it happens to you, realize that you don't have a problem; it's the company's. Remain positive, and tell yourself you are employable. Find a strong network of people who are willing to listen, show understanding, and give you support.

Have Your Landing Gear in Place

Don't wait until after you're laid off to redo your résumé. As a general rule of thumb, try to keep it updated every six months. The best time to look for a job is right after you get one. In addition, it's good to go fishing to see if your résumé will get you a bite. While you're looking for that new job, buckle up and fasten your wallet or purse. Have that cushion that's going to keep you on your feet and not knock you over with grief because you don't know if your next check is coming. One of the biggest setbacks to a layoff is not saving and putting away money for that rainy day. Remember, there's no such thing as being humble when the rent or mortgage has to be paid. Take a temporary or part-time job, work a night shift, or relocate. Have alternatives and use your network of connections.

Find Another Runway

Who says there can't be an upside to a downsize? Unfavorable industry conditions may not mean you have to look for the same or another dead-end job. If you've always hated what you're doing, make a transition or follow the steps of B. K., a former teacher. She always hated her field of teaching. In the past two years, she's been laid off twice. Each time she returned to her old profession. "It took one more layoff to steer me back to school and pursue my lifetime dream of writing," says B. K. A layoff can have benefits. It can get you to do what you always wanted and show you you're actually in the wrong industry. Use it as a time to do soul searching. Ask yourself, do you really like what you're doing?

Don't Lie Low

If a layoff does hit you, you may go through a period of withdrawal and retreat. Experts in the unemployment process describe this first stage as the period when there is shock and denial of what has occurred. S. H.'s friends often wondered when she was going to start looking for a new job after she lost her job. With a nice healthy severance based on three months of her $40,000 annual salary, she decided to just sit back and relax for a while. It was only a matter of time before her bank account began dwindling, and nervousness forced her to start looking for a new job. By the time she did, six months had passed and no one seemed as interested in helping her. The best thing you can do when you get that pink slip or notice is to not become too comfortable. The smart way to cope is to try and stay ahead of the game. Don't wait for a low bank account to catch up with you. Circulate and keep moving forward. Fight the urge to relax.

Look for an Escape Hatch

Just because you receive a notice, doesn't mean you have to accept a layoff. J. M., an employment specialist, didn't. She remembers the day management asked to meet with her. As she sat across from her manager, these were the words she heard, "The company's changing . . . We have to trim the budget. . . We've decided to eliminate your position." J. M. said it didn't register at first that she was being laid off. She thought, not me. Her only response to her manager was, "Okay." Once she left the office, she thought about all that she had contributed to the firm's goals. She mentally flipped through her Rolodex of contacts while at the same time recalling all the projects she had managed. With this in mind, she approached the vice president and talked him out of laying her off. She spelled out the company's current problems and discussed the good things she had done for the firm. The vice president's response was, "You gave me a lot to think about. Let me talk to the CEO and get back to you." One day later, not only was J. M. reemployed, but a new position with expanded responsibilities was created for her.

STEER CLEAR OF LAYOFF-PRONE ORGANIZATIONS

Read all you can about how a weakening economy is facing different industries. Watch for those organizations which are having the hardest times. Ones you may want to especially pay attention are service sectors like airlines, banking, commercial real estate, advertising, retailing, as well as defense and high-tech firms. Above all, don't cut yourself off from information sources, meetings, or announcements your company makes about their plans for the future. Be the one in the know. Look out for your firm's efforts at chipping away costs. Clues of cost-paring measures include everything from travel and expense reductions to not filling vacant positions.

Take Off on Your Own

A lot of newly unemployed persons find a layoff can promote opportunities for entrepreneurship. A. P., a former vice president at a large brokerage firm, found success through starting her own business. She started by compiling a list of her company's former clients and conducted an assessment of their needs. She had banked some favors with her previous contacts and used her layoff as a time to cash in on them. By using the skills she learned at her last job she created a thriving computer consulting business. Her list of clients is impressive and she trains their employees how to use various software packages. The key to her success, she says, was realizing that the expertise she gained from her last job was transferable into a money-making venture.

ADVICE FROM EXPERT PAUL FITZGERALD, VICE PRESIDENT, DRAKE BEAM MORIN ...

Note: Drake Beam Morin is an international career transition firm specializing in outplacement and job search, as well as selection and performance programs.

Who Fares Well When It Comes To A Layoff?

Success is achieved by those who in some way make themselves indispensable to the company. They may have handled responsibilities outside of their job description, taken advantage of company training programs to broaden their skills, or developed a loyal following of clients.

Those who fare well are also professionals who learn to toot their own horns, not in a brash or bragging way, but honestly and sincerely so that management is aware of their capabilities and achievements. When management decides who stays or who leaves, it is often this group who carries more value.

Realize We're in a Different Employment Age

Those who are aware that the age of permanent jobs has passed also tend to survive industry trimmings. They are people who realize that we have entered a new era of employment, and keep a sharp eye on where their next career move will be.

They, for instance, maintain current files of their skills and accomplishments. They update their résumés regularly, watch for opportunities to transfer or be promoted, and identify positions that are more "secure" (for example, those that contribute directly to the bottom line profitability). They also activity network with colleagues and professional associations, always keeping open lines of communication. They know that another key to their success is visibility.

At a time when many companies are changing rapidly, people who keep their career "running shoes" out of the closet are prepared for the starting gun.

Strategies or Steps for Coping After You've Been Hit

If the layoff is traumatic for you, work through the emotional pain *before* you start interviewing for your next job. Anger, bitterness, or hostility may come through to the interviewer if it hasn't been resolved.

Second, use your support system to help sustain you through this time of transition. Find one of two close friends who are good for venting and channeling your emotions to aid you in a positive way. Use exercise, good diet, and other stress management techniques to pull you through.

Third, conduct an assessment of your career up to this point. Decide what is going to be your next job target. Then determine what skills, achievements, and attributes will make you attractive to your next employer. Script a strong résumé to highlight your capabilities.

Finally, once your résumé and mind are focused on where you want to go, **network, network, network.** Ask for information and referrals rather than asking if someone has a job for you.

COMMON MISTAKES TO AVOID

1. Don't think of yourself as out of work. Your new full-time job is to find your next paying job. If you receive severance pay, treat it as your salary while you're locating your next position.
2. Don't rush to change your résumé too quickly and then contact everyone you know to ask about any job openings of which they are aware. First, you need to get organized so that when you turn to others, you'll be able to ask specific questions to obtain the help you need.
3. Don't take time off for an extended vacation or try to catch up on all those home projects you've been meaning to get to in the past. Keep in mind that securing your next job requires focused energy and continuous momentum.

Isabell Cottrell
President
Ethnic Gold Cosmetics
DeSota, Texas

While other women may tell you about garnering the right skills and being in the right place at the right time, I have a different piece of advice to sell. Mine is not about time nor place, but about not putting your dreams on hold and making sure your core is strong. Once you start believing in yourself, you can do whatever you set your mind to do. And it's not what you plan, it's what you do with the opportunities that present themselves.

My rise as an entrepreneur and to ultimately head my own company spans from a demand for products purchased in high numbers by ethnic consumers and not marketed properly to them, *for them*. Part of my quest to succeed also included learning how to nurture myself and returning to the basic values that my parents and godly grandparents instilled in me. They emphasized, "If you want something, you have to work hard for it." Those values have been critical to *who I am* and what I have become. By reaffirming my faith in God I have been able to set my own goals and accomplishing them up difficult mountains and down desolate valleys. Through those valleys, I never lost my vision of what I wanted for my life. From my youth I knew I would always be a businesswomen, as well as a good mother and wife. Such clear vision and exacting goals made my quest unrelenting.

Women cannot define **Success** in the same way as male society. We, whether collectively or individually, have to redefine what success is. If we don't, our children and our families are going to go down the tubes. We have different responsibilities and have to juggle a number of things at the same time in order to stay on top.

Everything that has occurred in my career has resulted from preparation and persistence. It's been shaped by strong, inner spiritual desires, recognition of my own potential and my willingness to grow. I think to be successful, one must also understand that life is a journey with many roads.

Out of my many experiences, I reclaimed me and saw that my dreams could become a reality. When the time was right, God gave me the plan to launch my own company. Having faith in God and belief in myself, education, respect for other people, perseverance, and hard work are key ingredients that I used to unlock the doors to pursuing my goals.

Sincerely,

Isabell Cottrell

Chapter 14

WHY DON'T YOU JUST MIND YOUR OWN BUSINESS?

IF you are:

Tired
of the office politics;

Weary
of navigating through troubled waters;

Reluctant
to start a job search;

Facing
another layoff or the possibility of a layoff;

Not interested
in being or remaining a corporate star;

BUT have:

A need to be on your own;
Balanced business experience;

Consider yourself to be a self-starter;
Are determined, enthusiastic, and independent;
Love hard work;
Need to control situations;
Feel self-confident;
Then your salvation may be to become self-employed.

ON YOUR OWN

Black women don't have to worry about squeezing out the competition when it comes to starting businesses of our own. We're the needle in the haystack. Of the estimated one million businesses that are started each year only about thirty thousand belong to black women. The opportunities are there. We just have to start collecting them.

You better hurry. The 1990s will be viewed as the decade for entrepreneurship, especially for women. Minority businesses are projected to increase rapidly from one in sixteen today to one in eight businesses by the year 2000. Federal legislation has committed millions of dollars to assist women in becoming business owners. The harvest is yours for the taking, and an array of programs linking successful women-owned businesses to fledging women-owned businesses have been established.

What About the Economy? Don't worry about it. In spite of the recession and economic slump, business opportunities can be successfully established now. According to *Money* magazine, the best business opportunities awaiting you are in health care, training and education, business consulting, environmental work, privatization, and retailing.

You may say to yourself, "I'm interested, but I can't afford to start my own business." Yes, you can. A business can be started with almost no money. Nancy Flake, Director of the Small Business Development Center at Howard University, says there are more than fifty business ventures requiring as little as two hundred dollars start-up capital. You have your pick of ventures from apartment preparation services to window washing. To give you some ideas as to what businesses are available, and in demand, check out the following list:

BUSINESS VENTURES REQUIRING $10,000 OR LESS START-UP CAPITAL

Venture	*Estimated Start-up*
Apartment Preparation Service	$ 500
Automobile Detailing	500
Burglar Alarm Sales and Installation	5,000
Carpet Cleaning Service	6,000
Catering	2,000
Child Care (in home)	500
Collection Agency	9,400
Computer Repair Service	6,400
Consignment Used Car Lot	9,000
Consulting Business	8,000
Coupon Mailing Service	4,000
Courier Service	3,000
Craft Business	4,300
Credit Consultant	1,000
Errand Service	1,000
Event Planning Service	5,000
Food Delivery	2,000
Freelance Writing	3,000
Furniture Restoration	2,000
Gift Baskets	2,500
Herb Farming	3,740
Home Computer	8,500
• Bookkeeping	
• Data Base Management	
• Desk Top Publishing	
• Tax Return Preparation	
• Word Processing	
Home Inspection Service	3,600
Hot Dogs/Hamburgers Business	9,000
House Painting	8,500
House Sitting/Home Care Service	7,000

Import/Export	Varies
Information Broker	3,500
Interior Designer	9,130
Janitorial Service	3,000
Kiosk & Carts Business	10,000
Maid Service	4,000
Money Broker	9,000
Multilevel Marketing	150
Newsletter Publishing	2,625
Parking Lot Striping Service	6,700
Personal Shopping Service	3,300
Pet Care Business	1,000
Pinball/Video Games Arcades	8,000
Pool Cleaning and Repair Service	9,600
Private Investigator	6,500
Private Mailbox Service	10,015
Résumé Writing Service	3,000
Secretarial/Word Processing Service	3,000
Specialty Advertising	5,000
Specialty Baked Goods	1,500
Street Vending Business	4,000
T-Shirt Shop	5,000
Tutoring Service	5,000
Used/Consignment Clothing	7,500
Utility Bill/Property Auditing Service	8,000
Wedding Planning	2,700
Window Washing Service	200

SOUNDS GOOD, BUT WHAT ABOUT FRANCHISING?

If the idea of starting from scratch doesn't appeal to you, then buy into someone else's formula for success. Purchasing a franchise may be exactly what you're looking for. But what is franchising? The International Franchise Association defines franchising as "a continuous relationship in which the franchisor provides a licensed privilege to do business, plus assistance in organizing, training, merchandizing, and management in return for a consideration from the franchisee."

With $600 billion total annual sales in 1990, and in excess of $758.5 billion in 1991, franchises are projected to be the primary method of doing business by the year 2000. Franchises have expanded way beyond the typical fast foods chains and automobile dealerships. Franchises can now be found across all industries and you can buy a franchise for as little as $1,000 or as high as $600,000. The table below illustrates the type of franchises available and the fees associated with their purchase.

SAMPLE FRANCHISES AND RELATED PURCHASE COSTS

	*Franchise Fee	**Capital Requirements
Alphagraphics Printshops Electronic graphics and print centers	47,900	260,000–320,000
Decorating Den Systems Residential and commercial interior decorating	7,900	15,000–30,000
Dunhill Personnel Systems Professional recruitment, office support, temporary services	12,000–25,000	60,000–75,000
Everything Yogurt Frozen yogurt, healthy light foods	30,000	56,000
Jani-King International Janitorial and commercial cleaning	6,500–14,000	3,000–14,000+
Jazzercise Dance fitness	625	2,000
McDonald's Hamburgers and fast food	22,500	40,000–265,000
Merry Maids Maid service	18,500	10,000–15,000
Petland Full service retail pet stores	40,000–50,000	125,000–250,000
Precision Tune Engine repair, tune-ups, oil and lube	20,000	147,000–164,000

*Franchise Fee—Initial fee paid to the franchisor for the right to use franchise name
**Capital Requirements—Initial investment amount

Acquiring a franchise has a number of advantages:

1. An established "formula of success." Offers the standards which have made the venture successful.
2. Services provided by franchisor: management and staff training, financial assistance, lease negotiations, financial projections.
3. Access to specialists to assist franchisee to improve business.
4. High customer recognition factor.
5. Federal and state laws require disclosure statements about earnings claims.

Before deciding to purchase a franchise you also want to examine the drawbacks.

1. The franchisor is paid first. Royalty fees set by the franchisor usually stipulate a percentage of the franchisee's sales, not profits.
2. Restrictions on how to operate the business. You may not be able to change location or the type of goods or services that can be sold.
3. Hidden fees. The franchisee may be required to buy all equipment or even the land from the franchisor.
4. Initial fees may be low, but hidden fees may escalate the stated capital requirements figure.

HOW TO BUY A BUSINESS

First, let's discuss why anyone would want to sell their business. The reasons for selling usually fall into two categories: visible and invisible. Reasons such as health problems, disinterest by children, death, divorce, marriage, and loss of a partner are considered visible reasons. These reasons are easily seen. On the other hand, the invisible reasons may be the real reason a seller fools someone into buying a business. For example, someone may unload their business onto you because it's in financial trouble or its future is in doubt even though new management or new funding could be injected into the business. Or, the business has potential but needs new management or funds to continue to be prosperous. Before putting your hands on a new business you will need to identify both the visible and invisible reasons that a seller is letting it go.

When's A Good Time To Buy?

When it's advantageous to you. There are a number of advantages to buying a business. The most significant advantage is that the business has a history and track record, both factors which can attract investors. In addition, through its financial track record, it is more likely to receive favorable treatment from lenders as banks are more likely to lend money to an existing business than to a start-up operation. Second, buying a business involves less risk than starting up a new business.

The major pitfall to look out for before you buy a business is that you might get stuck with a business that's a lemon, with no further potential to be profitable. Furthermore, you may buy a business that cannot be turned around even with a great amount of your potential or capital.

TAKING CARE OF BUSINESS

Besides analyzing the advantages and disadvantages of buying a business you will also want to do the following:

1. Develop criteria for the type of business in which you are interested.
2. Identify sources for locating a business to buy. Use trade journals and newspapers, business brokers, lawyers, CPAs, vendors, business listing services, and real estate agencies.
3. Make direct contact with the seller. Gather data. A rule of thumb is to examine companies which have been operating for at least two years.
4. Conduct a financial and market analysis.
5. Make an offer. Negotiate if necessary.

WINNERS AND LOSERS

It sounds so simple—a dream that could become a successful, profitable venture. It's yours and you're your own boss. Well, if it is so simple, then why do so many people fail in their attempts of acquiring their dream?

Losers in Business

Betting on the wrong business
Failure to develop a business plan
Mismanagement
Entered a market that is already crowded with competition

Did not offer what people wanted to buy
Failed to make appropriate changes in business operations
Lacked sufficient knowledge about the type of business
Limited understanding about business, industry or customers
Lack of sufficient capital
Inappropriate location
Wrong attitude
Poor quality product or service

On the other hand, if you don't intend to be a loser in business adopt these winning attributes:

Winners In Business:

Business start-up preparation
Experience with the proposed business
Managerial competence
Technical knowledge
Marketing expertise
Financial management capabilities
Well-defined business plan
Opportunity seeker
Goal-oriented
Risk taker
Aggressive
Good judgment
Ability to get things done through other people
Perseverance to always complete the task

STEPS TO TAKE BEFORE YOU PUT YOUR FINANCES ON THE LINE

Step 1—Conduct a Personal Assessment

The primary purpose of the self-assessment is to generate data to determine if you have entrepreneurial potential. Complete the questionnaire below:

ENTREPRENEURIAL PROFILE INVENTORY

	Yes	No
1. Are you a self-starter?	——	——

2. Do you have good health? ___ ___
3. Can you lead others? ___ ___
4. Can you accept responsibility? ___ ___
5. Are you a good organizer? ___ ___
6. Can people trust what you say? ___ ___
7. Are you able to juggle multiple tasks at once? ___ ___
8. Do you enjoy working independently? ___ ___
9. Are you willing to work long hours? ___ ___
10. Are you persistent? ___ ___

Scoring

Below
5   Think about sticking with a nine-to-five job, with the security of a regular paycheck.
5–7   You have entrepreneurial potential; however, you may want to consider a partner to help offset your weak areas.
8–10   Congratulations! You fit the entrepreneurial profile. You've got what it takes to operate a business. So get going!

Step 2—Identify the business product/service

What is your bright idea? Screen your big idea. You want to select a business that you will not only enjoy operating, but will also generate sufficient revenues, for a long, long, time.
Briefly describe your proposed product or service:

_____

_____

_____

_____

Now answer these questions:

1. Who would be interested in the product or service you are offering?
2. What similar product or service is already available on the market?
3. Why will the venture be successful?
4. How much money will be needed to start up the business? (If you are not sure, ESTIMATE!!)
5. How soon will you start the business?
6. Who are the competitors in the industry?

Step 3—Turn to the Experts

Seek out experts to give you advice in
  Preparing a business plan
  Securing capital
  Coordinating market research
  Identifying an attorney or accountant
  Determining an appropriate legal structure

LOCATING THE EXPERTS

Business assistance is available at the federal, state, and local levels. A variety of services exist which include written materials, counseling sessions, seminars and workshops. Costs for such services are minimal.

Federal Resources

The following programs are available specifically for women through the Small Business Administration (SBA):

WOMEN'S NETWORK FOR ENTREPRENEURIAL TRAINING

To be eligible as a WNET protege, your business must be at least a year old and poised for growth in sales, employees, location, or product lines.

WOMEN'S DEMONSTRATION CENTERS

New and experienced business owners can receive one-on-one counseling, business and financial planning assistance through these centers. Centers operate in the District of Columbia and eleven states: California, Colorado, Georgia, Illinois, Indiana, Michigan, Minnesota, Missouri, New Mexico, Texas, and Wisconsin.

OFFICE OF WOMEN'S BUSINESS OWNERSHIP

OWBO conducts Access to Capital conferences around the country, covering alternative financing sources for women business owners who can't get money from banks. Other federal programs include:

SMALL BUSINESS DEVELOPMENT CENTERS

SBDCs are open to anyone and are usually on college or university campuses. A typical program consists of one-to-one counseling, management help, seminars, and workshops. You can contact the local SBA office for a listing of SBDC's in your area.

U.S. SMALL BUSINESS ADMINISTRATION (SBA)

The SBA provides information ranging from how to start a business to sources of technical and financial assistance.
409 Third Street S.W., Washington, D.C. 20416 (202) 205–6906.

THE MINORITY BUSINESS DEVELOPMENT AGENCY OF THE DEPARTMENT OF COMMERCE

Funds about a hundred Minority Business Development Centers (MBDCs) across the country. MBDCs offer a variety of programs open to anyone. Counseling, management training, and marketing assistance are available. Contact (202) 377–1936 for the location of the nearest MBDC.

STATE AND LOCAL RESOURCES

Many states have women's business advocates or offices that assist women business owners. Contact your state or local economic development offices for assistance. See Appendix D, p. 277.

CITY AND COUNTY ECONOMIC DEVELOPMENT OFFICES

To obtain information concerning economic and business trends in your community, turn to city and county economic development office for information.

CHAMBERS OF COMMERCE, OR REGIONAL OR COUNTY PLANNING BOARDS

These organizations sponsor small business development programs.

ADULT EDUCATION PROGRAMS, COMMUNITY COLLEGE PROGRAMS, FOUR-YEAR COLLEGES AND OTHER EDUCATIONAL PROGRAMS

Conduct workshops on all aspects of starting and maintaining the small business.

LOCAL BANKS

They have it, you want it. Become friends with a banker. He/she will be crucial to the financial planning of your business.

MINORITY BUSINESS ENTERPRISE LEGAL DEFENSE AND EDUCATION FUND (MBELDEF)

Provides information and legal assistance in support of the development of minority-owned business.
300 I Street, Suite 200, Washington, D.C. 20002, (202) 543–0040

NATIONAL ASSOCIATION OF MINORITY CONTRACTORS (NAMC)

Disseminates information, including procurement opportunities of importance of minority contractors.
1333 F Street N.W., Suite 500, Washington, D.C. 20004, (202) 347–8259

THE NATIONAL FEDERATION OF INDEPENDENT BUSINESS (NFIB)

The nation's largest advocacy organization representing small and independent businesses.
600 Maryland Avenue, S.W., Suite 700, Washington, D.C. 20024, (202) 554–9000

NATIONAL MINORITY BUSINESS COUNCIL (NMBC)

Services the needs of minority-owned businesses with assistance procurement.
235 E. 42nd Street, New York, N.Y. 10017, (212) 573–2385

NATIONAL MINORITY SUPPLIER DEVELOPMENT COUNCIL (NMSDC)

Committed to matching minority-owned businesses with assistance in procurement opportunities, the NMSDC's data base includes information on more than 15,000 vendors certified by its 46 regional councils.
15 W. 39th Street, New York, N.Y. 10018, (212) 944–2430

SMALL BUSINESS SERVICE BUREAU

This national nonprofit small business service organization has over 35,000 members.
554 Main Street, P.O. Box 1441, Worcester, MA 01601, (508) 756–3513

THE INTERNATIONAL FRANCHISE ASSOCIATION (IFA)

The IFA publishes The Franchise Opportunity Guide, which lists IFA-member franchise companies by industry along with capital requirements and contact persons for those interested in purchasing a franchise.
1350 New York Ave., N.W., Suite 900, Washington, DC 20005–4709, (202) 628–8000 Fax (202) 628–0812

WOMEN IN FRANCHISING INC. (WIF)

Is a Chicago-based marketing and consulting firm with 21 franchising companies as corporate members. WIF holds "Franchising for Women and Minorities"; Seminar series are aimed at introducing participants to all aspects of franchising.
175 N. Harbor Drive, Suite 405, Chicago, IL 60601 or call (800) 222–4WIF

For More Information

MINORITY BUSINESS DEVELOPMENT CENTERS

With 107 different locations in the United States, these centers offer minority entrepreneurs one-on-one advice about their business plans and overall strategies for growth.

THE AMERICAN WOMAN'S ECONOMIC DEVELOPMENT CORPORATION

Offers 90-minute counseling sessions by phone, for tips on business topics such as plan structuring. Membership is $65 annually.
641 Lexington Avenue, 9th floor, New York, N.Y. 10022, (800) 222–AWED

Networking Groups

NATIONAL ASSOCIATION OF WOMEN BUSINESS OWNERS

600 South Federal Street
Suite 400
Chicago, IL 60605
(312) 922-6222

ASSOCIATION OF BLACK WOMEN ENTREPRENEURS

P.O. Box 49368
Los Angeles, CA 90049
(213) 660–6248

AMERICAN ASSOCIATION OF AFRICAN AMERICAN WOMEN ENTREPRENEURS

P.O. Box 13933
Silver Spring, MD 20910
(301) 565-0527

NATIONAL ASSOCIATION OF BLACK WOMEN ENTREPRENEURS

Box 1375
Detroit, MI 48231
(313) 341-7400

NATIONAL ASSOCIATION OF NEGRO BUSINESS AND PROFESSIONAL WOMEN'S CLUBS, INC.

1806 New Hampshire Avenue, N.W.
Washington, DC 20009
(202) 483-4206

NATIONAL ASSOCIATION OF WOMEN BUSINESS OWNERS

600 South Federal Street
Suite 400
Chicago, IL 60605
(800) 222–3838

NATIONAL ASSOCIATION FOR FEMALE EXECUTIVES

127 West 24th Street
New York, NY 10011
(212) 645–0770

NATIONAL ASSOCIATION OF MINORITY WOMEN IN BUSINESS

2705 Garfield
Kansas City, MO 64109
(816) 421-3335

If you have decided that minding your own business is the career path for you, remember to:

1. Assess your entrepreneurial potential.
2. Develop a list of possible opportunities and analyze the advantages and disadvantages of each.
3. Don't hesitate to ask for help—use the experts.
4. Network with other business owners and within business organizations.
5. Make a commitment to succeed in business.

Recommended reading

Bangs, Jr., David H. *The Start-Up Guide: A One-Year Plan for Entrepreneurs.* Dover, NH: Upstart Publishing Company, Inc., 1989.

Bermont, Hubert. *How to Become a Successful Consultant in Your Own Field.* Rockland, CA: Prima Publishing Company, 1989.

Blum, Laurie. *Free Money For Small Businesses and Entrepreneurs* (Revised and Updated). New York: John Wiley and Sons, Inc., 1989.

Brooks, Dr. Michael. *The Power of Business Rapport.* New York: HarperCollins, 1991.

Davidson, Jeffrey P., and George-Ann Fay. *Selling To The Giants: How to Become a Key Supplier to Large Corporations.* New York: Amacom, 1991

Diamond, M. R., and J. L. Williams. *How to Incorporate: A Handbook for Entrepreneurs and Professionals.* John Wiley and Sons, Inc., 1987.

Franchise Update Publishers. *The Executive's Guide to Franchise Opportunities.* San Jose, CA: Franchise Update Publications, 1991.

International Franchise Association. *The Franchise Opportunity Guide.* Washington D.C.: IFA, 1991.

Harper, Stephen C. *The McGraw-Hill Guide to Starting Your Own Business: A Step-by-Step Blueprint for the First-Time Entrepreneur.* New York: McGraw-Hill, Inc., 1991.

Hayes, John. *Franchise: The Inside Story.* New York: Harper and Row, 1991.

Kamoroff, Bernard. *Small-Time Operator: How To Start Your Own Small Business, Keep Your Books, Pay Your Taxes, and Stay Out of Trouble.* Laytonville, CA : Bell Springs Publishing, 1990.

Knight, Brian, and the Associates of Country Business. *Buy the Right Business—At the Right Price.* Dover, NH: Upstart Publishing Company, Inc., 1990.

Mancuso, Joseph R. *How To Write a Winning Business Plan.* Englewood Cliffs, NJ: Prentice-Hall, Inc., 1985.

Martin, Charles L. *Starting Your New Business: A Guide for Entrepreneurs.* Los Altos, CA: Crisp Publications, Inc., 1988.

Mucciolo, Louis, ed. *Small Business: Look Before You Leap: A Catalogue of Sources of Information To Help You Start and Manage Your Own Small Business.* New York: Arco Publishing Company, 1987.

Technology Management. *Planning and Financing Your New Business: A Guide to Venture Capital.* Warwick, RI: Technology Management, 1991.

RoAne, Susan. *How to Work a Room: A Guide to Successfully Managing the Mingling.* New York: Shapolsky Publishers, 1988.

Zuckerman, Laurie. *On Your Own: A Woman's Guide to Building a Business.* Upstart Publishing Company, Inc., 1990.

Deborah G. Sims
President
Sun Valley Ford–Lincoln–Mercury
Douglas, Arizona

When *Essence* magazine featured a story about my automobile dealerships, I received a lot of inquiries about how I started my business. I was surprised by the number of young people who, for whatever reason, wrote wanting to hear about how the process can be shortened. They weren't interested in knowing how the process includes working in a store for "X" number of years or the best way to learn the car business. They were more concerned with what it takes to instantly become a dealer.

It's ironic how people tend to think that successful black women just got here, that it didn't take work, effort, maneuvering, heartaches, or tears to get to where we are.

If there's one issue I want to stress, it's that nonminorities often have the avenue already paved. They have the road, the avenue, the stop sign, the red light. However, as black women we often have to pave our own road and put up our own signs. And it's not anything that comes that easily. Success takes work. When I say work, I'm talking about working smart, not staying on a job for long hours from eight to eight, seven days a week. To me, that's something that should occur in the early stages of getting a business started or when beginning a new job.

My driving force has been determination. The reason I chose the route I did was because I always liked cars. In college, I decided I didn't want to work in the school cafeteria. I wanted to be outdoors. My father always had a fanatical interest in cars. That lured me to the race track or compelled me to hide behind the seat of his car while he was drag racing someone down the street. Just from being around cars and a family of car buffs, I got involved with something that interested me.

For you, too, there's got to be an interest. Your career should involve something that you really want to do. Otherwise, you'll be among the many people who dwell in job situations, for years, that they'd really prefer not to be in. So, the main thing is to look at your situation and see where you can advance from it. Is there any potential there? If not, move on to something that you'd like to do.

A large majority of black women are not really doing what they'd like to do or being what they'd like to be. This may be for reasons of discrimination, education, etc. But I look at discrimination in terms of what can I do to overcome it. Recognize that some segments of society can't look beyond color. But you must. I think we have to do everything we can to not give people an *excuse* to criticize our credibility, aggressiveness, goals, or successes. In the car industry, as in any other industry, I've learned that if you're successful you will continue to be successful as long as you focus on keeping the right chemistry around you.

The best piece of advice I'd like to leave you with is a recommendation that you look at yourself and figure out what direction that you want to go in. If you don't know, at least start somewhere to find out. JUST START!! A lot of the time, people procrastinate or are afraid to make a decision. But it's okay to make a mistake (not the same mistakes). At the same time, most people do want to go in the right direction, but they are looking for someone else to tell them what their destiny should be. You have to lead and direct yourself. It's about self-empowerment. It's your spiritual key.

With black women, we're so afraid of failure, we don't start anywhere. I started out washing cars while in college, thinking I was going to be an attorney solving all the problems of the world. But I realized how to make the most of a situation and use it to advance my career. After college, I went back to selling cars. The college placement office was showing me jobs that were paying less than what I was making selling cars, part-time. So, I told myself if I work full-time I should be able to double that.

It wasn't long before I progressed from sales to management, and then entered the Ford Minority Dealership Program. I had been in the business for eight years before they actually approached me. I knew not only how to sell cars but how to handle customers and had a greater understanding of the business. What sold Ford on me was my reputation for being an experienced car person. That was reinforced by my dealer who kept talking about this young black girl who was at his store kicking butt.

My secret card was credibility. When you are doing things right and have a lot going for you, eventually someone else will hear about it. Though I was fast becoming a shaker, there were days when I was miserable and my feet hurt, but I consistently prayed and hoped that I could be like my boss and go home every day at five and have financial freedom. I began telling myself, *One day that's going to be me.*

Persistence does pay off. Those who aren't persistent usually don't have an aggressive attitude about their career or bettering their personal life. They constantly have fears. For whatever reason, they look for everyone's advice instead of just going out and making small changes in their daily activities. They don't want to take the risk of making a mistake. But people who are successful have done things wrong, a lot of things wrong, but through experience they learn from their mistakes.

Do something for your career! Don't just sit there waiting for everyone else's advice. Eventually, if you're out there striving, you're going to get something. Someday, somewhere. Just don't ever, ever, ever, give up!

Sincerely,

Deborah Sims

Cathy Jessie Bell
Owner/Operator
McDonald's Franchise
Columbia, Maryland

What a blessing it is to be able to share a word of advice to the working women of the world. I don't profess to have all of the formulas for success. However, I can speak from personal experiences on what has worked for me. Throughout my professional career, as well as during my current business stint, my foundation has been built on three basic thoughts. Through my faith and confidence in myself, I have never had a fear of failing. I have never been afraid of pursuing or asking for the things that I want. Last, but not least, I have always used the simple to most complicated things to which I have been exposed to broaden my personal level of qualifiable experience.

Before you can concern yourself with not being a failure, you have to genuinely possess the desire to take on the task at hand. You need to be confident in yourself and your ability to perform. Once you have assessed your desire, confidence, and ability levels, and find all is intact, you need to make the commitment. Sisters, at this point, there is no stopping you. What is there to fear? Nothing beats a failure but a try. Many times we are fearful of jeopardizing our current career/ financial status for something we view as an unknown. This applies to most situations whether they involve a job change that is being sought or a plunge into the world of being an entrepreneur. I understand, because I have been on both sides of the equation.

As a typical young adult graduating from college, I felt that all I needed to do was land a good job in corporate America. I also thought that once I became employed, with an acceptable salary and nice perks, I would be in dreamland forever. My dreams almost shattered when I joined a major Fortune 500 company, which was initially reluctant to hire me. The problem? I was black and female. They tried to discourage me by offering me a job contingent on my ability to relocate. Now, I have to let you know that they didn't expect that a two-week newlywed would just pack up and leave without her husband. But they didn't know we had made a commitment to support each other's goals. When I accepted the position, with a relocation, they suddenly discovered that a job did exist in the state where I was living. Unfortunately, they offered me a job in the most racist, redneck section of the town.

I was being set up to fail. I was sent to market consumer products in a midwestern town that had a sign which read, "God Bless A Nigger After Dark" (I'm not kidding). People followed me around, threatened my life, and did everything but try to kill me. When I finally felt enough was enough I approached my employer and said, "I will be successful, and you're going to have to reassign me." Taking a stand and not letting fear bring me to my knees led to a long list of promotions. That one experience taught me to never allow being a woman and black to be a crutch. I've always felt that I could do anything that I put my mind to and that I could hang with the best.

To get ahead, you need not only to have the right mindset, but to put fear where it belongs. Second, you've got to work with what you've got and be willing to make sacrifices. When my husband and I decided that we wanted a McDonald's franchise, we quickly learned that our success was going to be dependent on our commitment and what we were willing to give up. Not only did I have to do eighteen months of training, but I had to relocate without my husband, quit my job, sell my house, pack up my car and move to Florida. And I didn't become an instant owner. I did everything from scrubbing toilets to mopping floors to flipping burgers. To be in business you have to know that business from the inside to the outside. That isn't to say that a franchise isn't attainable to anyone. It is, but you have to be willing to make a total commitment to the business. Just because you hang the golden arches doesn't mean you'll make the money. When it comes right down to it, it's not the price that someone pays for your product that makes you money, but your desire to succeed and dedication.

Prior to McDonald's, we went on a search for something bigger and better and looked at numerous opportunities. Being with a major corporation, in a relatively high visibility position, I was afforded some valuable opportunities to make contact with individuals that were in decision-making positions. While still working, but searching, this was the exact series of events that led to my franchise opportunity. I was at a job fair recruiting for my employer when I became involved in a conversation with a national licensing manager for a major company that was into franchising. I felt through the course of the conversation that this would be my grand opportunity. I went for the gusto, giving up my job security and all the perks that went with it. I never once feared that I would fail. I was confident in my ability to be an outstanding owner/operator. And I knew, based on all the past exposure that I had in handling various business transactions as a small business owner, that I was ready to deal.

In closing my letter, I would just like to say to all of my sisters that you too can do whatever you want to do. It doesn't matter if it's a $10,000, $100,000, or $1,000,000 desire. It is all relative. Though I might be considered seasoned, I am by no means done. In the words of Ray Kroc, founder of McDonald's, "When you are green you are growing, but when you are ripe you rot." May God continue to bless us. Good luck.

Sincerely,

Cathy Jessie Bell

Chapter 15

BLACK WOMEN CAN WIN!

Black Enterprise describes them as a "new breed of corporate achievers." *Ebony* says they are the "most promising." *Essence* categorizes them as "stars" and "power players." *Dollars & Sense* refers to them as the "best and brightest." People also regard them as "powerful and influential," while others say they are women "who dream worlds and are changing America." They do it all. They command some of the best salaries. They oversee million-dollar budgets. They represent a vast array of fields and industries. They are recognized as pioneers, gatekeepers, trailblazers, and trendsetters. What's interesting is not just where they are, but how they got there.

WHY HER?

We don't know about you, but when we read about the careers of successful black women like Barbara Jordan, Oprah Winfrey, Maya Angelou, Wilma Rudolph, Dorothy I. Height, Eleanor Holmes Norton, or Shirley Chisholm we ask, "What made their route different from ours?" Really, doesn't it make you jealous? How is it that they took the high road while some of us took the low road? Was it planned, or was it by accident? Look around your job. Did the woman opposite you move up, and if so, why her instead of you? What made you feel trapped, but why didn't she? She was so self-assured, but you weren't confident. Could it be that she gathered skills you didn't know you were supposed to have? Or, did she find her claim to fame through a mentor while you had no one to give you direction? Why do some women know where they're going, yet you feel lost? Do such women have something that you don't? If they achieved it, why can't you?

BY PLAN OR BY ACCIDENT?

When celebrities are asked how they rose to the top, their answers will range from chance encounters with the right people to being in the right place at the right time. In the workplace, however, few successful black women happened to just run into stardom. They won't all tell you stories of blood, sweat, and tears, but many will tell you that their climb to the top was not by accident. They also didn't audition to get ahead, but most certainly had to give every job their best performance.

There's no rule that says you can't have your chance to win the corporate spotlight. Think about the privileges. It may not get you chauffeur-driven limousines or people begging for your autograph, but you wouldn't complain about the respect, professional recognition, a healthy paycheck, or other perks. Better yet, you could use the sense of accomplishment and achievement that comes from others' seeking your advice as opposed to your having to seek theirs. It sounds so attractive, especially when you throw in high-level decision making and opportunities to climb to the height of your profession.

Interested? Every company has its stars and there's no reason why you can't be one. There's still room at the top for black women. Black women are not in short supply.

How She Got Over

They say stars aren't born, they're made. It's no different in the workplace. Taking a leading role, versus being an understudy, depends on the same things that turn unknowns into celebrities—talent, brains, and someone to discover you. Most successful black women will also tell you there were at least five major personal prerequisites to beginning their career climb to corporate success.

1. Faith In Herself

Every successful black woman we talked to emphasized that to get ahead you have to love yourself. Even your mother might have said, "If you don't love yourself, no one else will." To get ahead, you have to believe that you're capable of reaching your goals. You can't expect anyone else to, if you don't. There's a lot of power in having faith. So, don't tell yourself what you can't do. Inside you is a successful black woman waiting to be nurtured. To nurture that positive you, plant seeds of success. Treat yourself to new attitudes, new ideas, and new experiences. Talk to yourself. Look into your mirror everyday and ask yourself, "Who's the most important person?" Then answer the question. Say, "I AM!"

Well, do you? Do you believe in yourself? It's too bad that a significant number of black women don't. They're hard on themselves and won't give success a chance. When someone tells them what they can do, they respond, "Yeah, right!" Their motto is "Why bother?" In spite of having other black role models, they tell themselves, "I don't have what she has." But what someone else has doesn't really matter. What does matter is if they've done it, so can you.

2. Desire To Succeed and High Expectations

You've got to aim if you want to hit something. Success is a destination. You can't walk around in a circle claiming it. It just doesn't work that way. What does work is having a burning desire to do well in whatever you set out to do. Strive to be the best that you can be. Don't settle for less. Always go for the next rung up the ladder. Urge yourself to keep moving, don't become too comfortable. Tell yourself there's more for you to achieve. Be a dreamer. Think BIG! And keep saying, "I'm gonna make it. All I have to do is try."

3. Willingness To Face Tough Challenges

Many black women will tell you that being black is a tough challenge. In the workplace, you're going to face all kinds of obstacles. People will misjudge you. They'll assume wrong things about you, just because you're black and a woman. They'll try to push you to the edge and test you. But never let that stop you from getting what you want. Remember, you can't climb a smooth mountain. Keep telling yourself, "No matter what happens, I can get through this."

4. Tireless Work Ethic

When asked about how they reached their goals, successful black women often say they had to work hard at it, nonstop. They also made their hard work count. That may have required going the extra mile, doing more than was expected, and sometimes putting in longer hours. When the going got tough, they kept on going. When they felt like they could no longer go on, they kept on pushing themselves along.

5. Commitment To Professional Excellence

Has anyone ever said to you, "If you're going to do it, do it right"? If you're serious about succeeding, strive for professionalism. Don't just talk the talk. Walk the walk. Work like a professional. Look like a professional. Think like a professional. Got it? Good, go get it!

THE SECRETS OF SUCCESSFUL BLACK WOMEN

You have to agree that successful black women did or are doing something right. Aren't you curious about how they achieved penthouse careers while you're barely getting past the first floor? Aren't you tired of hearing about what they have, instead of how they got it? What's her secret?

She's got personality. She's well liked, but she maintains a professional distance. She recognizes that success in the workplace often comes down to whether or not you're liked. D. W., a vice president of human resources, began her career with her current firm as a clerk. She captured the attention of management by her charisma and congenial personality. No matter how bad situations became, she maintained her composure. Yes, she was inspiring. Her personality helped promote cohesiveness, and management asked her to join their ranks as a supervisor. She eventually became a customer service manager and then moved into her current position. According to her boss, there isn't anyone who doesn't like her. When first approached above moving into management, she didn't have the degree or the experience. But that didn't count her out. Her boss's boss told her, "With your people skills, there's already a slot with your name on it."

She's got great connections. She knows it pays to be nice to people and recognizes the power of networking. She also connects with people inside and outside her organization who have the inside track to information and opportunities. She also believes in having a mentor and finding people in the company who can act as her sponsor—those who are willing to back her quest for advancement to higher positions. K. C., director of operations, believed in the power of the Christmas card and staying in touch with former bosses. As a result, a former manager contacted her about a management position when he was offered a vice presidency in another company. "He told me that he always remembered how hard I worked as an assistant supervisor in one of the departments he had directed."

She's in the right place at the right time. Some black women share that significant turning points in their careers occurred purely by accident. C. R., a business development manager, loves to tell how she was chosen to fill a key position at a time when a company for which she worked needed a black. She says, "Some people called me a token. But I didn't care. I've learned that you have to make the most of your opportunities." Other successful black women also share that they stepped into prime positions by default. They explained that there were times when the sudden departure of a superior left them next in line for consideration for a position. They emphasized that timing was everything, but they also learned the importance of being prepared at all times. They feel that the company's decision to promote them was also measured by their past and a proven record of achievements.

She accepts temporary detours. Successful black women don't believe in dead ends. They know it's important to have a good route. When they do go down the wrong road, they don't use the same road back. They use back alleys and jump fences, if necessary. They also don't view backtracking as delaying their progress. They accept lateral moves and takes steps down. They know there's more than one way to move ahead. They are willing to change career paths but also recognize the importance of determining when they are going down a wrong path. When they experience setbacks, they rise to the occasion instead of letting it get them down. They don't lose sight of what they want. They evaluate a job to determine if it is carrying them to where they want to go. A. P., a former broker, explained that there are events in her career that she didn't want to happen. She says, "A forced relocation was one thing that worked to my advantage. I went into a new city and joined a new department, which gave me greater opportunities. But initially, I didn't see it that way." A factor in making her decision was asking herself what was the worst that could happen if she moved.

She's a risk taker. Most successful black women have had to take gambles in order to make things happen. By taking risks, they found that they had what it takes. At the same time, they also look for opportunities where they have the best chance to succeed. They extend themselves further than what is expected. They recognize that for black women to get someone's attention, they must be dynamic and do something out of the ordinary. They learn how to force their way up and don't always try to get their promotions by the book. They don't wait their turn or for a job posting before they ask to be moved ahead. D. M., a sales manager, explains that black women have been programmed to accept less and expect less. She says, "When a black woman's been smacked down, it makes it doubly hard for her to gamble and take risks."

She knows how to position herself. Black women target positions they want, and go after them. They accept jobs that will break them into new fields. They look for opportunities to be seen and get the attention of key company players. They not only read people well, but the politics of their work environment. They identify what doesn't work in order for them to excel. They also position themselves by establishing kinships with colleagues and bosses. They are careful about whom they are seen with, and they look for ways to stand out and give their careers altitude. J. B., now a bank manager, positioned herself to move up by volunteering to be her company's United Way chairperson. As chairperson, she was able to demonstrate leadership and organization skills that would otherwise have gone unnoticed in her position as a bank teller.

She challenges the system. Successful black working women fight the resistance of others' trying to prevent them from breaking through the "glass and concrete" ceilings. Barriers are not obstacles, in their eyes, but challenges. They know when to rock the boat and when confrontation is better than a compromise. They cope by reminding themselves that they are deserving and continually moving forward. J. W., a pharmaceutical sales rep, says "Black women are usually hired in the most menial positions. We're given fancy titles, but have no power for decision making. As a result, we sometimes have no other choice but to buck the system to help ourselves."

She is resilient. She has a stick-to-it-ness and strong survival instincts. Although she experiences the frustrations associated with her race and being a woman, she adapts to its ups and downs. She knows if she doesn't bend, she may break her career. She constantly surrounds herself with people who keep her thinking positive. She doesn't dwell in self-pity. She also doesn't expect a harvest without doing the preparatory work that leads to it. She places more emphasis on "motive action" than "motivation." S. W., an office manager, says,

"We have to have a strong desire and determination. That enables us to be flexible, as well as take the actions needed to make our careers successful."

She understands that the working world is a different world. Successful black women say the first lesson in coming to the workplace is to deal with the change in culture. They recognize that adaptation is necessary. B. M., a senior claims adjustor, says, "The hardest thing for me has been learning how to fit in and work with people who spend more time trying to figure out how I can wear my hair in ten different ways." Black women like B. M. also share that getting ahead requires having an awareness of the games which go on and how to play them. They feel that all black women must recognize that because black women are still thought of as primary nurturers, the demands on their careers are greater.

She is an agent of change. She doesn't have a crystal ball, but she keeps her eye on the future. She's a visionary and a futurist. She monitors industry trends and keeps up with the mission of her organization. She consistently thinks about tomorrow's challenges. She doesn't wait for things to happen, but creates her own opportunities. L. D., a personnel administrator, grew tired of waiting for management to approach her about a promotion. "I decided I had to move my own mountains," she said. L. D. campaigned for advancement by planting small seeds. She proposed changes to her company's workflow based on rumors that they were looking for ways to streamline the operations. Once her ideas were accepted, she laid the groundwork for other projects which eventually led to a major promotion.

She makes smart choices. In a way, she's calculating, because she counts the cost of every action and doesn't move about her career haphazardly. She's shrewd and views every move she makes as an investment in her future. She also weighs every decision carefully. M. C., a consultant, explains it best. "When you're advancing, you have to be analytical. You can't jump to decisions too quickly. If a company recognizes that you are a thinker, and a person with problem-solving skills, you're going to make it."

She knows information is power. She stays in the know. But she doesn't rely on other people to keep her informed about what's happening in her workplace. S. L., a lawyer, says, "I've always felt it's critical for black women to remain close to the activities that are closest to their company's heart." Successful black women also say that anyone who totally depends on secondhand information may find out that the information is unreliable. Black women, they say, must therefore stop removing themselves from direct sources of information. J. D., a human resources administrator, adds, "Some of us hurt ourselves by not attending meetings or other social gatherings where information is being passed around."

She walks in beauty. She's got the whole package and all nine yards. Finesse, high self-esteem, intelligence, and plenty of confidence. She sports a look that makes a statement that she is definitely a professional. When your read her lips, you know she's all about business. C. K., an image consultant, says, "Black women must understand how dress and appearance define the kind of professional she'll be viewed as."

WHAT IS WINNING AND HOW DO YOU MEASURE SUCCESS?

It really depends on where you start in life. If you start behind your would-be contemporaries, don't become discouraged. Be appreciative of where you are. Although your race may be longer for the moment, it doesn't mean that you can't catch up. Examine all your options, and elect the best choices. Don't program yourself to accept or expect less. Develop a winner's mentality. Rely on yourself, and don't let your career be dictated by other people or which way the wind blows. To succeed, your career requires your full participation. So, get off the sidelines and get into the race.

Barbara Bates
President
BAB Designs
Chicago, Illinois

Believe it or not, I didn't go the typical route to becoming a fashion designer. I had no formal schooling nor aptitude for drawing. I was always gutsy, had a good mind and great vision for what men and women should wear. Sheer career misery and a love for clothes put me on the road to becoming a fashion designer. What further established me as a woman with great designs had more to do with great taste in fabrics and a keen eye for pulling together the right wardrobe. Just think. It all started because someone happened to think I dressed well. There was no strategy. Ironically, design schools often ask me to talk to their students about my start. Surprise. Surprise. I can read the probing thoughts in their eyes when the students learn that I was a single parent at fifteen, entered the business at thirty; an unhappy secretary for ten years; unskilled and uneducated. As if their lives weren't already complicated, they then wonder why they're spending money to attend school. But I never leave them with a wrong message. I always share that my way was just another route.

My way. Simply, I'm a self-taught designer. Without the traditional tools of education, I relied on what little I knew about sewing, an eye for fabrics, and people who helped sew the designs I visualized. Even before I hung my designer shingle, I was shopping and selecting outfits for friends and others. There was only one problem, I was providing a service for which I didn't have a name. I was afraid to say I was a designer.

After a few years of store-to-store shopping and constantly bidding others to sew for me, I realized I had a small business. I was selling to friends, and friends' friends, and many others. Being a real fly-by-the-seat-of-the-pants person, I quit my job and continued working out of my home.

I knew that I had a potential clientele and that it would continue to grow by word of mouth. So, I took another risk and opened a small tailoring shop. I placed an ad in the paper for employees. Literally knowing nothing about what kind of machines to buy, I depended on the advice of other local designers and people who were sewing for me. Everything else I did during those growing years was a result of trial and error.

Lucky me. A client offered to put up part of the money if I included him as a partner. At the time, it sounded like a good idea. But after a year, he wanted his money back. Lucky me, again. I was able to repay him in only two months. In the meantime, I was building an impressive list of clients, all purely by accident.

A significant turning point in my career came when I flew out to Las Vegas to attend a friend's wedding. While there, I stopped in a store on the main strip in Caesar's Palace with two friends who were wearing some of my designs. Impressed, one of the salespersons asked where we had purchased the clothes. Thank God for good friends. They bragged that I had made them. That chance encounter resulted in a meeting with the owner who decided to carry my line.

At the same time that I was in Las Vegas, I called a guy I knew in Texas. He had previously contacted me because he had seen my designs on men in Chicago. That day, I became a designer on the run. He flew me to Houston to take his measurements. While there, he also accompanied me to a local shopping center to show me his style preferences. Sam Perkins, an NBA player, entered the store as we were leaving and my new client gave him my card. Two months later, he became one of a growing list of great connections. Through him, my clients started stretching across the NBA population.

Now, my clients have gone beyond the basketball court to include such well-known celebrities and entertainers as Oprah Winfrey, Hammer, Whitney Houston, Bobby Brown, Mike Tyson, and the Winans.

As trite as it sounds, you, too, can follow your dream, even if you feel you're in the twilight of your career. I won't lie to you. It takes hard work, persistence, and putting your all into it, along with many sacrifices. But believe that it can be done. And if you feel unsure, just try it, if you don't do anything else.

Sincerely,

Barbara Bates

Eldoris Mason, R.N.
Executive Director
BRASS (Behavior Research and Action in the Social Sciences)
Chicago, Illinois

I began my career as a surgical nurse at Cook County Hospital after completing my education there. I say education rather than "training" because students at County were expected to be leaders. Soon I was "scrub" nurse to the famous surgeon, Karl Meyer, and for heart surgery. County has played a large role in my life, even though I didn't spend most of my professional life there. I taught student nurses there, and later returned there as Associate Director of Nursing Services. I've always been proud to have been a "County grad," partly because of the excellent student-centered curriculum, and partly because they had a quota system. Very few Negro students were accepted in any class and even fewer graduated in the 1950's.

It seems that I was always being asked to do things that I had never done before: administering a long-term care facility, direct planning for a comprehensive mental health center, lead-conducting a feasibility study to establish an optometry center. I learned a lot by doing "ghost writing" for presenters at conferences, and sometimes for legislators. The research involved expanding my general knowledge in many areas. For twelve years, I worked for the Chicago Public Schools as a teacher-nurse. It was the best arrangement for trying to raise three children.

Three things that I will always be grateful for are the love that I received from my parents (my mother is my best friend, and someone who is a terrific role model); my faith in God (which she helped to nurture by her quiet example. I've always believed that God answered her prayers for me); and starting my college education in a liberal arts curriculum.

When I came to BRASS Foundation, Inc., fourteen years ago, I had no idea that I would stay so long. But there have always been new challenges. I had no idea that the organization was held in low regard, as were all of the administration and services which had black administrations. Today, BRASS administration and services are recognized as leaders in the field throughout Illinois, and even nationally. It is gratifying to be asked to serve on various committees and boards which set policy, and to receive public recognition that means that you made a significant contribution, and that others care how you think about an issue.

Advice:

Never believe that being black will prevent you from achieving your goals. I've never met anyone who I thought was superior to me because they were white. Recognizing that racism does exist means being in touch with reality, but it isn't a valid reason for not working for success.

It is important to make a commitment to whatever you undertake. That means giving it your best, always. Loyalty is a reflection of our own character. If you can't be loyal to the leadership, then it is best to walk away. It is okay to want the boss's job, but competing for it against the boss is destructive. Remember, that job descriptions are usually statements of "minimum requirements." Don't define yourself or limit your participation by it. Opportunities frequently come because you have interest, and show it.

Involvement with the broader issues that affect your organization will facilitate networking and cooperation and will stimulate continued growth in many areas. I've always avoided cliques because they limited my ability to experiment and change courses when I thought it necessary. I think of this as "enlightened self-interest."

The saying that "no man (woman) is an island; no man (woman) stands alone..." is true. We all need support and to develop and treasure those relationships that nurture our humanity.

Most important, recognize that whatever paths we take, life will not be easy; challenges come every day. But if you find your "center," you will weather the storms. As we go through life, we change with time. Change is ever-present. Nothing alive stands still, no matter how imperceptible the change. My goal is to direct the movement forward.

Sincerely,

Eldoris Mason

Chapter 16

ONE LAST LAP TO GO!

If you were told that you have one year remaining until your worklife ends, how would you react? Would you spend the rest of it in disappointment and have a long list of "if only's?" Or, would you have no regrets?

You may have cruised through this book and recognized some familiar situations in your own career. By now, you've caught on that there's no generic prescription or "1-2-3" plan for success. There are no simple answers, and career solutions can't all be consolidated into one book, but we do believe, as our mother religiously told us, that everyone can do something, whether it's small or large. You just have to be willing to try.

Achieving a successful career is tough, and for a black woman getting ahead is more challenging in today's society. Tradition makes us avoid, as we read in Terry McMillan's *Waiting To Exhale*, "the road less traveled." But we hope *Work, Sister, Work* will help you find a better road to a successful career.

The first step begins with you. Walk with your head up, and dream your dreams. A wise woman once told us, "Your badge of identity is not a burden or a plus." She also said, "Although race and gender may limit your mobility, don't let it limit your ability, and just because someone says no to you doesn't mean it's racism."

There's another reality that we don't want you to forget. As long as you are working, you'll always be at someone else's beck and call. If you can't handle it, develop your "my freedom plan." Consider ownership and setting your own rules. Don't remain on a job to just take up space. Be willing to follow your dream. Have a statement of purpose about your career. Hold on to it, but don't be afraid to modify it. Pursue that dream with intensity. Go after what you want every day. Determine where your priorities lie. Talk to yourself, and remind yourself of your goals.

Search for a workplace that is interested in your journey. If not, think about a transition. If there's an ambivalence about moving minorities, or a secondary system "for men only," then consider moving on to a less restricted environment. And get help when you need it. Find a mentor, someone who is singularly interested in your plight. Don't restrict him or her to the same race, same sex, or same journey.

As you are progressing, monitor and track your accomplishments. Maintain a career diary. Remember, certain people tend to get amnesia when you work for them. Use your diary to refresh their memories. At the same time, stay away from disbelievers. People will try to pull you down. But don't **you** be guilty of putting down someone else's success. It will only make you look smaller. So, stand behind others, too. There's a great deal of strength in working together.

Yes, "to thine own self be true." But know your level of ignorance and limitations. There are times when you will need to ask for assistance or to have certain skills in place *before* you can do anything? That's why it's important to do self-analysis. Ask yourself: What do I need? What can I do differently? What can I do better, and what can I do that's unique? When you find yourself saying, "I just have to be me," then ask, "Who is me?" Some of us really don't know.

By the way, about this issue of image. Image is not about what is; it's about what is perceived to be. Keep that in mind when you're caught up in the wrong politics, misread the environment, or make a mistake in dress or habit. Be creative in your packaging. Find your points of strength. Maintain a high profile. Get your name on the right people's lips. If they don't know your name, advertise and influence the people who report the names to those up top.

Keep in mind that you don't get ahead in name only. Your skills will also determine where you will be used best. Make a list of the qualities that you've got going for you. Consider the ways that you can get people to notice you. Remember, there are a lot of bodies competing for only a few positions. So, be a winner, and set the tone that if someone follows you they're in trouble.

One final set of thoughts. Become introspective and in tune with yourself. Also, learn when to replenish yourself. Just like a car, we all need to put back in the things that keep us running. Change your old habits. And remember, the hardest place to make a change is usually in your mind. So, stay at it. Practice setting goals and limits. Treat yourself like your own best friend. Refocus and let your needs come to the front. And if your friends and family aren't with you, tell them to get out of your way!

Well, that's about it. We wish you much success in your journey through the workplace. In the meantime, we hope you enjoy *Work, Sister, Work!* Write us, and tell us about you, your experiences, and how you're doing. And let us know if there's other information that we missed.

Enjoy,

Cydney & Leslie
11421 Lockwood Drive, #401
Silver Spring, Maryland 20904

APPENDIX A

Image Source List

Association of Image Consultants International
250 W. 57th Street
New York, NY 10019
(212) 642-9009

Color One Associates, Inc.
c/o JoAnne Nicholson, President
2211 Washington Circle, NW
Washington, DC 20037
(202) 293-9175

Image Industry Council International
P.O. Box 422643
San Francisco, CA 94142
(415) 905-5727

Kaufman Professional Image Consultants
c/o Karen Kaufman
200 Locust Street, 3B
Philadelphia, PA 19106
(215) 592-9709

APPENDIX B

JOB SHOPPING RESOURCES

Published Information Sources

There is a wealth of published materials useful for job hunting. Your research should help you to identify not only potential employers, but also fields that you may be interested in pursuing. A good place to start is with *How to Find Information About Companies* and the *Encyclopedia of Business Information*. A list of other valuable resources is provided below.

Government Publications

Occupational Outlook Handbook
Published by the U.S. Department of Labor (DOL) every two years. Surveys over 200 career areas. Provides clear descriptions of each job, including working conditions, education and training requirements, salaries, and prospects for the future.

Dictionary of Occupational Titles
Considered the reference bible for occupational information. Published by DOL. Includes over 20,000 job titles which are annotated, organized by major job categories, and cross-referenced by industry and title.

Guide for Occupational Exploration
Published by DOL. A key guide to finding the best job options. Assists individuals in determining the right jobs for them. Lists more than 20,000 jobs by occupational clusters, skills required, job title, and industry groups.

Corporate and Industrial Directories

Dun and Bradstreet Million Dollar Directory
Lists 16,000 public and private companies with a net worth of at least $500,000.

Standard and Poor's Register of Corporations, Directors and Executives
Includes corporate listings for over 45,000 firms and 72,000 biographical listings.

Directory of Corporate Affiliations
Provides information on "who owns whom" of major U.S. corporations.

Thomas Register of Manufacturers
Use this directory to create your own list of U.S. manufacturing firms making a specific product. Provides information on a wide variety of products and companies which are leaders in their field.

MacRae's State Industrial Directory (directory for each state)
Listings by company name, trade name, and product class.

Moody's Manuals
A series of eight separate manuals on current information about public companies.

Other Valuable Resources

The Career Guide—Dun's Employment Opportunities Directory
Describes career opportunities in more than 5,000 U.S. companies including information on the requirements and hiring practices of these employers.

Annual, 10Q and 10K Reports
Includes information about publicly owned companies. Particularly useful if you have interest in a company's operations.

Directory of National Trade and Professional Associations of the United States and the *Encyclopedia of Associations*
Two guides that list more than 14,000 national associations with all contact details. These groups are invaluable for names for networking contacts.

The Guide to American Directories
Offers descriptions of more than 6,000 directories which will lead you

to addresses, membership names, and titles of people covering a wide
range of industrial and professional activities throughout the U.S.

American Almanac of Jobs and Salaries
Provides descriptions of various jobs and salary levels in specific
industries.

The Directory of Executive Recruiters
Lists names and recruiters who specialize in particular fields.

Stay on top of your industry. READ the following magazines:

Barron's
Black Enterprise
Business Week
Business World
Entrepreneur
Forbes
Fortune
INC.
Nation's Business
Venture

And don't overlook specific trade magazines and newspapers covering
your particular profession.

APPENDIX C

CAREER RESOURCES TARGETED FOR MINORITIES AND WOMEN

Action Alliance of
Black Managers
P.O. Box 15636
Columbus, OH 43215
(614) 860-9388

Alliance of Black
Entertainment Technicians
8306 Wilshire Boulevard
Suite 130
Beverly Hills, CA 90211
(213) 299-0617

American Association of
Black Women Entrepreneurs
814 Thayer Avenue
Suite 202
Silver Spring, MD 20910
(301) 565-0527

American Association of
Blacks in Energy
1220 L Street, N.W.
Suite 605
Washington, DC 20005
(202) 898-0828

American Business Women's
Association
9100 Ward Parkway
P.O. Box 8728
Kansas City, MO 64114
(816) 361-6621

Association of Black
Psychologists
P.O. Box 55999
Washington, DC 20040
(202) 722-0808

Association of Black
Sociologists
c/o Dr. Sandra Walker
Ass't Dean, College of
Arts and Sciences
Univ. of Missouri
Kansas City, MO 64110
(816) 276-2736

Association of Black
Women Entrepreneurs
P.O. Box 49368
Los Angeles, CA 90049
(213) 660-6248

Association of Black
Women in Higher Ed.
Brooklyn College Provost
Bedford Avenue and Avenue H
Brooklyn, NY 11210
(718) 780-5864

Association of Women in
Science
1522 K Street, N.W.
Suite 820
Washington, DC 20005
(202) 408-0742

American Society of Women
Accountants
2313 N. Tracy Street
Alexandria, VA 22311
(703) 938-7114

Black Caucus of the
American Library Association
Central University Library
C–075–R
University of CA–
San Diego
La Jolla, CA 92093
(619) 534–1258

Black Data Processing Associates
P.O. Box 2420
Washington, DC 20013
(202) 659–5367
Black Filmmakers
Foundation
80 Eighth Avenue
Suite 1704
New York, NY 10011
(212) 924–1198

CAREER RESOURCES TARGETED FOR MINORITIES AND WOMEN

Black Human Resources
Network
1900 L Street, N.W.
Suite 500
Washington, DC 20036
(202) 775–1669
Black Psychiatrists of
America
P.O. Box 370659
Decatur, GA 30037
Black Women Can Win!
11421 Lockwood Drive #401
Silver Spring, MD 20904
(301) 681–2320
Black Women In Publishing
P.O. Box 6275
FDR Station
New York, NY 10150
(212) 772–5951
Blacks In Agriculture
817 Fourteenth Street
Suite 300A
Sacramento, CA 95814
(916) 444–2924

Blacks In Government
1424 K Street, N.W.
Suite 604
Washington, DC 20005
(202) 638–7767
Chicago Women In Trades
37 S. Ashland Avenue
Chicago, IL 60607
(312) 942–1444
Coalition of Black
Professional
Organizations
P.O. Box 76685
Washington, DC
(202) 310–1983/1948
Conference of Minority
Public Administrators
of the American Society
of Public Administrators
1120 G Street, N.W.
Washington, DC 20005
(202) 968-7072

EDGES
(consortium of black
business professionals)
333 Atlantic Avenue
Brooklyn, NY 11201
(718) 797-1223
Executive Leadership
Council
Suite 711
444 North Capitol Street, N.W.
Washington, DC
(202) 783-6339
Federation of Organization
for Professional Women
1825 Connecticut Ave., N.W.
Suite 403
Washington, DC 20009
(202) 328-1415
Inter America Travel
Agents Society
2000 Lee Road
Cleveland, OH 44118
(216) 932-7151

International Black
Writers
P.O. Box 1030
Chicago, IL 60690
(312) 995-5195
National Action Council
for Minorities in
Engineering
3 West 35th Street
New York, NY 10001
(212) 279-2626
National Alliance of
Black School Educators
2816 Georgia Ave., N.W.
Suite 4
Washington, DC 20001
(202) 483-1549
National Alliance of
Postal and Federal
Employees
1628 Eleventh Street, N.W.
Washington, DC 20001
(202) 939-6325

CAREER RESOURCES TARGETED FOR MINORITIES AND WOMEN

National Association of
Black Accountants
300 I Street, N.E.
Suite 107
Washington, DC 20002
(202) 543-6656
National Association of
Black Consulting
Engineers
6406 Georgia Avenue, N.W.
Washington, DC 20012
(202) 291-3550

National Association of
Black Journalists
Box 17212
Washington, DC 20041
(703) 648-1270
National Association of Black-
Owned Broadcasters
1730 M Street, N.W.
Suite 412
Washington, DC 20036
(202) 463-8970

National Association of
Black Reading and
Language Educators
P.O. Box 51566
Palo Alto, CA 94303
(415) 322-7239

National Assoc. of Black
Real Estate Professionals
Box 21421
Alexandria, VA 23320
(202) 624-1719

National Assoc. of Black
Social Workers
642 Beckwith Court, S.W.
Atlanta, GA 30314
(404) 584-7967

National Assoc. of Black
Women Attorneys
3711 Macomb Street, N.W.
2nd Floor
Washington, DC 20016
(202) 966-9691

National Association of
Blacks In Criminal
Justice
P.O. Box 66271
Washington, DC 20035
(202) 829-8860

National Association of
Colored Women's Clubs
5808 16th Street, N.W.
Washington, DC 20011
(202) 726-2044

National Assoc. of Female
Executives
127 W. 24th Street
New York, NY 10114
(212) 645-0770

National Assoc. of Health
Services Executives
1101 14th Street, N.W.
Suite 1000
Washington, DC 20005
(202) 289-1030

National Assoc. of Media
Women
157 West 126th Street
New York, NY 10027
(212) 675-0975
(212) 666-1320

National Assoc. of
Milliners, Dressmakers, and
Tailors, Inc.
157 West 126th Street
New York, NY 10027
(212) 666-1320

National Assoc. of
Minority Political Women,
USA, Inc.
6120 Oregon Avenue, N.W.
Washington, DC 20015
(202) 686-1216

National Assoc. of Negro
Business and Professional
Women's Clubs
1806 New Hampshire Avenue,
N.W.
Washington, DC 20009
(202) 483-4206

CAREER RESOURCES TARGETED FOR MINORITIES AND WOMEN

National Assoc. of Real
Estate Brokers
4324 Georgia Avenue
Washington, DC 20011
(201) 289–6655

National Association of
University Women
1501 Eleventh Street, N.W.
Washington, DC 20001
(202) 232–4844

National Association of
Urban Bankers
122 C Street, N.W.
Suite 580
Washington, DC 20001
(202) 783–4743

National Bar Assoc.
1225 Eleventh Street, N.W.
Washington, DC 20001
(202) 842–3900

National Beauty
Culturists League
25 Logan Circle, N.W.
Washington, DC 20005
(202) 332–2695

National Black Coalition
of Federal Aviation
Employees
9470 Timberleaf
Dallas, TX 75243
(214) 343–2668

National Black MBA Assoc.
180 North Michigan
Suite 1820
Chicago, IL 60601
(312) 236–2622

National Black Media
Coalition
38 New York Avenue, N.E.
Washington, DC 20002
(202) 387–8155

National Black Nurses
Association, Inc.
P.O. Box 1823
Washington, DC 20013
(202) 393–6870

National Black Police
Association
1919 Pennsylvania Ave., N.W.
Washington, DC 20006
(202) 457–0563

National Black Public
Relations Society
6565 Sunset Boulevard
Suite 525
Los Angeles, CA 90028
(213) 962–8051

Nat'l Black Women's
Health Project
Self-Help Division
1237 Gordon Street
Atlanta, GA 30310
(404) 758–9590

National Coalition of
Black Meeting Planners
50 F Street, N.W.
Suite 1040
Washington, DC 20001
(202) 628–3952

National Coalition of 100
Black Women
50 Rockefeller Plaza
Concourse Level
Suite 46
New York, NY 10020
(212) 838–0150

National Conference of
Black Lawyers, Section on
the Rights of Women
126 W. 119th Street
New York, NY 10026
(212) 864–4000

National Conference of
Black Political
Scientists
Dept. of History and
Political Science
Albany State College
Albany, GA 31705
(912) 439–4870

CAREER RESOURCES TARGETED FOR MINORITIES AND WOMEN

National Council of Negro
Women
1211 Connecticut Ave., N.W.
Room 704
Washington, DC 20036
(202) 659–0006

National Dental Association
5506 Connecticut Ave., N.W.
Suite 24–25
Washington, DC 20015
(202) 244–7555

National Displaced
Homemakers Network
1411 K Street, N.W.
Suite 930
Washington, DC 20005
(202) 628–6767

National Economic Assoc.
c/o Dr. Gus T. Ridgel
Southern University
Baton Rouge, LA 70813
(504) 771–2809

National Forum for Black
Public Administrators
777 N. Capitol Street, N.E.
Suite 807
Washington, DC 20002
(202) 408–9300

National Funeral
Directors and Morticians
Association
1615 Saint Paul Street
Suite 100
Baltimore, MD 21202
(301) 547–0700

National Medical
Association
1012 Tenth Street, N.W.
Washington, DC 20001
(202) 347–1895

National Network of
Minority Women In Science
c/o AAAS, Directorate for
Education and Human
Resources Programs
1333 H Street, N.W.
Washington, DC 20005
(202) 326–6670

National Newspaper
Publishers Assoc.
529 14th Street, N.W.
Suite 948
Washington, DC 20045
(202) 622–7323

National Optometric
Association
2830 South Indiana Avenue
Chicago, IL 60616
(312) 791–0186

National Organization for
the Professional
Advancement of Black
Chemists and Chemical
Engineers
c/o Dept. of Chemistry
525 Howard Street
Washington, DC 20059
(202) 269–4129

National Organization of
Black Law Enforcement
Executives
908 Pennsylvania Ave., S.E.
Washington, DC 20003
(202) 546–8811

National Organization of
Minority Architects
57 Post Street
Suite 804
San Francisco, CA 94104
(415) 989–3830

National Pharmaceutical
Assoc.
P.O. Box 934
Howard Univ.
Washington, DC 20059
(202) 636–6544

National Society of Black
Engineers
4200 Wisconsin Avenue, N.W.
Washington, DC
(202) 660–9866

CAREER RESOURCES TARGETED FOR MINORITIES AND WOMEN

National Technical Association
P.O. Box 20038
Washington, DC 20038
(202) 829–6100

Nontraditional
Employment for Women
243 W. 20th Street
New York, NY 10011
(212) 727–6252

Sisterhood of Black
Single Mothers
1360 Fulton Street
Suite 423
Brooklyn, NY 11216
Tradeswoman
P.O. Box 40664
San Francisco, CA 94140
(415) 821-7334

Wider Opportunities for
Women
1325 G Street, N.W.
Washington, DC 20005–3104
(202) 638-3143

APPENDIX D

BUSINESS PROGRAMS BY STATE

State	Name of Business Program	Contact Person and Phone Number
Alabama	Office of Minority Business Enterprise	Jack Crittenden (800) 248–6889 (out of state, (800) 248–0033)
Arizona	Governor's Office of Women's Services	Harriet Barnes (602) 542–1755
California	Office of Civil Rights, California Department of Transportation	Tille Boranian (916) 445–2276
Colorado	Women's Business Development Program, Office of Business Development	Charlotte Redden (303) 892–3840
Connecticut	Office of Small Business Services, State of Connecticut Economic Development	Leslie Twible (203) 258–4272
Delaware	Delaware Development Office	Gary Smith (302) 739–4271
Illinois	Minority and Female Business Enterprise Bureau, Department of Central Management Services	Sharon Matthews (800) 356–9206 (in Chicago, (312) 814–4190)
	Department of Commerce and Community Affairs	Mollie Cole (312) 814–6111
Indiana	Small Business Development Corporation, Women and Minorities in Business	Ann Neal-Winston (312) 264–2820

State	Name of Business Program	Contact Person and Phone Number
Iowa	Small Business Section, Iowa Department of Economic Development	Toni Hawley (800) 532–1216 (out of state, (515) 242–4758)
Kansas	Office of Minority Business, Department of Commerce	Antonio Augusto (913) 296–3805
Louisians	Division of Minority and Women's Business Enterprise, Louisiana Department of Economic Development	Angelisa Harris (504) 342–5373
Maryland	Office of Minority Business Assistance	Mitchell Smith (301) 333–2459
Massachusetts	State Office of Minority and Women Business Assistance, Business Affirmative Action Agency	Executive Director (617) 727–8692
Michigan	Business Women Services	Owner Barbara Gentry (517) 335–2166
Minnesota	Department of Administration, Customer and Vendor Services	Dorothy Lovejoy (612) 296–2600
Mississippi	Office of Minority Business Enterprise, Department of Economic and Community Development	Elliott Travis (601) 359–3449
Missouri	Women's Council on Economic Development and Training, Missouri Department of Economic Development	Sue McDaniel (314) 751–0810

Nebraska	Assisting Business Division, Nebraska Department of Economic Development	Steve Williams (800) 426–6505 (in Lincoln, (402) 471–3782)
New Jersey	Division of Development for Small Businesses and Women and Minority Business, Office of Women Business Enterprise	Cindy Conrad (609) 292–3860
New York	Governor's Office of Minority and Women's Business Development	Stephanie Brown (518) 474–6342
North Carolina	Minority Business Development Agency, Department of Economic and Community Development	David Soloman (919) 733–2712
Ohio	Women's Business Resource Program, Ohio Department of Development	Melody K. Borchers (800) 282–1085 (out of state, (800) 848–1300)
Oklahoma	Women-Owned Business Assistance Program, Department of Commerce	Marketing Head (405) 841–5242
Oregon	Office of Minority, Women, and Emerging Small Business	Susan Panek (503) 378–5651
Pennsylvania	Bureau of Women's Business Development, Department of Commerce	Lenore Cameron (717) 787–3339
Rhode Island	Office of Minority Business Assistance, Department of Economic Development	Issac Wallace (410) 277–2601

State	Name of Business Program	Contact Person and Phone Number
South Carolina	Governor's Office of Small and Minority Business Assistance	Adriene B. Wright (803) 734–0657
Tennessee	Office of Minority Business Enterprise, Department of Economic and Community Development	John Birdsong (800) 342–8470 (out of state, (800) 251–8594)
Texas	Disadvantaged Business Program, Office of Small Business	Rose Reyes-Pitts (800) 888–0511
Utah	Women's Business Development Office, Department of Community and Economic Development	Kathy Thompson (801) 538–8700
Vermont	Governor's Commission on Women	Billi Gosh (802) 828–2851
Wisconsin	Women's Business Services, Wisconsin Department of Development	Mary Strickland (800) 435–7287

APPENDIX E

In the February 1992 issue of Black Enterprise *the editors identified the twenty-five leading corporations that offer the best opportunities for black professionals. The best places for blacks to work are:*
Ameritech, Chicago
AT&T, New York
Avon Products Inc., New York
Chrysler Corp., Highland Park, Michigan
Coca-Cola Co., Atlanta
Corning Inc., Corning, New York
E. I. du Pont de Nemours & Co., Wilmington, Delaware
The Equitable Life Assurance Society, New York
Federal Express Corp., Memphis
Ford Motor Co., Dearborn, Michigan
Gannett Co. Inc., Arlington, Virginia
General Mills Inc., Minneapolis
General Motors, Detroit
International Business Machines Corp. (IBM), Armonk, New York
Johnson & Johnson, New Brunswick, New Jersey
Kellogg Co., Battle Creek, Michigan
Marriott Corp., Washington, D.C.
McDonald's Corp., Oak Brook, Illinois
Merck & Co. Inc., Rahway, New Jersey
NYNEX Corp., New York
Pepsi-Cola Co., Somers, New York
Philip Morris Cos. Inc., New York
Teachers Insurance and Annuity Association (TIAA-CREF), New York
UAL Corp., Chicago
Xerox Corp., Stamford, Connecticut

INDEX